A Cognitive Approach to Genericity in Norwegian

Anna Kurek-Przybilski

A Cognitive Approach to Genericity in Norwegian

Jagiellonian University Press

Reviewer
dr hab. Agnieszka Gicala, prof. UP in Krakow

Cover design
Sebastian Wojnowski

This work was supported by the National Science Centre – Preludium – under grant number 2017/25/N/HS2/00003.

ISBN 978-83-233-5054-5
ISBN 978-83-233-7281-3 (e-book)

JAGIELLONIAN
UNIVERSITY
PRESS

www.wuj.pl

Jagiellonian University Press
Editorial Offices: Michałowskiego 9/2, 31-126 Kraków
Phone: +48 12 663 23 80
Distribution: Phone: +48 12 631 01 97
Cell Phone: +48 506 006 674, e-mail: sprzedaz@wuj.pl
Bank: PEKAO SA, IBAN PL 80 1240 4722 1111 0000 4856 3325

For Henry

Table of contents

Acknowledgements

The project described in this book sums up four years of my PhD studies at Adam Mickiewicz University in Poznań. I would not have been able to finalise the research without the help and advice of many people.

First of all, I would like to thank my supervisor, Prof. Dominika Skrzypek, who has helped me enormously. Her support and professional advice have always motivated me to research and broaden my knowledge, not only on the subjects in question. Moreover, Prof. Skrzypek encouraged me to apply for funding for this project, which resulted in a grant from the National Science Centre (grant no. 2017/25/N/HS2/00003).

I would also like to thank Prof. Iwona Kowal and Prof. Eystein Dahl for their detailed and earnest feedback on my PhD dissertation. The suggestions were most helpful when I revised the text for publication. Prof. Dahl also contributed greatly to conducting the first part of the research. Thanks to his involvement in proofreading the survey texts, the study has evolved into a comprehensive data set on Norwegian generics.

I would not have been able to conduct the technical part of the whole study without the enormous help and advice of my husband, Henry Przybilski. Apart from being the best technical support for the whole project, Henry has showed unbelievable patience and peace of mind, which kept me sane through all those years. I will never be able to thank you enough for this.

Last but not least, I thank all the anonymous respondents who have devoted their precious time to filling in the two surveys. This has provided priceless language data for this project.

Introduction

This is a revised version of my doctoral dissertation *Generics in Norwegian – A Cognitive Analysis*. I defended the thesis in October 2020 at Adam Mickiewicz University in Poznań. The goal of this book is to show how genericity functions in the Norwegian language and how it is rendered in the cognitive framework.

Genericity as a language phenomenon is regarded as the ability to talk about kinds and to make generalisations about people, objects and events. The possibility to make such generalisations is known to be present in all languages (see Chapters 1 and 2). However, the way it is expressed may vary from language to language. In Germanic languages, and therefore also in Norwegian, genericity is expressed mainly with the use of different noun forms. When it comes to Norwegian, there are five noun phrase (NP) types that can be used generically and these are: bare noun, indefinite singular, definite singular, indefinite plural, and definite plural.

All of the forms listed above can be used in a number of contexts, not only the generic ones. In this study, a number of generic texts are analysed, together with feedback from native speakers of Norwegian, in order to determine whether there are certain contexts in which given NP types occur as generic. In the last section of the book, a cognitive model of such contexts was created (see Chapter 7), based on the models of Radden 2009, Pettersson 1976, and Leslie et al. 2011.

The study focuses on *bokmål*, one of the two written variants of Norwegian. Bokmål is used by the majority of the Norwegian population (see the discussion in Chapter 7), whereas the other variant, *nynorsk*, is slightly less popular in written use. Due to this fact, the study was designed based on texts written in *bokmål*.

The data collected for this study consists of three sets: Survey 1, the corpus texts and Survey 2. The first survey was conducted in 2017 and consists of 30 generic texts with gaps to fill. The specialised corpus of generic texts contains 170 texts, divided into five thematic categories. The second survey was created with 20 generic sentences (test items) and five non-generic sentences (filler items) retrieved from the specialised corpus. Such a wide variety of data collected for this study made it possible to conduct a comprehensive empirical analysis of the phenomenon.

The cognitive models used to analyse the material were based on the studies of Radden 2009, Pettersson 1976, and Leslie et al. 2011. The models were adjusted to the Norwegian data, which later led to the creation of the cognitive model of Norwegian generics. Since the vast majority of the available methodologies concerns English, adapting the chosen models to the Norwegian data was necessary. Apart from the cognitive analyses, a number of statical tests were conducted on each of the data sets. The tests included, among others, the analysis of variance (ANOVA), the Kruskal–Wallis test and a number of post hoc tests, such as Tukey HSD and Dunn's test. Complementing the cognitive analysis with quantitative tests provided a detailed view on Norwegian generics.

The book is divided into seven chapters. Chapter 1 presents general remarks on theory of genericity and Chapter 2 focuses on most influential theoretical approaches to the phenomenon, with a detailed description of the cognitive models used in this study. Chapter 3 is an overview of the literature on genericity in Mainland Scandinavian languages. Chapters 4, 5 and 6 describe the data analyses—Survey 1, the corpus and Survey 2, respectively. Chapter 7 contains conclusions, discussion and implications for further research within the field.

The existing research on genericity in Norwegian is limited to the analyses of individual generic sentences (see Borthen 2003 and Halmøy 2016). The study presented in this book is the first empirical study on Norwegian generics, conducted with the use of cognitive methodology and quantitative tests. The project described in this book is meant to bridge the gap in research on genericity in Norwegian, as well as contribute to the cognitive approaches to genericity.

1. Genericity as a language phenomenon – introductory remarks

> Les baobabs, avant de grandir, ça commence par être petit.
> Antoine de Saint-Exupéry, *Le Petit Prince*

Human language not only makes communication between people possible and effective, but also very diverse. We can talk about something concretely and literally, but we can also construct abstract and ambiguous utterances or generalise over something. For instance, saying that baobabs are small before they grow tall is a generalisation, as shown in the popular quote from *Le Petit Prince* above. Generalisations that refer to a whole species or to a group of individuals or objects are called generic.

Expressions of genericity are as diverse as the phenomenon itself. Depending on the language group and the context in which generic sentences appear, they can include generic noun phrases (NPs) and can be written in either present or past tense. Furthermore, certain predicates promote generic readings by referring to whole kinds, e.g. *to be numerous.* Those are called kind-predicates and can only be used with plural NPs or NPs denoting kinds.[1] In research on genericity the focus is usually on a few main areas, such as theoretical studies, corpus linguistics, and cognitive or experimental approaches that combine two or more of the aspects of the phenomenon. Each of these has proved to be successful in studying genericity. For instance, purely theoretical studies such as Carlson (1977, 1982), Carlson and Pelletier (1995), and Mari et al. (2013a)

---

[1] The verbs *to refer to* and *to denote* are used interchangeably in this book, though in philosophy these two notions are distinct. This project presents a purely linguistical approach to genericity, and therefore no distinction between the two notions will be made.

have contributed greatly to the development of the applied terminology. Corpus studies such as Oosterhof (2008) have made it possible to outline the NP types that have generic meaning in certain languages, whereas experimental approaches to the phenomenon have shown that genericity might be not only a linguistic but also a psychological matter (see e.g. Gelman and Tardif 1998; Leslie 2007; Leslie et al. 2011; Ionin et al. 2011).

The research on generics in different languages is abundant. The phenomenon has been studied from a cross-linguistic perspective (e.g. Chierchia 1998), in whole language groups (e.g. the account of genericity in Romance languages given by Kabatek [2013]), and in individual languages (e.g. Karczewski's [2016] account on generics in Polish, Carlsson's [2012] analysis of Swedish, the comparative study of Hungarian, English, and French generics by Farkas and de Swart [2009], or Molnár's [2014] account of Hungarian and German generics).

When it comes to empirical studies on genericity in Mainland Scandinavian languages, and in Norwegian in particular, a comprehensive analysis is lacking.[2] The goal of this study is therefore to provide such an account of Norwegian generics. Since the phenomenon is rather diverse, the main research question of this study concerns the way generics can be rendered in Norwegian, particularly the NP types used in generic texts and sentences. Moreover, the role of context and speakers' cognition in expressing genericity will be the main aspects of this study.

1.1. Generic reference

Making a generalisation about a given object, a species, or a group of people requires that a speaker *refers* to it. In the scholarly literature, genericity is therefore seen as a type of reference. Reference, as used in a linguistic context, assigns a feature or a set of features to a given object (Lyons 1977: 177–197). In other words, a proposition, when uttered, creates a link to an element of the world – it refers to it by picking out certain features that define the object being described.

For example, in Sentence 1 a speaker may mean that barking is a feature characteristic of most (or maybe even all) dogs, based on one's proposition.

---

[2]   In Chapter 3, I provide an overview of the existing studies on Danish, Norwegian, and Swedish.

(1)   Dogs bark.

On the other hand, a receiver of such information might still classify a non-barking dog as a dog, even if it happens that a given animal may not match the characteristics from Sentence 1. Referring to all dogs in this case is a way of assigning barking to the whole kind, not only to a given group of animals.

As Lyons points out, reference is an utterance-dependent notion (Lyons 1977: 180), not an NP-dependent one. This means that in Sentence 1 it is not the noun form itself that refers to all dogs, but rather the whole sentence that promotes such a reading. Assigning the act of barking to the species makes the receiver of the information connect it intuitively to all individuals from the group 'dogs'. One can also imagine that in a different context one might refer to some particular group of dogs that tend to bark, without stating the fact that most or all dogs do so. Additionally, it seems crucial that the speaker chooses an appropriate referring expression in order to achieve a desired meaning of a given sentence. Such an expression might come in the form of a proper name, a definite noun phrase, or a pronoun (Lyons 1977: 180).

Generic reference is often context-bound, as its interpretation may vary when used in different contexts. Such dependency also implies that both the speaker and the hearer interpret a given sentence in the same way. Whether an NP, a sentence, or a text is considered generic is often a matter of judgement and language intuition.

An interesting aspect of different reference types, including the generic one, is the use of tenses. Lyons (1977: 194) points out that generic sentences, with certain exceptions, are not only timeless but also *tenseless* and *aspectless*. Timelessness and aspectlessness mean that a given sentence holds true irrespective of time, as is illustrated in (2). Lions being friendly beasts is not associated with any particular point in time, despite the fact that all the sentences are written in present tense.

(2)   a.   The lion is a friendly beast.
       b.   A lion is a friendly beast.
       c.   Lions are friendly beasts.

The *tenselessness* of generic references is manifested in the fact that the truths they express hold true irrespective of the tense they are uttered in. The tense used in such expressions is sometimes called the generic tense

(Dahl 1975: 99). According to Dahl, stating something in generic tense – be it in past, present, or future – means that a state, a law, or a characteristic feature is true at a certain time and is not valid for all times (Dahl 1975: 103). 'A certain time' implies that the fact, for instance, that cows have four legs holds true for the time being, but also leaves open the possibility that the situation may change – perhaps in the future most cows will have five legs due to genetic modifications. The potential changes in meaning which are implied by generic present, past, and future were illustrated by Dahl (1975: 103) in the following example:

(3)   When I was a boy, I wrote with my left hand, but now I write with my right hand, although I will probably write with my left hand again when I grow older.

All sentences in (2) can be perceived as tenseless, since the present tense in generic sentences is neutral in relation to time (Lyons 1977: 194).

(4)   The dinosaur was a friendly beast.

However, an example such as Sentence 4, even though written in the past tense (generic past), can still be interpreted as tenseless and timeless. The use of past tense in this example is connected to the fact that the speaker knows that dinosaurs are extinct. Nevertheless, the part of the proposition that marks the tense does not bear the generic reading – that reading is rendered by the predicate and the NP (Lyons 1977: 194).

1.1.1. Generics and genericity

Even though it has been a known fact that language users can speak about kinds as well as individuals and that the two uses of nominal and verbal expressions may differ to some extent, for a long time coherent terminology to describe this fact was lacking. This inspired the Generic Group, consisting of Gregory N. Carlson, Gennaro Chierchia, Manfried Krifka, Godehard Link, Francis Jeffry Pelletier, and Alice ter Meulen,[3] to publish *The Generic Book* in 1995. Their main goal was to 'develop a terminology to be recommended for

---

[3]   The researchers from this group are also known for developing Carlson's division into generics and kind-reference. According to some researchers, such a division is present in

use by other researchers' (Carlson and Pelletier 1995: viii). The notions established by the Generic Group have been widely used in numerous publications on the subject since 1995, but not all linguists have adopted the terminology proposed by Carlson and Pelletier. For the most part, the notions I use in this book are those proposed by the Generic Group, unless they are terms coined after the publication of 1995, such as the generic generalisation types proposed by Leslie et al. (2011).

In English, one can differentiate between generics and genericity. Both notions are used in several works on the phenomenon (see e.g. Carlson and Pelletier 1995; Mari et al. 2013a), often without a very clear distinction between the two. It might therefore seem that the notions (at least to a certain degree) designate the same matter in linguistics, but when it comes to the philosophy of language this is not necessarily the case.

There are at least three main words that appear in discourse on the matter, namely *genericity*, *generics*, and the adjective *generic*. The distinction between the first two notions that is present in English does not seem to be the case in Norwegian, for instance. The two words connected to the phenomena in Norwegian are the noun *generisitet* and the adjective *generisk*. In the French literature on the subject, one comes across the nouns *la généricité* and *le générique*, as well as the adjective *générique*. German terms include the noun *der Generizität* and the adjective *generisch*. German and Norwegian show the same structure of the notions connected to genericity – there is no equivalent to the English *generics*, whereas in French one might suppose that *le générique* (sometimes also used in the plural form *des génériques* – see Dahl 1985: 57) is indeed such an equivalent.

Since the majority of the works on genericity are written in English, the notions *genericity* and *generics* appear quite often. Moreover, some researchers differentiate between the two. Nickel, for instance, claims that 'generics (linguistic phenomenon) exhibit genericity (not obviously a linguistic phenomenon), and though a theory of generics is closely connected to a theory of genericity, the two are distinct' (Nickel 2017: 437).

As Nickel postulates, the difference between the notions is purely conceptual. The term *generics* is related to natural languages in a strictly linguistic sense, not in an abstract one. It simply designates the ability to create and utter generic sentences (Nickel 2017: 437). Generics could therefore be

---

certain languages (for Norwegian, see e.g. Halmøy 2016), whereas in other works such semantic division is absent. In this book I treat kind-reference as generics.

considered as *actual realisations* of genericity in the same way as utterances are actual realisations of abstract units – sentences. The idea of assigning features to kinds only, is connected to the conceptual level of genericity. At that point, the speaker assigns a given feature to a given kind – a feature that cannot be connected with an individual – in order to utter it afterwards with the use of language. Such features, when expressed in a form of generic sentences, then become generics in a given language. For instance, Sentence 5 contains a kind-restricted predicate (also called kind-predicates; in this case 'to be extinct'):

(5)   Dodos are extinct.

These predicates can only apply to whole kinds, not to individuals of a particular kind (Nickel 2017: 437). One cannot for instance say that 'a lion is extinct' or that 'a sparrow is widespread' (Lyons 1977: 196). Sentences containing kind-restricted predicates are considered classic examples of generics – they do not allow for any interpretations other than generic ones. They also limit the choice of NP types that can be used in such utterances, as shown in the example above.

Nickel also points out that even though some generics are indeed very clear when it comes to their interpretations, sentences of this kind are still highly context-bound (Nickel 2017: 438). This applies particularly to sentences which do not contain kind-restricted predicates:

(6)   a.   Ravens are black.
      b.   Dogs bark.
      c.   Cows have four legs.

This context-dependence does not allow for any statistical approach to the issue, as the variability of the phenomenon is too great and is additionally connected to truth-conditions. Every person has some knowledge about the world and can therefore judge whether a given sentence is probable (true) or not. Generics depend greatly on truth-conditions and the plausibility of a given feature occurring in real life. Sentences 7a and 7b illustrate this dependency:

(7)   a.   Ravens are black.
      b.   Ravens are white.

Most speakers, referring to their general knowledge about the world, would probably not consider the second sentence to be true or generic. This is because generics that do not contain kind-restricted predicates imply that a generalisation or a feature from the sentence concerns most individuals from a given group – most, but of course not necessarily all, as in some very particular cases one could utter Sentence 7b as a true sentence, for instance when talking about albino ravens (Nickel 2017: 438). The problem with such an interpretation, though, is that the probability of an albino raven occurring in the real world is very low and most speakers would not allow for a generic sentence about such a limited group.[4] An albino raven would still be classified as a raven, but uttering a generalisation about an exception to the rule does not seem acceptable to most speakers. If it was acceptable, other examples of this kind would have to be considered true as well:

(8)   a. Cows have three legs.
       b. Frenchmen do not drink wine.

Both examples could be true in some particular contexts, but they cannot be considered generic in the classic meaning of this term as described above. In order to create a generalisation about a kind or a group of objects or people, one needs to refer to a quality that the majority of this kind/group would possess. Moreover, this type of generics, namely generalisations without kind-restricted predicates, is not prone to any statistical analysis and cannot therefore be evaluated this way (Nickel 2017: 439).

There are two main types of sentences that can have generic meaning. One of them is kind-referring sentences as discussed above, whereas others are much more context-dependent and therefore connected to the conceptual level of the notion (habitual sentences, also called characterising sentences in the literature on the subject [Krifka et al. 1995: 3]). The first type might therefore be connected more to the notion of *generics*, whereas the latter matches a slightly broader notion of *genericity*.

Since the meaning and use of generics is probably the most direct evidential connection we have to genericity, it's only natural to frame a theory of genericity as a theory of the truth-conditions of generics (Nickel 2017: 441).

---

[4]   See also the so-called false generalisations in Section 2.5.3.

The distinction of generics and genericity, as important as it is, does not seem to pose difficulties in the analysis of the phenomena in a language. Both terms are used interchangeably in many publications in linguistics. Some researchers opt for one of the notions, others for the others, whilst others still do not differentiate between them at all and use them interchangeably. Also, the most comprehensive work on the topic, *The Generic Book*, contains both names in seemingly similar contexts (see e.g. Krifka et al. 1995: 1–124; Dahl 1985: 412–415).

1.2. Two senses of genericity

In the literature on the subject, it is often mentioned that genericity has two senses – one being expressed through kind-referring sentences and the other through habitual sentences (Krifka et al. 1995: 2–4). Kind-referring sentences, as the name suggests, refer to kinds, as shown in the examples below.

(9)   a.   Beavers build dams.
      b.   Foxes are mammals.

Other predicates often utilised in kind-referring sentences are called 'kind predicates' (Krifka et al. 1995: 10; known also as kind-restricted predicates, as mentioned above). Those include constructions such as 'to be extinct', 'to be rare', 'to be numerous', etc. Kind-predicates may be used only with NPs that designate kinds and are most often bare plurals. Indefinite and definite singular nouns are unacceptable and somewhat awkward, as shown in the examples in (10) below.

(10)   a.   Pandas are rare.
       b.   Lions are numerous in Africa.
       c.   ? A panda is extinct.
       d.   ? The lion is rare.

The two forms above identified as unacceptable can occur in generic contexts. Hawkins perceives such sentences as indefinite and definite generics (Hawkins 2015: 214) and provides the following examples:

(11)   a.   A lion is a noble beast.

     b.   The lion is a noble beast.

     c.   Lions are noble beasts.

     d.   The lions are noble beasts.

The four sentences presented above differ from the examples in (10) in that they do not include kind-referring predicates. Therefore, it is fully acceptable to form generic sentences with indefinite and definite singular forms without them sounding awkward or unnatural. Moreover, Hawkins' examples show that both singular and plural forms can be used in generic sentences – in singular and in plural. This view differs slightly from other theories in which the plural definite form is completely excluded or, as we shall see in Section 2.5.1., reserved for humans.

It is also worth mentioning that whilst all NP types technically have the potential to take on a generic reading, not all forms use this potential, or not in all contexts, and above all not in all languages. As Behrens states, in most languages all *generic* NP types[5] are ambiguous, as they always have another possible reading (Behrens 2005: 276). Furthermore, 'it is never the case that all different generic types permitted in a language would be intersubstitutable in all possible (generic) contexts' (Behrens 2005: 276).

The nature of definite and indefinite reference allows for both generic and specific uses of each of the NP types. The indefinite article still refers exclusively and the definite article inclusively within pragmatically defined parameters. It is therefore no accident that one and the same morpheme can perform both functions. Again, locatability and grammaticality facts prove the fundamental similarity between generic and non-generic reference (Hawkins 2015: 214).

Apart from the fact that the same morpheme can take on more than one function, context remains the decisive factor in interpreting a given sentence. This is particularly visible in the case of indefinite reference. If indefinite reference is used specifically, it is only the speaker who knows which entities of a group the sentence concerns, whereas in the case of generic indefinite reference, both the speaker and the hearer are able to identify the referents (Hawkins 2015: 215).

---

[5]   In none of the languages studied does there seem to be a noun form reserved only for generic references (Behrens 2005: 277). Therefore, stating that a noun form is generic means that it has such a reading in a given context, not by default.

Whether the speaker uses a definite or indefinite form, the interpretation of such reference has to be verified by the context. Reference can be specific, when the speaker means a given entity or group of entities, or generic, when the entities identified in the sentence represent a feature or features of a larger group. Hawkins calls generic references *non-specific* references used in *specific* contexts (Hawkins 2015: 215). Those *specific* contexts can be an effect either of the speaking situation, when the speaker is able to point at something and refer to it specifically, or of the predicates used in the sentence (for example, kind-predicates), as well as a wider context in which a given sentence appears. It is therefore possible that a sentence analysed out of context would have a specific reading, whereas in a wider context it might be interpreted as generic (Behrens 2005: 279).

A similar ambiguity in interpreting the sentences depending on their form can be observed in habitual sentences as well. This is particularly visible in languages that have a formal distinction when it comes to functions of particular noun phrases. Behrens refers to French, where the reading of habitual sentences depends highly on the context, as both in habitual and non-habitual sentences it is possible to use definite forms which are also applied in generic constructions (Behrens 2005: 285):

(12) a.

Jeanne	mange	*les*	*pommes.*
Jeanne	eats	the	apples.

Jeanne eats the apples.

      b.

Jeanne	mange	*des*	*pommes.*
Jeanne	eats	PL.IND	apples.

Jeanne eats apples.

Habitual sentences, also called characterising sentences, express the second meaning of genericity (cf. Carlson and Pelletier 1995), namely regularities and the characteristics of someone or something. Characterising sentences do not need to include generic noun phrases or even to make generalisations about kinds to be considered generic. As Behrens claims, 'habitual sentences … resemble traditional generic sentences in that they express a typical characteristic of their subjects' (Behrens 2005: 288). Let us consider the following examples:

(13) a. Yesterday, we had a very interesting discussion *about the potato.* (The teacher told us that it was first cultivated in South America.)

    b. John smokes a cigar after dinner.

    c. I love *beavers.*

    d. *The beaver* has always fascinated me. (Behrens 2005: 289; emphasis in original.)

Sentence 13b is a *classic* characterising sentence – it states a characteristic feature about John, the subject of the sentence (cf. Behrens' definition above). Sentence 13c can also be interpreted as habitual since it states a generalisation about the speaker. On the contrary, Sentences 13a and 13d contain generic noun phrases but do not make generalisations about kinds. Nevertheless, they are considered generic habitual sentences. The interpretation of habitual sentences as generic or non-generic depends on the notion of genericity that one applies. Behrens therefore proposes to distinguish between *generic sentences* and *generic phrases* (Behrens 2005: 289), which will be discussed in greater detail in Chapter 2.

1.3. Design of the study

The goal of this project is to provide an empirical account of genericity in Norwegian from a cognitive perspective. In order to verify which NP types appear in generic contexts, three different data sets were collected. The sets include data from two surveys and a corpus of generic texts.

The first survey (called 'Survey 1' throughout the book) consists of 30 generic texts with gaps and was conducted among 599 native speakers of Norwegian. The corpus contains 170 generic texts divided into five thematic categories ('people', 'animals', 'plants', 'tools', and 'other'). All of the corpus texts were retrieved from an online encyclopaedia, *Store norske leksikon*, and are written in the *bokmål* variant of Norwegian. The last data set of the project was a second survey (called 'Survey 2' throughout the book), which consists of 20 test items and five filler items. All survey sentences were retrieved from the corpus previously constructed for the project. Detailed descriptions of each data set are provided in Chapters 4 through 6.

When choosing a study design for this project, the goal was to describe genericity from the point of view of cognitive linguistics and combine it with quantitative methods. The design of the study was crucial in order to obtain credible and representative data. To this end, a mixed methods research (MMR) approach was utilised. There are numerous reasons for the popularity of MMR in recent years, such as the *triangulation* and *complementarity* of the data (Hesse-Biber 2010: 3–4). *Triangulation* allows a research question to be approached from many different perspectives, which are then combined in the final analysis. Such an approach provides more credible results than single-method studies. The *complementarity* of such projects means that one analysis strengthens the other, for instance the quantitative description (QUAN) is supported by the qualitative one (QUAL), or the other way round, depending on the research question and the field of study.

The use of MMR not only allows a given phenomenon to be studied from different perspectives in one research project, but it also provides a broader understanding of the problem in question. In contrast to multimodal methods, which utilise either qualitative or quantitative tests (Hesse-Biber 2010: 3–4), MMR relies both on qualitative and quantitative data analyses. Such methodology is known as the 'third methodological movement' or the 'third research paradigm' (Creswell and Clark 2018) – the other two being qualitative and quantitative paradigms.

There are numerous study designs within the MMR paradigm and the strategy must be chosen in accordance with a given research question. For the empirical part of this project, a concurrent triangulation mixed methods design was chosen. The strategy combines two types of data analysis, namely qualitative and quantitative, which are performed simultaneously and then combined in order to provide a more detailed account of the phenomenon (Riazi 2016: 47).

The MMR design of this project does not exclude or interfere with the cognitive framework applied for the interpretation of the findings. The qualitative part of this project consists in analysing the material from the point of view of cognitive linguistics and the models described in Chapter 2. The QUAL analysis is crucial in order to show how genericity can be expressed in Norwegian and what cognitive status is assigned to the phenomenon. The QUAN part, on the other hand, presents a number of statistical tests through which the data can be structured and its distribution visualised and provides numerical data that support the descriptive analysis.

The quantitative analysis performed in this project consisted of statistical tests. First, I provided descriptive statistics for all data sets, which allowed me to examine the distribution of the data in a given set. Second, according to the data distribution, further statistical tests were performed. When the data were distributed normally, parametric tests were chosen. When the data were not normally distributed throughout the set, non-parametric tests were utilised.

Parametric tests, such as the analysis of variance (ANOVA) used in this project, can only be performed when certain requirements are met. In the case of ANOVA, the following restrictions apply:

1. normal distribution of the data,
2. homogeneity of variance,
3. comparability of the groups.

If one or more of the requirements of ANOVA are not met (this can be verified with Levene's test and the Shapiro–Wilk test), a non-parametric analysis should be performed (Mertens et al. 2017: 148).

ANOVA is used when more than one group (data set) is being analysed. It allows the differences between the groups to be evaluated (Mertens et al. 2017: 10). In this study, the groups in the model are always five NP types. ANOVA, as with other statistical models, relies on the null hypothesis. The null hypothesis is a reference point where all tested groups are equal (Mertens et al. 2017: 9). If the null hypothesis is rejected after performing ANOVA, it means that there are statistical differences between the tested groups. However, ANOVA does not show where the differences are or whether one or more groups are different from the others. Performing only ANOVA is therefore insufficient and further tests are needed. The method used by many researchers and in this study are post hoc tests, which can determine which groups score differently, while still taking into consideration the main assumptions of the analysis (Mertens et al. 2017: 12). The post hoc test that is used throughout this book in the case of ANOVA is Tukey HSD.

When a given data set does not meet the requirements of ANOVA, non-parametric tests must be used. In this project, the non-parametric test of choice is the Kruskal–Wallis test; an accompanying post hoc test is Dunn's test. The purpose of non-parametric tests is the same as for ANOVA: they can determine whether there are differences between the tested groups, without indicating where potential differences are. Non-parametric tests are utilised when the distribution of the data is not normal or when the requirement of homogeneity of variance is not met. The results provided by non-parametric tests are as valuable as those that can be obtained through ANOVA. Due to the lack of requirements (parameters) that must be met, non-parametric tests can be utilised with different data sets and in different types of projects.

In each of the analyses performed in this project, the notions of p-value and F-statistic are used. In short, a p-value is used 'to indicate statistical significance, not the effect size or importance of the hypothesised theoretical relationship' (Mertens et al. 2017: 152). Typically, the p-value should be below 0.05 in order for the results to be considered significant. However, the value is used in many different analyses and tests in statistics, and it can differ depending on the particular analysis and its purpose.

The F-statistic is used in ANOVA to indicate potential differences between the tested groups. The F-statistic does not suggest where the differences are located, what their values are, or whether certain groups differ more from others (Mertens et al. 2017: 12). However, most of the computer programmes report both the p-value and the F-statistic, as these two indicate whether the results are statistically significant or not. All the statistical tests in this project were conducted and graphically depicted in R software.

2. Theoretical models of genericity

In every language that has been studied to date,
generics have the least marked surface forms;
it is natural to conjecture that this is a linguistics universal.

Leslie 2007: 382

Approaches to genericity can be divided into three main categories, based on their origin. The three main groups of 1) Carlsonian theories, introduced by Carlson and other researchers from the Generic Group, 2) neo-Carlsonian theories, developed by some members of the Generic Group and other researchers, and 3) recent cognitive and experimental theories.

The first and second approaches can be perceived of as the *core* or somehow *classic* research on the matter, as those theories were developed first. A more unified methodology and terminology was introduced, which was in fact the main purpose of *The Generic Book* published in 1995. Cognitive research in the field has shed new light on the notion of genericity, and has allowed for a more interdisciplinary approach. In the latest experimental studies on genericity, researchers turn often to psychology and the theories used in disciplines such as cognitive linguistics or neurolinguistics. Regardless of the approach one chooses when researching genericity, a distinction between generic NPs, generic sentences, and generic texts needs to be made. The different levels at which genericity is expressed can sometimes influence the choice of research strategy.

2.1. Generic NPs

Genericity can be expressed at both the NP level and the sentence level. Generic NPs need not occur in generic sentences and vice versa: generic sentences need not contain generic NPs to be interpreted as generic (Behrens 2005: 288). In English, generic NPs can technically occur in all possible forms (definite and indefinite, singular and plural), but it is always the context and the reading of a given sentence that plays the central role in its interpretation.

Certain NP types tend to have a generic reading in most cases (for instance, bare plurals), whereas others depend on the context in which a sentence is uttered or on the form of the subject of the sentence (e.g. definite plural generic). Moreover, when it comes to habitual sentences, the NP type does not seem to play the central role, whereas in *classic* (kind-referring) generic sentences the form of the NP and its role seem to influence the reading of a sentence. On this basis, one can differentiate between two main analysis methods. One way of analysing generic sentences is the *bottom-up* strategy, where linguists look rather at the forms of NPs, definiteness, and their function in the sentence. The other strategy, the *top-down* approach, focusses on generic sentences and their structure rather than on the functions of each element of the sentence (Behrens 2005: 287).[6] Generic NPs can occur in different forms, definite or indefinite:

> One obvious difference between definite and indefinite noun-phrases, used generically, is that, with definite noun-phrases, both a collective and a distributive interpretation is possible, but with indefinite noun-phrases (in the singular) the collective interpretation is excluded. (Lyons 1977: 196)

According to Lyons, English native speakers are rather consistent when it comes to the interpretation of NPs. For instance, bare plurals will most of the time be considered generic, whereas definite plural nouns will, for most English speakers, designate a specific group of entities.

Languages can show different levels of grammaticalisation when it comes to generic NPs and their form. For instance, the most used NP types in English generic sentences are bare plurals, singular definites and singular indefinites,

---

[6]   In the analysis presented in further chapters of this book, I employ both strategies. In order to properly analyse the two surveys and the corpus texts, it is necessary to look at both levels of genericity – the NP level and the sentence level.

with very few exceptions. The exceptions allow for more liberty in the choice of NP types in such utterances and are, of course, context-dependent. Such a wide variety of choices might not be the case in every language though.

French, on the other hand, is an example of a language with fully grammaticalised articles, where the singular bare noun is considered incorrect in generic contexts, even when it comes to mass nouns that tend to occur as bare nouns in English and Norwegian, for example. Furthermore, the French indefinite singular article seems to be the only indefinite form acceptable in a generic context (Galmiche 1985: 2).

The most often used forms of a generic NP are the definite ones – singular and plural – with a very limited use of indefinite forms:

(14) a. Le   lynx   a   une   vue   perçante.
          The   lynx   has   a   vision   sharp.
          The lynx has a sharp eye.

      b. Les   lynx   ont   une   vue   perçante.
          The   lynxes have   a   vision   sharp.
          The lynxes have a sharp eye.

      c. Un   lynx   a   une   vue   perçante.
          A   lynx   has   a   vision   sharp.
          A lynx has a sharp eye. (Galmiche 1985: 2)

The rule seems to be consistent and applicable to most (if not all) generic readings. Generic interpretations are of course context-dependent and prone to numerous readings, including non-generic ones. Nonetheless, there are some exceptions where an indefinite form would indicate a generic reading without the possibility for different interpretations:

(15) Un lapin albinos est en voie d'extinction (l'albinos des Pyrénées).
      A   rabbit albino is   on way to extinction (the albino of the Pyrenees).
      The albino rabbit is about to go extinct (the albino of the Pyrenees).
      (Galmiche 1985: 9)

The 'albino rabbit' in the sentence above is understood generically as it is a subspecies. Therefore, one can imagine saying that 'a rabbit species' [*une espèce de lapin*], namely the albino of the Pyrenees, is about to go extinct (Galmiche 1985: 9). It is worth mentioning that in English one would rather opt for a definite form when talking about subspecies (Mari et al. 2013b: 77), but both indefinite and definite forms are substitutable in such contexts (cf. Lyons [1977: 196]).

A particular type of generic NPs are the so-called well-established kinds (WEKs). Another category that is closely connected to WEKs are familiar nouns. Even though some familiar nouns may be WEKs, the two notions are sometimes used synonymously.

The interpretation of WEKs and familiar nouns is very much dependent on one's language intuition, the context in which the noun appears, and the predicate in a given sentence (cf. e.g. Pettersson 1976; Carlsson 2012). Thus, the notion of a well-established kind is not a well-established concept itself. Such NPs are regarded as familiar to the speakers of a given language, which can be the result of either one's general knowledge or the cultural context one lives in (different cultures might have different WEKs and familiar nouns). As cited Borthen (2007: 156 [Gundel et al. 1993]) puts it:

> [t]he notion of being 'well-established' is a bit vague in the existing literature, but it seems reasonable to assume that *well-established* means *familiar* in the sense of GHZ (1993).

The publication mentioned by Borthen refers to the so-called Givenness Hierarchy (Borthen 2007: 144). In short, the classification allows English NPs to be identified, according to their grammatical form (emphasis added):

in focus > activated > **familiar** > uniquely identifiable > referential > type identifiable

Each of the descriptions presented in the model above receive a certain cognitive interpretation, e.g. familiarity is described as the ability to re-call a representation of an object from one's memory, based on discourse (Borthen 2007: 144). Familiarity is perceived by Borthen on a par with being well-established. Both notions are connected to speakers' knowledge about the world and their ability to interpret the discourse.

In English, familiar nouns are definite singular, as in the examples in (16) (Borthen 2007: 148):

(16) a. *The coke bottle* has a narrow neck.
      b. *The blue whale* is the largest animal on earth.
      c. Bell invented *the telephone.*

'The coke bottle' and 'the blue whale' are examples of noun phrases that function as kinds, whereas 'the telephone' can be understood both as a concept of the device and a specific reference, depending on the context. In Norwegian such nouns are definite (singular or plural) but they can also occur as bare nouns.

2.2. Generic sentences and generic terms

The opposition between generic sentences and generic phrases was introduced by Behrens in her work on the typological aspects of genericity. The two notions are applied in a slightly different manner, opening them up to a broader and more precise analysis of generics, without classifying characterising sentences as non-generic (Behrens 2005: 288–289).

The argument often used against analysing habitual sentences as generics is that the characteristics expressed in them often concern individuals, rather than whole kinds. This way, characterising sentences cannot be analysed as generic, as they do not state anything about kinds – only about some, or even one member of a given group. Behrens calls this a broad sense of genericity (Behrens 2005: 289). In order to also account for those sentences, she then proposes a *broad* approach in which the notion *generic phrase* is used. Generic phrases are not bound by any syntactic restrictions (Behrens 2005: 289) and could therefore be used in all instances that are not considered *classic* generic phrases, namely kind-referring phrases.

Generic phrases, according to Behrens, can, but do not have to, occur with kind predicates such as *be extinct* and *be rare*. They can also occur with predicates that presumably are not generic but in certain contexts do acquire a generic reading, as in the examples below:

(17) a. Polar bears are mammals.   (kind predicate)
      b. Polar bears are dangerous.   (non-generic predicate)

The fact of being dangerous can be used in both specific and generic reference. In specific reference it indicates that somebody or something is dangerous at the moment of speaking about it [non-generic predicate]. Used with a kind-referring expression, the predicate – still being non-generic – expresses a generalisation over most or all members of the kind, as in Example 17b. On the contrary, being a mammal is not a feature that can be acquired for a certain period of time or that can apply only to some entities of a given kind.

Generic sentences and phrases discussed by Behrens (2005) are not new notions in research on genericity. Since the very beginning of such research, linguists have brought about a number of notions with quite a similar meaning. Carlson (1982), for instance, refers to generic terms and generic sentences (Carlson 1982: 145). Carlson perceives generic sentences in a similar way as Behrens does, namely as *classic* kind references. Carlson (1982: 145) does seem to differentiate between kind-referring sentences and habitual sentences, proposing various notions used in philosophy and linguistics to describe them. Nevertheless, the examples proposed by Carlson are rather generic sentences in the classic meaning of the term, whereas habitual sentences are perceived as a separate category.

Likewise, the notion *generic terms*, coined by Carlson, seems to be synonymous with generic NPs and kind-denoting NPs. As examples of generic terms, Carlson lists 'dogs', 'mountains', and 'unfriendly policemen' (Carlson 1982: 146). He then discusses whether it is plausible to say that generic terms denote kinds or, citing Twardowski, *genera* (Carlson 1982: 146).

Generic terms cannot be perceived as notions that exclusively denote kinds. Carlson and other researchers have pointed out that this would imply, for instance, that the term *dogs* holds for all dogs in the world, not allowing any exceptions (Carlson 1982: 146). This, as we have seen in (6c), is a false approach. Moreover, perceiving generic terms as solely denoting kinds would mean that there are categories devoted to generics only. In none of the languages studied so far has such a category been found (cf. Behrens 2005).

Carlson (1982: 148) points out that even though kind predicates can only be attributed to kinds and not to members of a given kind, this does not mean that generic terms denote. However, predicates do not divide in only two categories (kind denoting and *regular*). They do express rather complex semantic relationships, such as the ones in the examples below:

(18)   a.   Dogs are mammals. (*all*)
       b.   Dogs eat meat. (*most*)
       c.   Dogs give milk to their young. (weaker than *most*) (Carlson 1982: 148)

Examples such as those in (18) will be discussed further in the following sections of this chapter. It is worth mentioning here that throughout this book the notions of *generic terms, kind-denoting NPs,* and *generic NPs* will be treated as synonyms. As stated above, after *The Generic Book* was published a number of studies were conducted. However, many researchers still utilise different notions to refer to the same concept. When quoting or making references to these studies I follow the original terminology (as above in the description of Carlson's discussion on generic terms and sentences), but the preferred notions used in this research are kind-denoting NPs and generic NPs.

Generic terms are also said to function similarly to proper names, especially in 'so-called' constructions (Carlson 1982: 150). The examples in (20) sound awkward because they do not contain proper names, whereas the sentences in (19) are correct (Carlson 1982: 150). The same concerns generic terms: in certain sentences non-generic terms would sound awkward, just like the examples below without proper names do.

(19) a. Giorgione is so-called because of his size.
      b. Cardinals are so-called because of their colour.
      c. Machine guns are so-called because they fire automatically.

(20) a. The man over there is so-called because he is over there.
      b. Most machine guns are so-called because they fire automatically.
      c. All devilfish are so-called because of their satanic appearance.

In his analysis Carlson also discusses kind-denoting predicates, mentioning that they do not need to occur in sentences with natural kinds or nominal kinds (Carlson 1982: 153). On the contrary, they are restricted to kinds and cannot denote members of kinds.

The notions *generic sentences*, *generic phrases*, and *generic terms* are closely related and their application in generic constructions are also similar. Generic sentences, as stated both by Behrens and Carlson, are sentences that express generalisations – either about kinds (*classic* generics) or about individuals (habitual sentences, also called characterising sentences). *Generic terms* are a notion utilised by Carlson concerning NPs that denote kinds, such as 'dogs' or 'cats'. *Generic phrase*, on the contrary, is a term coined and used by Behrens. It concerns phrases used in habitual sentences, which are also considered generic.

2.2.1. Generic anaphora

Genericity can be expressed not only in statements that contain generic NPs or kind-restricted predicates. The phenomenon can occur also in anaphoric expressions, which can be generic. Carlson (1977: 425) mentions generic anaphora in examples such as the sentences in (21):

(21) a. Kelly is seeking a unicorn, and Millie is seeking *it*, too.
      b. Kelly is seeking a unicorn, and Millie is seeking *one*, too.
      c. Queenie is seeking *unicorns*, and Phil is seeking *them*, too.

The examples above illustrate that both the indefinite singular form and the bare plural form can serve as antecedents in anaphoric expressions, as well as those which are interpreted generically. In his further discussion Carlson mainly analyses the use of bare plurals (BPs) in this function, showing that not all expressions of this kind are interpreted in the same manner. The opposition is particularly visible when it comes to transparent and opaque readings.[7] Referential opacity is also present in generic anaphora, where the pronouns may refer to their generic counterparts but could also convey transparent readings. The nature of the antecedent determines what kind of reading a statement has. For instance, an antecedent that is a mass noun, such as 'furniture' in (22) favours an opaque reading, whereas the antecedent from (21a) does not (Carlson 1977: 425–426).

(22) Cedrick is seeking furniture, and Hiram is seeking *it*, too.

Even though the anaphoric expression in (22) might be seen as referring to the same piece of furniture that Cedrick is seeking, this is not the case (Carlson 1977: 426). Example 21c, on the other hand, refers rather to the activity of searching for unicorns than looking for a particular group of such animals. The BP 'unicorns' is a generic antecedent and the pronoun 'them' therefore has a generic reference.

---

[7] The notion of referential opacity was coined by Quine (2013) in his seminal work, entitled 'Word and Object'. Referential opacity is presented as a way of interpreting expressions. The reading of a given expression can be either opaque or transparent. If the reading is opaque it implies that the expression is ambiguous to some extent and can be interpreted in more than one way, depending on the speakers intentions and knowledge (Quine 2013: 131).

According to Carlson (1977: 432), 'a generic may serve felicitously as antecedent for an existential'. The examples of generic anaphora in such contexts are numerous and he provides some (Carlson 1977: 433):

(23) a. My mother hates *raccoons* because *they* stole her sweet corn last summer.

   b. *Raccoons* have stolen my mother's sweet corn every year, so she hates *them* a lot.

(24) a. My brother thinks *snakes* are nasty creatures, but that hasn't stopped me from having *them* as pets my whole life.

   b. I've had *snakes* as pets my whole life, but my brother still thinks *they*'re nasty creatures.

(25) a. Martha told me that *beans* don't grow as well in this climate, but *they* grew well for me last year.

   b. *Beans* grew quite well for me last season in spite of Martha's warning that *they* can't grow in this climate.

(26) a. I didn't believe that *goats* liked *tin cans* until I actually saw *them* eating *them* last week.

   b. Before I actually *saw* goats eating tin cans last week, I didn't believe *they* liked *them*.

What all the sentences above have in common is the fact that in each of them the generic noun phrase serves as the antecedent for the anaphoric expression. The examples contain indefinite plural forms which, according to Carlson and many other researchers in the field, are the most frequently used generic nouns.

2.3. Generic texts

In analyses on genericity, two linguistic levels are usually taken into account, namely the NP level and the sentence level discussed above. Behrens (2005) proposes a new level of analysis: generic texts. Generic texts present generalised knowledge about kind or a particular stereotypical situation (Behrens 2005: 289). In generic texts one finds more generic noun phrases than in non-generic texts, but

[t]his does not imply that a generic text contains only generic sentences of the classical type or that every mention of a linguistics expression allowing reference to the topic of a generic text is in actual fact to be interpreted as a generic NP. (Behrens 2005: 290)

The fact that generics are present in a given text, e.g. in a novel, does not mean that the whole text is therefore generic. Since generic texts state generalisations over kinds or refer to stereotypical situations, it is rather non-fiction texts that contain numerous generic sentences. Nevertheless, this is not the rule. Behrens (2005) herself has analysed a fiction text, namely *Le Petit Prince*, in French, English, German, Hungarian, and Greek. This proves well that even literary texts can be considered generic, even though this genre is not usually recognised as generic by its nature. A number of Swedish generic texts were analysed by Carlsson (2012). The texts utilised for the analysis on genericity in Swedish were encyclopaedia texts about natural kinds.

In her study on genericity Behrens proposed two approaches, namely heuristic and interpretative ambiguity tests. The first approach is the one often used in the analysis of individual sentences and in corpus-based studies. The researchers base their judgements on their own linguistic intuition (Behrens 2005). This approach is quite common and can be found in most works on genericity, for instance in Carlson's and Chierchia's analyses, as well as in *The Generic Book* and the like.

The interpretative approach is a strategy used in survey-based studies (Behrens 2005: 291), such as this one. It requires that the researchers consult native speakers of a given language and take into account their judgement of generics. In this project I apply both strategies, heuristic in the case of the corpus and interpretative in the case of the surveys. An interpretative ambiguity test is often based on actual utterances, not necessarily sentences created for the sake of analysis. This way the respondents' judgements can be analysed as those occurring in a spoken language.

The approach proposed by Behrens is new in two ways. First of all, the third linguistic level, separate from the NP level and the sentence level, was not considered in previous analyses. Generic texts defined by Behrens allow linguists to study genericity in a wider context than a noun phrase or a sentence. The second innovative aspect is the approach to the analysis itself. One can either analyse sentences based one's own language intuition, ask native speakers of a given language for judgement, or combine the two strategies.

2.4. Formal and modal approaches to genericity

The notions described in previous sections and the classification of generic sentences into two main types (kind-referring and habitual sentences) are parts of the formal paradigm of genericity proposed and developed by the researchers from the Generic Group and their successors. The approach they proposed is very complex, and an exhaustive description of these theories lies outside the scope of this work. I will briefly characterise the main assumptions of the formal and modal theories, since this paradigm has served as the foundation for all modern accounts of genericity.

The Generic Book, published in 1995, was the first compilation of the existing research on genericity. The work standardised and unified the terminology that had been in use from the 1970s. Moreover, the work of Carlson and Pelletier (1995) was a milestone in the research on the subject, as it also developed new theories and approaches whilst taking into account older assumptions. This section consists of two main parts, in which I will discuss the Carlsonian approaches to genericity (started by Carlson in his numerous publications on the matter and continued later by others) and the neo-Carlsonian theories (introduced by Chierchia and others) that arose in the years after *The Generic Book* was first published.

Both Carlsonian and neo-Carlsonian approaches are based on the Logical Form (LF) and are considered to be of a rather formal character. The theories are also said to be modal, as they often propose models for analysis of generic utterances which are perceived to be quantificational in nature (Lazaridou-Chatzigoga et al. 2015: 470).

Since there are numerous models and operators connected to the semantics of genericity, I shall only focus on the most acknowledged ones and those that are considered somehow *classic* in the literature on the subject. The main focus of this thesis is the cognitive approach to genericity in language, and I will not apply LF analysis in my research. Nonetheless, the achievements of Carlson, Chierchia, and their successors are crucial in understanding the phenomenon.

2.4.1. Carlsonian theories

Many of the theories on genericity are based on Carlson's work, starting in 1977, when the article entitled *A unified analysis of the English bare plural* was published. Later, Carlson took up the issues of temporal expressions and genericity (Carlson 1979), generic terms and sentences (Carlson 1982), and the logical form of generic utterances (Carlson 1983). All these papers and theories have contributed to the major study on genericity, namely the publication of *The Generic Book*.

Carlson's take on genericity relies greatly on phonologically null generic operators, such as *Gn* (Carlson 1977, 1982), which was later developed into the widely used and acknowledged GEN operator (see e.g. Carlson, Pelletier 1995; Mari et al. 2013b). In short, both the Gn operator and GEN can be assigned to a given predicate in order to obtain a generic reading, as shown in the examples below (Krifka et al. 1995: 22):

(27) a. John smokes.   Gn(smoke)(John)
      b. Italians smoke.   Gn(smoke)(Italians)
      c. Italians know French.   Gn(know.French)(Italians)

In his seminal work from 1977, Carlson mainly analyses the generics of English bare plurals, but a short description of other NP types in such contexts is also given. For instance, the hypothesis is made that the indefinite singular form with the article 'a'/'an' might, in certain contexts, function as a counterpart of bare plurals. In order to support for this, Carlson gives examples of generic sentences where both noun forms can be used and interpreted in a similar manner (Carlson 1977: 415):

(28) a. *A mammal* bears live young.
      b. *Mammals* bear live young.

Later in his work, he explains that such a hypothesis might be neglected and that BPs 'cannot be plural of "a"' (Carlson 1977: 429). The assumption was later discussed by numerous linguists and agreed upon, for instance, by Mari et al. (2013b: 25):

kind-referring definite singulars in languages like English are **not** trivial variants of kind-referring bare plurals. (emphasis added)

In Carlson's analysis from 1977, the opacity phenomena were introduced. The notion of referential opacity, as mentioned before, was first introduced by Quine and was discussed by numerous linguists afterwards (see e.g. Lyons

1977: 192). Carlson analyses *opaque* sentences, the meaning of which can be ambiguous, as in the example below:

(29)   Minnie wishes to talk with a young psychiatrist. (Carlson 1977: 417)

The opacity of Sentence 29 (the opaque reading) makes it impossible to interpret it in only one way. A recipient might then presume that Minnie wishes to speak with *any* psychiatrist, as long as it is a young psychiatrist. When the transparent reading of Sentence 29 is taken, though, Minnie might in fact have in mind a particular psychiatrist she wishes to speak to (Carlson 1977: 417).

Sentence 29, according to Carlson, can have at least two different semantic structures:

(30)   a.   (Epl x) (young psych. (x) & M. wishes M. talk with x)
        b.   M. wishes (Epl. (x) (young psych. (x) & M. talk with x)

where (30a) represents the transparent reading and (30b) shows the opaque interpretation (Carlson 1977: 417). Interestingly, the use of the indefinite article 'a' in (29) does not in fact exclude a narrow meaning where Minnie has in mind one particular psychiatrist (Carlson 1977: 417).

One of the most important claims made by Carlson is that there is a semantic difference between individuals and the stages of individuals. His hypothesis was formulated as follows:

The stages aren't simply the things that *are*; they are more akin to things that *happen*. That is, stages are conceived as being much more closely related to events than to objects. (Carlson 1977: 448)

'Stages' are closely connected and perhaps even synonymous to 'properties' (Carlson 1977: 448-449), as they both characterise an individual but are not a part of it. These can be observed in the examples in (31), where different stages (properties) of Jack are listed.

(31)   a.   Jack is intelligent.
        b.   Jack is tall.
        c.   Jack likes wine.

As can be seen, the fact of being intelligent, tall, or liking wine does not mean that without those features Jack would not be Jack. Those are therefore only his stages, which can last for a period of time, be applicable at any time, or even be replaced by other stages. Such an approach to analysing generic sentences might suggest that genericity can in fact occur both at the NP level (individual) and at the sentence level (stages of individual). Since stages relate to events, one might suppose that these will appear in habitual sentences, rather than in kind-referring sentences, where generic NPs denote kinds seen as individuals in Carlson's analysis.

In his later work, Carlson further modified the theory and also focussed on atemporal clauses with 'when', such as in the examples below:

(32) a. Giraffes are intelligent when they are tall.
      b. Cats are intelligent when they have blue eyes. (Carlson 1979: 52)

Even though the sentences in (32) may sound awkward to speakers of English, the use of 'when' does not exclude a generic reading of them. Carlson (1979) discusses the existence of what he calls 'a generic verb phrase operator' which seems to exclude any temporal references from sentences such as those in (32). A number of restrictions are given in order to support the atemporal 'when' hypothesis and analysis. The restrictions concern the structure of the main clause, the use of NPs, and the generic interpretation (Carlson 1979: 51–53).

An interesting claim made by Carlson in his work from 1979 is that he sees kinds 'not as being sets of objects, as is commonly supposed, but rather as being individuals themselves' (Carlson 1979: 54). Another category of entities was also proposed, namely stages, which Carlson calls subtypes of entities and 'time-space slices of individuals' (Carlson 1979: 54). Such an approach was novel in many ways, mostly because most researchers perceived – and still do perceive – kinds as collections of individuals.

For each of the claims made, Carlson proposes semantic structures that illustrate the theory. Apart from the LF, he makes and confirms a number of hypotheses in the paper, one of them being the claim that most predicates apply to stages and to kinds themselves (Carlson 1979: 56). His main focus falls on the generic operators, which influence the reading of a given sentence. If the operator is present, a generic reading is preferred, whereas the lack of the Gn operator in a sentence suggests a specific or *event-type* reading.

The theory of the Gn operator accounts for ambiguities of sentences which can arise when the generic reading is unavailable in a given context. In this sense, a generic reading seems to be more straightforward than a non-generic one. This dependency is best seen in the semantic structures proposed by Carlson, where the presence or absence of the Gn operator allows one to interpret a given sentence in a generic or non-generic way. Interestingly enough, cognitive linguists also seem to be searching for the difference between these two readings, though by the use of different tools. Instead of marking genericity at the semantic level, cognitive approaches focus on the speakers' language intuitions (see Section 2.5.).

In yet another of his works, an article from 1982, Carlson delves further into the matter of generic sentences. This time it is not only the semantic structure of an NP or a DP that is taken into account, but a much wider scope in which generics are analysed as a sentence-level phenomenon. The two main issues of this study are 1) the interpretation of generic terms and 2) the truth-conditions of generic sentences (Carlson 1982: 145). Such an approach lends a more ontological character to the study, which is also one of the main features of most formal theories of generics.

The truth value of a given generic sentence is certainly important when interpreting it, but it does not exclude a generic meaning. This means that if a generic claim is made, such as that in (1) – assigning a feature of barking to all or most dogs – the claim can still be considered generic even if it does not hold for each and every dog in the world. Carlson himself points out that one can easily find an exception to the rule that, for instance, all dogs bark, and yet most people would still be willing to ascribe the feature *dog* to a non-barking individual of the kind *Canis lupus familiaris* (Carlson 1982: 147).

Another point that Carlson makes is that some predicates cannot occur in a sentence with individual objects, but can only refer to whole kinds. These were mentioned before as kind-referring predicates – predicates that can only describe the whole species. In contrast to those, another type of predicate is discussed, namely the one that refers to less than 50% of a kind – a minority – and is yet used generically. An example of such a predicate can be 'to give milk', as in the example below:

(33)   Dogs give milk to their young. (Carlson 1982: 148)

Even though it is only female dogs at a certain age and under certain situations, Sentence 33 would be interpreted as generic by most speakers.

A similar issue was discussed by Leslie et al. (2011) in their study on the Generic Overgeneralisation (GOG) effect (see Section 2.5.3.), where the sentence 'Ducks lay eggs' was given as an example of GOG.

Another issue discussed by Carlson are kind-denoting terms and entity-denoting terms. All predicates that can apply to entity-denoting terms will also apply to kind-denoting terms as each entity is a part of a kind (Carlson 1982: 158).

The ambiguity concerning the use of different tenses in generic sentences is presented in the examples below:

(34)   a.   Dogs barked.
      b.   Dogs bark.
      c.   Dogs will bark. (Carlson 1982: 165)

Each of the sentences above has a generic reading and it is only the situation in which they could be uttered that accounts for their meaning. For instance, in (34a) the use of past tense might suggest an episodic reading or, if the species was extinct, a generic reading. Sentence 34b is the *classic* generic example, whereas (34c) could have been uttered before the kind 'dog' existed and if somebody was able to predict the future and state that dogs will be able to bark (highly improbable truth-conditions, but a possible generic reading).

All sentences in (34) are habitual sentences – the type that by some linguists are considered generic; these, according to Carlson, can be analysed in a similar matter as kind-referring sentences:

> the analysis of generics should, if possible, be assimilated to the analysis of habitual sentences (to the point where we treat generics and habituals as subclasses of a more general category we will call *gnomic* sentences.) (Carlson 1982: 165)

Even though Carlson's claims from his early work seem to be well-grounded, the theory has evolved and Carlson himself introduced minor changes and new aspects. In an article from 1983 he focussed on the LF of natural kinds and nominal kinds. The former were described as either subsets or supersets, where all entities share exactly same features. *Nominal kinds*, on the other hand, are seen as group of entities, the majority of which share a given feature (Carlson 1983: 300). Predicates that refer to natural kinds must therefore be true for all individuals of that group, for instance, the predicate 'to be a mammal' will be true for all cats, whereas the predicate 'to have four legs' might refer to a majority of that kind but not necessarily to each and every individual.

Theories including generic operators were further developed and modified by other researchers from the Generic Group. The work of Chierchia, which will be discussed in greater detail in the next section, has contributed to the development of the neo-Carlsonian theories. This proves that Carlson's original claim, even though slightly modified and proved insufficient for a comprehensive analysis, has remained an important element of the study on generics. As Mari et al. (2013b: 8) summarised, 'Carlson's analysis is very elegant: it presents a unified analysis of English bare plurals and predicts the correct existential and generic readings.'

Carlson's approach to genericity can indeed be seen as *elegant*, but recent research has shown that the formal analysis might not be sufficient when it comes to interpreting generic sentences in different contexts. Since formal and modal approaches focus mainly on sentences constructed for purposes of the analyses, they do not take into consideration the wider context of the utterances, nor do they account for different possible readings that depend highly on the context (Lazaridou-Chatzigoga et al. 2015: 471). This does not mean however that modern approaches to genericity can neglect the achievements of formal linguists. It is in fact quite the opposite:

> [T]he literature on the processing and acquisition of genericity has often ignored or misrepresented the relevant linguistic analyses and stands to benefit from the wealth of insights and the systematicity found in the theoretical linguistics literature. (Lazaridou-Chatzigoga et al. 2015: 471)

The theories presented in the preceding section are much more complex and this short description was certainly not meant to exhaust the subject. For a more detailed discussion of the Carlsonian approaches to genericity, see for instance Carlson and Pelletier (1995), Carlson (2010), Pelletier (2010), Mari et al. (2013a), Lazaridou-Chatzigoga et al. (2015), and others.

2.4.2. Neo-Carlsonian theories

The importance of Carlson's theories and approaches has motivated many researchers to develop and better adjust the claims so that new analyses and models may be introduced. The linguist who has contributed the most by far to the development of neo-Carlsonian theories is Chierchia. Since *The Generic*

Book was published Chierchia has continued his research, which in 1998 led to his seminal work on genericity, *Reference to kinds across languages* (1998).

One of the central points in Chierchia's analysis is its cross-linguistic perspective – something missing in Carlson's theoretical studies on genericity. Chierchia's interest falls on the role and functions of generic NPs in languages such as Chinese, English, Italian, and other Germanic and Slavic languages. Apart from this multilingual perspective, Chierchia follows Carlson in some ways and disagrees with him in others. Mari et al. (2013b: 9) have meticulously analysed the differences between Carlsonian and neo-Carlsonian approaches.

There are quite a few differences between Chierchia's approach to genericity and Carlson's. I shall briefly analyse the neo-Carlsonian theories started by Chierchia in 1998, focussing on the main differences between the two contrasting views, as they were pointed out by Mari et al. (2013b).

The main element of Chierchia's study is the Nominal Mapping Parameter. Put simply, the theory of the Nominal Mapping Parameter concerns the features of an NP that allow it to denote certain objects or groups of objects. When a given NP denotes an individual, *clusterings* of these denoted objects are created in the semantic structure (Chierchia 1998: 358). As Chierchia points out, depending on the language under analysis, a given NP can create different clusterings. A particular mapping parameter might be considered characteristic of one language group, and a different one for another language:

> Given certain assumptions on the nature of the domain of quantification, minimal changes on what NPs can denote (which we will call the 'Nominal Mapping Parameter') lead one to expect certain clusterings of properties of bare nominal arguments. Such clusterings appear to be exactly what differentiates important language families. (Chierchia 1998: 358)

According to Chierchia, the Nominal Mapping Parameter and the neo-Carlsonian approach could solve the issue of BPs' ambiguity in English. The ambiguity is that English BPs can denote kinds (see Sentence 1: *Dogs bark*) and they can favour a specific reading of a given utterance (such as *Dogs are in the garden*). The generic interpretation of BPs is the one suggested by Carlson. The second reading, a specific one, is also possible but depends highly on the context.

Chierchia's work appeared exactly 20 years after Carlson's seminal paper on genericity. The differences that emerge from Chierchia's view in comparison to the original theory by Carlson are therefore apparent, especially when it comes to the understanding and analysis of English kind-referring NPs. Chierchia points out the main differences between the neo-Carlsonian approaches and suggests that most objections to the Carlsonian model can be rejected when it comes to the neo-Carlsonian approach thanks to the new analysis model.

First of all, Chierchia allows for the generic use of definite article in his analysis, calling it Singular Generic 'The' (Chierchia 1998: 379). He agrees that the singular definite form of a noun might well be interpreted generically, for instance in Sentences 35a and 35b:

(35) a. The tiger is rare.
      b. The tiger roars. (Chierchia 1998: 379)

This assumption is proven by the fact that both sentences are correct and considered natural for English speakers. As Chierchia himself points out, a corresponding mechanism was also observed by Krifka et al. (1995), where the main focus of generic definite nouns concerns the WEKs.

The use of the definite form is justified by Chierchia and depicted in his analysis model with the use of generic operators. He proposes his own analysis models and operators, which do not stem from Carlson's analysis but which do rely heavily on his main assumption, namely that generic sentences always have phonologically null operators in their semantic structures. Since Chierchia's analysis methods are based on Universal Grammar and LF, I shall not delve further into the matter here.

On the contrary, the use of a plural definite form would not be possible in such sentences, as that would imply an episodic reading, which normally does not occur with kind-predicates such as 'be rare':

(36) a. *The tigers are rare.
      b. *The tigers roar.

As shown in the examples above, English, unlike the Romance languages, 'has the definite article, but disallows generic or kind-oriented uses of it' (Chierchia 1998: 393). As we shall see in the following sections and chapters, Norwegian seems to accept definite plural forms in generic sentences, even though such uses of definite forms are rare and reserved for certain types of NPs.

As has been mentioned before, Chierchia's paper can be seen as ground-breaking, mostly because of its cross-linguistic approach, which seemed to confirm the correctness of the proposed theory. Contrasting approaches to genericity in Germanic (English) and Romance (Italian) languages are presented, as well as a brief reference to Chinese and Russian. Such a wide perspective provides the reader with a broader scope of Chierchia's study, as well as the evolution of the Carlsonian approach in favour of the new hypotheses and theories.

2.5. Cognitive approach to genericity

The cognitive approach to genericity has made it possible to study the phenomenon in many different languages, very often in a form of cross-linguistic studies and with the focus on the cognitive status of generics (e.g. the theory of 'generics as default' coined by Leslie). When it comes to formal and modal theories presented in the previous sections, most of them concerned widely-studied languages and might therefore not be fully compatible with other language groups. Cognitive linguists have proved that a more psychological approach allows for a much broader perspective in research, which has resulted in various studies being published, not only on English but also, for instance, Mandarin Chinese (see e.g. Gelman and Tardif 1998) or Polish (Karczewski 2016), among many other languages. In the following sections I shall focus on the notion of a generic reference as it is understood by cognitive linguists and presented in numerous publications on English and other languages. Since this study is based on both surveys and a corpus analysis, a wide scope of approaches is needed in order to structure the data collection and the analysis. However, the cognitive analysis remains the main core of the projects and is only complemented by quantitative methods.

The cognitive view on generics has been described in many studies, one of them being Lakoff's book *Women, Fire and Dangerous Things* (1990). The author proposes his own view on genericity, as well as focuses on many cognitive publications on the subject, referring for instance to Eleanor Rosch and her theory on categorisation. Lakoff himself perceives categories as structures that should be correlated with one's conceptual systems (Lakoff 1990: 58). Such systems, as shall be presented in this book, can be captured in a form of models that provide a set of *default* generic contexts. Genericity is also one of the categories that functions in a language and in one's cognition. Creating a model of generics can therefore help to understand how the phenomenon is presented both from a cognitive and a linguistic point of view.

Understanding a reference as generic does not necessarily mean that the whole kind or all of its members possess a given feature. The cognitive approach to categories and generics allows for prototypes, which are understood as *best examples* of a given feature (Lakoff 1990: 41). In other words, generic meaning can be achieved by referring to a single member of a kind or a single event. Such references create prototypes which are representative and can be used to make generic generalisations.

The theory of prototypes is closely connected to the mechanism of categorisation. Categories can be understood in a very classic sense when they group people, objects or event in certain categories based on the similarities between given objets. However, the cognitive research on categorisation has showed that categories are always coded for a given language and a given culture, rather than being universal for all languages and cultures (Rosch 1978: 28). Rosch says that *maximum information with least cognitive effort is achieved if categories map the perceived world structure as closely as possible* (Rosch 1978: 28). Categories are aligned with one's cognitive systems, language knowledge and culture a person identifies with. This approach is particularly useful when analysing genericity in different languages.

As shall be presented in the following chapters of this book, Norwegian generics are often expressed with the NP types that are not associated with genericity in other related languages (e.g. definite plural in English and German). This shows that certain categories, such as some plants (see Chapters 5 and 7), are categorised in a given way, according to the cultural and linguistic taxonomy, rather than the biological one. Models presenting different generic contexts and their representation in Norwegian are be provided in Chapters 5, 6 and 7.

In the following parts of this chapter, a cognitive approach to genericity will be presented, with a special focus on the theories proposed by Radden and Driven (2007), Pettersson (1976) and Leslie (2011).

2.5.1. Understanding the generic reference

As mentioned before, genericity can be understood in two ways—as a classic generic reference to kinds and as habituals. In cognitive linguistics, generics and habituals are considered to be very similar when it comes to their meaning, since they do not refer to any particular kinds or events but rather describe generalisations about given kinds and events (Langacker 1997: 192).

In his study, Langacker proposes that events or features limited to a single member should be considered as habituals, whereas those referring to kinds as generics (1997: 195). This view is coherent with the earliest theories on genericity and the classic approach to the notion (see previous sections of this chapter). In the following parts of this chapter, I shall focus on a few cognitive models of genericity in order to create a theoretical framework for the analyses presented in Chapters 4–7.

Radden and Dirven (2007) propose a model of different types of reference, where both the indefinite and the definite forms are listed as generic. According to them, generic reference in English can only be expressed with four different NP types, excluding bare nouns (BNs). The examples provided in this model can be found in (37).

(37) a. the life of a tiger   (indefinite singular)
      b. Boys don't cry.   (indefinite plural)
      c. The tiger has stripes.   (definite singular)
      d. The poor suffer.   (definite plural)

The proposed model does not apply to all Germanic languages. Norwegian, for instance, seems to follow that pattern only to some extent – singular and plural forms of generic nouns are allowed, but so are BNs, which are not taken into account in the paradigm proposed by Radden and Dirven (2007).

One of the most crucial claims of cognitive grammar when it comes to generic references, is that categories differ from classes (Radden and Dirven 2007: 106). Categories are seen as abstract representations of kinds, whereas classes are actual, physical entities. Moreover, both classes and categories have their members. Members of a category are all sub-kinds, as 'Bengal tiger' and 'Siberian tiger' belong to the category 'tiger' (Radden and Dirven 2007: 106). When it comes to members of a class, those are all individual entities of a given group; for example, each and every dog on this planet can be considered a member of the class 'dogs'.

Radden and Dirven compare generic reference to specific reference (called also individuative reference), where a speaker must select an entity from the world of categories and make a mental connection to it. In the case of generic reference, that entity is the whole kind (Radden and Dirven 2007: 106).

One of the main characteristics of a category in a generic sense is that all or most of its members should share the majority of the features typical of that category. This would be, as Radden and Dirven call it, an ideal situation. Nevertheless, it is very rarely the case. Generic references are often subjected to overgeneralisations, which means that a feature which is characteristic of only half or less of the population tends to be assigned to the whole species, as presented in the examples below:

(38) a. Mammals give milk to their young.
      b. Ducks lay eggs.

Radden and Dirven point out that generic reference is, from a grammatical point of view, not very different from individuative reference since all languages that have been studied to date seem to be using the same referring expressions when talking about kinds as they do when referring to specific objects. This claim has been confirmed by all linguists in the research on genericity.

Further in their analysis, Radden and Dirven give a short description of each of the NP types used in generic contexts. They stress the fact that not all of the forms convey the same meaning and that their individuative counterparts also bear different semantic functions.

Indefinite singular generic

The indefinite singular generic is a counterpart to individuative reference when used in this form. It is then *an element for its class*, meaning it is an entity that bears the features of the whole class but can be referred to with the use of the singular noun form. The similarity is that in both individuative and generic references, a speaker must select an entity that he has in mind in order to refer to it (Radden and Dirven 2007: 108). In the case of generic reference, that entity is the whole kind, for instance all birds or all Italians, as shown in the examples below:

(39) a. A bird has a beak, wings, and feathers.
      b. An Italian is a native, citizen, or inhabitant of Italy.
      c. ? An Italian is fond of children.

Examples 39a and 39b are perfectly correct, whereas Example 39c sounds rather awkward. The reason for this is that the first two examples capture the *essence* of the whole group. Assigning this essence to one entity from a given group does not exclude the generic reading (Radden and Dirven 2007: 108). The third sentence, on the contrary, cannot be seen as correct since being fond of children is not considered an *essence* of all Italian people. However, the interpretation of whether or not something is considered an essence of a person/object depends very much on the context, as well as on one's world view and even general knowledge. Example 39c does not suggest that being fond of children is a characteristic feature of a given nation, as such features are often stereotypes connected with a given culture (e.g. being fond of pizza, gesturing while speaking, etc.). Furthermore, the essence might not be interpreted in exactly the same way by all speakers of a given language.

Some predicates can only be used with generic NPs, for instance, 'be extinct', 'be rare', 'be numerous', and others. It is therefore important to note here that English indefinite singular nouns cannot occur with kind-predicates, as such predicates can only refer to absolutely all members of a category, not merely some or even the majority (Radden and Dirven 2007: 108). That is also why the sentences in (40) cannot be considered correct or even acceptable in the English language:

(40)   a.   * A sparrow is extinct.
       b.   * A dog is rare.
       c.   * A tiger is numerous.

Kind-predicates can occur with a singular form of a noun, but it needs to be the definite form and even then the use of such constructions is quite limited. Radden and Dirven (2007: 108) give an example of a subspecies such as 'the Balinese tiger' in Sentence 41:

(41)   The Balinese tiger has been extinct for 50 years.

Indefinite plural generic

In generic reference, the indefinite plural NP type represents *indeterminate elements for their class* (Radden and Dirven 2007: 108), namely some entities from a category, not necessarily all or the majority of them, which represent the whole category:

(42)   The large majority of *Italians* are Roman Catholics and for centuries, this
has affected their art. *Italians* are proud of their artistic heritage. (Radden
and Dirven 2007: 108)

The example above shows two different interpretations of BP, namely the
first sentence states it clearly that the fact of being Roman Catholic applies
to the vast majority of the population. The hearer will therefore assume that
it is not the whole nation that can be identified this way. In contrast, the
second sentence implies that being proud is somehow the essence of Italians.
As Radden and Dirven summerise it:

> People tend to generalise on the basis of relatively few experiences, and the in-
> definite plural provides the adequate referring expression to do so: it conveys
> generalisations based on vague, impressionistic judgements and allows for ex-
> ceptions. (Radden and Dirven 2007: 108–109)

Indefinite plural, called also for bare plural, is said to be the most common
NP type used in generic sentences (see for instance Carlson 1977; Krifka et al.
1995; Chierchia 1998; Mari et al. 2013a). As has been mentioned before, BPs
are most likely to be interpreted generically among all available NP types in
English but even despite this fact they are not free of ambiguities.

Definite singular generic

The definite singular form is seen by Radden and Dirven (2007: 109) as a 'prototypical element for the class as such' in generic contexts. It can, for instance,
refer to sub-kinds as we have seen in the section above, but the definite
singular is also seen as being somehow characteristic and representative of
the whole category that a speaker refers to.

Also in this case, individuative and generic references share some features,
namely they refer to particular entities. In individuative reference, that entity
is one element, known both by the speaker and the hearer, and in generic
reference that one particular entity is the whole kind (Radden and Dirven
2007: 109). Similar observations have been made by other scholars as well (see
e.g. Carlson 1977; Chierchia 1998).

Definite plural generic

The definite plural generics stand for 'many elements for their class' (Radden and Dirven 2007: 109). Compared to inviduative reference, which concerns all elements from a given set, definite plural generic reference makes a generalisation about, presumably, the majority of entities from a given group, but not necessarily the whole category (Radden and Dirven 2007: 110).

(43)   a.   *The Italians* are generally not inhibited when interacting with the opposite sex.
     b.   Football is the main national sport and *the Italians* are well known for their passion for this sport. Italy has won the World Cup four times.

Sentences 43a and 43b show how the definite plural form refers to the majority of individuals, making it a generalisation over the whole category of Italians. One must also bear in mind that this type of generic reference seems to be reserved for humans only and using definite plural form in order to refer to animals, plants, or objects might yield incorrect and/or awkward sounding utterances (Radden and Dirven 2007: 110).

Since 'people typically generalise on the basis of many individuals that share a salient attribute' (Radden and Dirven 2007: 110), the use of the plural definite form is possible: a generalisation does not need to apply to all members of the category to be understood generically by most speakers of a given language. Another particularity of this generic NP type is that it clearly allows for exceptions, whereas in individuative reference the use of this NP type does not:

(44)   a.   Open the boxes. = Open all of the boxes.
     b.   The Italians are friendly. = Most/ some/ all Italians are friendly.

Sentence 44a states clearly that all of the boxes a speaker refers to should be opened. Individuative reference makes it explicit with the use of the definite plural form, which normally does not allow for any exceptions. Sentence 44b, however, might mean that either most, some, or even all Italians are friendly and that the hearer is unable to judge how many Italians the speaker actually has in mind. Most likely, he or she has only met a few Italians, who turned out to be friendly people, and he or she made an assumption on this basis. Since the generalisation concerns humans and the sociocultural differences between them, such an utterance is considered perfectly clear and unambiguous (Radden and Dirven 2007: 110).

Another aspect of generic human groups is that they can be referred to with the use of adjectives, such as 'the poor', 'the old', or 'the young' (Radden and Dirven 2007: 110):

(45) a. *The old* are still running the country.
      b. *The young* will take over soon.

Both sentences refer to all members of the relevant category. Radden and Dirven (2007: 110) call this process the metonymy property of 'a thing for the thing', which will be discussed in more detail in the following section. In short, we can say that referring to 'the old' means in fact pointing out many members of the category, stating something about them and in this way creating a valid, generic reference. The same concerns Sentence 45b and any other utterance we can imagine where a generalisation over a human group would be made.

Interestingly enough, there seem to be a limited number of adjectives that can function that way. One cannot say, for instance, 'the happy', 'the new', or 'the thirsty' (Radden and Dirven 2007: 110).

Radden and Dirven (2007: 111) give an overview of all generic reference types and how they function. The indefinite singular form is an essential attribute that needs to be assigned to one particular entity in order for it to be understood generically and to represent the whole category. With the indefinite plural form, on the other hand, a speaker indicates many entities from a given category and assigns to them a characteristic feature. The feature does not need to apply to all members in order to be understood as generic. This is one of the main characteristics of the indefinite plural form in English. The BP form is most common in generic contexts, as has already been pointed out by numerous scholars.

The use of definite forms is slightly more restricted, however. The singular form is used either when a speaker talks about a distinctive attribute that can be assigned to a kind, or when the attribute concerns a sub-kind, such as the Balnese tiger mentioned in Example 41.

On the contrary, the plural definite form is reserved almost entirely for humans and it can be understood as a reference to *all* members a speaker might have in mind and not necessarily to all members of a given category, as such a generalisation would be difficult to make. When talking about humans one does not usually need to refer to all people in the world, but rather to different sociocultural groups inside the category 'human' – for instance, 'the Italians' mentioned in the examples before.

A similar categorisation of generic reference types was proposed by Pettersson (1976) in his work on definite and indefinite forms in Swedish. The model seems to align more with the Norwegian language, mainly due to the fact that bare nouns are presented as possible generic forms.

Pettersson divides generic nouns as either having the property 'limited +' [*begränsad +*] or lacking it [*begränsad –*]. Non-generic nouns are always specific (Pettersson 1976: 121) and those are associated with either an indefinite form or a bare plural. Non-specific reference can be rendered with a bare noun, which was not depicted in the model for English above. English and Mainland Scandinavian languages do share a lot of features, but what is correct and accepted in Scandinavian languages does not necessarily occur in English as well, as is the case with generic bare nouns.

The property depicted in the scheme as 'limited +' can be associated with definite nouns, whereas 'limited –' suggests indefiniteness. By using a definite noun, the speaker delimits the number of antecedents. This is not observed in the case of an indefinite noun (Pettersson 1976: 122).

The 'bare' form proposed by Pettersson occurs in the case of non-specific reference. This element was missing in the models presented above, which all concerned English. In Swedish – and Norwegian, as will be presented in the following chapters – the bare noun is quite frequent in generic contexts and not only in the case of uncountable nouns.

An interesting aspect can be also observed in the case of limited reference, both generic and non-generic – those are rendered with the use of definite forms. As has been seen before, definite plural generics in English are used exclusively to talk about people. However, this is not the case in Norwegian – or Swedish for that matter. The definite reference is still limited in its scope, but its usage is wider in Swedish and Norwegian than in English.

2.5.2. Metonymy and generics

In recent years, various works have been published on genericity, seen from a cognitive point of view. One of the seminal works on the topic, where different types of generic references were given, is the one by Radden (2009). In his study on generics in English, Radden proposes different analysis methods than those presented before in this chapter, namely 'a metonymic and conceptual blending analysis', and makes the three following claims:

1. Generic reference applies to types, where the type is invoked by way of an instance. Generic reference thus involves the metonymy instance for type.
2. The characterising type of generic reference allows for exceptions, i.e. it applies to a subtype of the type. Generic reference may thus also involve the metonymy type for subtype.
3. Generic reference involves the conceptual blending of instance and type. (Radden 2009: 202)

In Radden's analysis, generic NPs substitute either some, the majority of, or all members of a given category. As in his work from 2007, different types of generics are also considered with the emphasis on their conceptual role in semantics. Generic reference, as presented by Radden, is understood in a broader sense, not only as a kind-reference. As the author says himself, 'genericity is … much rather to be seen as forming a cline from full to marginal genericity' (Radden 2009: 199), indicating that both senses of the phenomenon, as discussed by Carlson and Pelletier (1995), are on the same spectrum.

Radden's claim that 'the type is invoked by way of an instance' implies that the singular instance influences the type and that both determine the generic meaning (Radden 2009: 204). This way the first claim can refer to kind-generics, where exceptions are not allowed: saying that a cat is a mammal implies that all cats are mammals, even though the feature was asserted to an instance only.

When it comes to individuative and generic references pointed out by Radden, metonymic reasoning is needed in order to differentiate between the two types. Metonymic reasoning means that both a speaker and a hearer are able to correctly identify whether an instance one is speaking about is a type or an instance. For example, 'this jacket' in Sentence 46a is an instance (one particular jacket), whereas 'this jacket' in Sentence 46b refers to a type (all jackets of this particular style):

(46) a. I really like *this jacket*.
      b. *This jacket* is our best-selling item. (Radden 2009: 201)

Usually it is the context in which an utterance is produced that determines the reading of an NP. Nevertheless, ambiguities may arise when a non-linguistic aspect, such as gesturing, plays a role in a speaking situation, for example, when a seller in a shop actually points at a given jacket and utters Sentence 46b. In such a case, an individuative reference is used in order to illustrate the generic meaning of the utterance (Radden 2009: 201). Most speakers will certainly understand that it is not in fact this particular jacket that was sold many times, but a number of different items that looked exactly like the model that the seller is pointing at.

What happens in a situation such as the one described above is a process of metonymy called instance for type (Radden 2009: 201). This metonymic reasoning means that people are able to correctly distinguish generic generalisations from individuative references where an instance represents the whole category (type). Other studies conducted on this matter also seem to confirm this thesis (see e.g. Gelman and Tardif 1998; Leslie 2007; Leslie et al. 2011).

In metonymic analysis, special attention is given to characterising sentences which clearly allow for exceptions. The well-known example about a lion implies that lions *usually* have such tails, whereas in reality the sentence applies only to male lions (Radden 2009: 201):

(47)   A lion has a bushy tail.

The sentence is said to represent the metonymic relation where a type (lion) stands for a subtype (male lion).

A similar relation can be observed when the category one is referring to stands for a subcategory. An example of (linguistic) subcategory for category metonymy can be the expression 'housewife mother', which in fact refers directly to the category 'mother', irrespective of whether she is a housewife or not (Radden 2009: 201–202).

Radden (2009: 224) proposes four generic types: 1) the representative generic, expressed with the indefinite singular, 2) the proportional generic, expressed with the indefinite plural, 3) the kind generic, expressed with the definite singular, and 4) the delimited generic, expressed with the definite plural.

Each of the generic reference types proposed by Radden and Dirven (2007) and Radden (2009) have their own semantic roles. The indefinite singular, called the representative generic, is used when an instance evokes a type (instance for type, cf. Radden [2009: 202] and the discussion above), that is to say, speaking about 'a lion' means referring to the type 'lion'. This metonymy works when a given instance possesses distinctive attributes that can also be assigned to the whole category (kind-reference).

The second type of generic reference, the proportional generic, is in most cases an exclusive relation and can be observed in sentences such as (48):

(48)   Hedgehogs are shy creatures. (Radden 2009: 224)

The example shows an exclusive metonymy since there might be exceptions from the rule of hedgehogs being shy creatures. However, the representative generic can be used in an inclusive manner when sentences with kind-predicates are formed:

(49)   Horses are mammals. (Radden 2009: 224)

Proportional generics are also interpreted as instance for type metonymy. In Example 48 the bare plural form refers to numerous members of the category, but presumably not to each and every one of them, making it the same type of metonymy as in the case of the representative generic. The same cannot be said about Example 49, which clearly evokes an inclusive relationship – *being a mammal* is a kind-predicate and therefore can only refer to whole kinds, not only to certain members of a given species.

Radden perceives the definite singular form as kind generic, in contrast to proponents of formal theories, who claim the bare plural to be model kind genericity (see e.g. Carlson 1977; Carlson and Pelletier 1995; Chierchia 1998). What is similar in Radden's and the Generic Group's analyses is the claim that the definite singular form is most often used with WEKs. 'The kind is, however, constrained with respect to the level within its taxonomy and the Great Chain of Being' (Radden 2009: 224). This type of generic reference can involve either instance-for-type or type-for-subtype metonymy.

(50)   a.   The tiger hunts by night. (instance for type)
       b.   The albatross lays one egg. (type for subtype)

A delimited generic is an inclusive reference, reserved mainly for humans and more precisely to well-defined human groups (Radden 2009: 224), such as pasta-loving Italians in Example 51a or 'the rich' in Example 51b:

(51)   a.   The Italians love pasta.
       b.   The rich are controlling the country.

Delimited generics imply that the use of such sentences in the meaning of 'all', 'every', and so on is not possible. However, if such a reference was feasible, for instance in a different language, one could perceive it as a regular reference, not a generic one. The issue of definite plural reference in the context of generics will also be discussed in the empirical chapters of this book – 4, 5, and 6.

2.5.3. Types of generic generalisations

Among the many works on generics in English presented above, one finds multiple types of generic NPs, generic sentences, and even generic texts. An overview proposed by Leslie et al. is an attempt to comprehensively describe this diversity, based on a large number of papers and studies. Leslie et al. (2011: 19) propose the division of generic generalisations. The categories and examples representing them can be found in (52).

(52) a. Triangles have three sides.   (quasi-definitional)
      b. Tigers have stripes.   (majority characteristic)
      c. Lions have manes.   (minority characteristic)
      d. Cars have radios.   (majority)
      e. Pit bulls maul children.   (striking)
      f. Canadians are right-handed.   (false generalisation)

According to this classification, generic propositions are ordered by the meaning of predicates used in such sentences. The scale ranges from quasi--definitional generics, to which there seems to be no exceptions.

The former category asserts a property that is crucial and *universally true*. This means that quasi-definitional generics are always true and there are no exceptions that could be categorised in this way. An example given by Leslie et al. (2011) is Sentence 53:

(53) Triangles have three sides.[8]

No person familiar with the basics of geometry would ever accept or utter a statement such as 'Triangles have four sides.' A figure having four sides simply cannot be a triangle, as having three sides is a distinctive feature of

---

[8]   All examples in this section come from Leslie et al. (2011), unless otherwise specified.

each and every triangle. Generic sentences of this type are quite rare since distinctive features are usually widely known to speakers of a given language. Quasi-definitional generics might occur most often in conversations with children or among children them (see for instance e.g. experiments conducted by Gelman and Tardif [1998], as well as Gelman and Bloom [2007]).

Sentences which present a majority characteristic are a widely used generic sentence type. They assert a feature that is true for the majority of group members or elements from a given set. Such a feature can be, for instance, possessing stripes as in the example below:

(54) Tigers have stripes.

The difference between quasi-definitional predications and majority characteristics is the fact that the latter allow for exceptions. We could imagine a tiger without stripes (for instance, the very rare pure white Bengal tiger), even though this would imply some sort of anomaly. Nevertheless, classifying such an animal as a tiger would probably not pose a problem to most speakers.

The third category presented in the table above concerns an interesting phenomenon, namely generic statements that are based on features possessed by the minority of a given group. It might seem that such sentences are not very common, but in fact they occur quite often, especially when talking about natural kinds. Minority characteristics can concern, for instance, methods of nourishing offspring or physical features:

(55) Lions have manes.

The features presented in this category are so essential to the members of the group that possess them that exceptions – though numerous – are not taken into account by most speakers. The experiments conducted by Leslie et al. (2011) have shown that people are prone to overgeneralise, especially when it comes to this type of generics. It is fully acceptable to say Sentence 56:

(56) Ducks lay eggs.

This is a valid sentence even though it is only females of a certain age and at certain times that do so. Nevertheless, the feature itself is so central to the kind that the exceptions from this rule do not make such generics false.

Majority predication, in contrast to majority characteristics, represents features that occur very often in a given group but are not principled. Example 52d states that most cars in fact do have radios, but this feature does not define the car in any way – any car can be constructed without a radio and it will still fit the category 'car' without being an anomaly, as in the case with the albino tiger.

The fifth category of predications used in generic sentences are striking features, assigned to the minority of the group. Such predications concern usually something dangerous and controversial:

(57) Pit bulls maul children.

Mauling children is not a characteristic feature of this dog breed, not is it central to the kind. Nevertheless, the act of attacking someone – and especially children – is considered striking and therefore such a characteristic might be interpreted as generic. Moreover, the feature could be easily assigned to a different kind where the number of members possessing the feature would be equally low:

(58) Lions maul children. (author's example)

The fact that any lion would be able to maul a child is obvious, but since it does not happen as often as in the case of pit bulls, the sentence would be considered true, yet awkward. Another known example of such generics is the sentence below:

(59) Mosquitoes carry the West Niles virus. (Leslie 2007: 376)

Mosquitoes do not possess any distinctive feature that would make them carry the West Nile virus. Many different species are capable of doing so, but the fact that some mosquitoes can be so dangerous is shocking and therefore the generalisation is assigned to the whole kind.

The last type of predicate discussed by Leslie et al. (2011) is false generalisations, as the predication made about Canadians in the example below:

(60) Canadians are right-handed.

Even though right-handedness is prevalent and could probably be assigned to the majority of the Canadian population, the alternative (being left-handed) is too common to be ignored. In the case of false generics the statistics do not matter, but the property itself makes a given statement false. Technically, minority characteristics could be eliminated in the same way. The only difference is that in the case of characteristics of natural kinds, one does not focus on ducks that do not lay eggs, for instance, to describe the whole kind. There seem to be no alternative methods of gestation – if a given kind bears their young in the womb, one would not consider egg-laying as an alternative and the other way round. One kind cannot have two methods of gestation, so generics concerning that feature will always be based on a minority characteristic, not false generalisations.

Examples and categories presented by Leslie et al. (2011) show that predications do matter when it comes to the reading of certain generics, but it is in fact the cognitive abilities of each speaker that seem central in interpreting such statements. Based on the experiments conducted in their research, Leslie et al. were able to test two hypotheses, namely the generics-as-default hypothesis (GAD) and the generic overgeneralisation effect (GOG). For a detailed account of these the reader is referred to the original paper.

2.6. Analysis model of the project

In the light of the different research methods and theories presented above, it is clear that genericity is a complex phenomenon that can be analysed with the use of different methods and approaches. Since the nature of this study is two-fold (based on surveys and corpus research), the use of cognitive approaches to the subject seems justified.

The theories used for analysing the data are the cognitive models proposed by Radden and Dirven (2007) and Radden (2009). The matrix of generic references and their conceptual implications presented in Radden and Dirven (2007) serves as a basis for the description of reference types in Norwegian. The conceptual blending analysis proposed by Radden (2009) is utilised to analyse the distribution of NP types in the Norwegian material, as well as to study the cognitive status of generics in the language. Finally, a unified model for Norwegian generics based on the collected data will be proposed and contrasted with the original views based on the English data.

The model of generic generalisations proposed by Leslie et al. (2011) is utilised in the interpretation of generic texts from the first survey (Chapter 4) and the sentences from the second survey (Chapter 6). Since the main part of the project – namely the corpus analysis – concerns longer generic texts, the analysis models proposed by Radden and Dirven (2007), and Radden (2009) seem more suitable, as they can be used to build a paradigm of the generic NP types used in Norwegian.

3. Genericity in Mainland Scandinavian languages

There is abundant research on genericity, presenting both theoretical and empirical approaches. Even though the great majority of the studies concern English, one can still find publications about different language groups and individual languages. In this chapter I shall look into the existing research on genericity in Scandinavian languages. The main focus remains on the Mainland Scandinavian languages only, since the morphosyntactic structures of Danish, Norwegian, and Swedish differ significantly from those in Faroese and Icelandic. Expressions of genericity are strongly dependent on the NP structure, as well as the semantics of a given language. Therefore, the analysis of genericity in North Germanic languages such as Icelandic and Faroese is beyond the scope of this project.[9]

3.1. Danish

Among the works on generics in Danish, the normative Danish grammar, *Grammatik over det Danske Sprog* (Hansen and Heltoft 2011), and Hansen's article (1994) on generic nouns are the most detailed. In Hansen (1994) we can find general rules concerning article use in generic contexts, whereas Hansen and Heltoft (2011) provide a detailed description of generic nominals, as well as a discussion on the functions of each of the generic NP types.

---

[9] For a broader account on typological aspects of genericity see Behrens (2000). Dialectal differences in expressions of genericity in Mainland Scandinavian languages can be found in Dahl (2015) and Delsing (1993).

When it comes to countable nouns in Danish, one differentiates between four NP types that can take on a generic reading. The forms are the indefinite and definite singular as well as the indefinite and definite plural. A bare noun as a grammatical form cannot occur in generic contexts with countable nouns (Hansen and Heltoft 2011: 500). The examples of all possible NP types are presented in (61).

(61) a. En   tulipan   kræver   fugtig   jordbund
          a   tulip   needs   humid   soil
          Tulips need humid soil.

      b. Trompeten   er   et   blæseinstrument
          trumpet-DEF   is   a   brass.instrument
          A trumpet is a brass instrument.

      c. Klæder   skaber folk
          clothes-Ø make   people
          Clothes make people.

      d. Japanerne   spiser   med   pinde
          Japanese-DEF   eat   with   chopsticks
          The Japanese eat with chopsticks.   (Hansen and Heltoft 2011: 137)

Even though each of the NP types presented above can occur in a generic sentence, it does not mean that the forms are interchangeable irrespective of the context or the noun used in a given sentence. Hansen and Heltoft provide a number of restrictions concerning the use of each of the NP types and their meaning in generic contexts.

Indefinite generics are discussed in detail in *Grammatik over det Danske Sprog*, since indefinite forms are used in a number of different contexts, including generic ones. The indefinite NPs have multiple readings and some of them include generics, e.g. the uncountable nouns for 'dust' and 'concrete'. The authors take into account the differences in meaning between non-generic and generic nouns, focussing on the markedness and the categories countable/uncountable.

Ved et generisk nominal forstås et nominal hvor substantivet i sammenhæn-gen betegner en hel art af genstande eller individer, ikke enkelte eksemplarer. (Hansen and Heltoft 2011: 500)

With a generic nominal, one understands a nominal where the noun in the context refers to a whole kind of objects or individuals, not single specimens.

A definition of generics, though simple and rather general, can provide the reader with the knowledge necessary to follow the discussion. At this point, the difference between *classic* generic sentences and habitual sentences is not crucial, as the general guidelines concerning article use in generic contexts focus on generic nominals. Habitual sentences, on the other hand, do not need to contain generic nominals since predicates in such sentences might provide a generic interpretation.

The opposition of definite/indefinite and one/many is not the same in the case of generic and non-generic reference in Danish. Generic forms might sometimes be interchangeable (with a slight change in meaning in certain contexts), which cannot be said about the same forms in non-generic contexts (Hansen and Heltoft 2011: 501). As the authors point out, certain contexts are unavailable for some of the NP types, as in the examples in (62).

(62)   a.   Skrivemaskinen/*en skrivemaskine blev opfundet i slutningen af for-
             rige århundrede.
             The typewriter/*a typewriter was invented at the end of the previous
             century.
       b.   Et kæledyr/*kæledyret kræver megen pasning.
             A pet/*the pet needs a lot of attention.
       c.   Forkundskaber/*forkundskaberne er nyttige.
             Prerequisites/*the prerequisites are useful.

In the first example, the noun 'a typewriter' is unavailable in a generic context, which can be due to the predicate used in the sentence, namely 'to be invented'. Certain predicates do not allow the use of indefinite singulars, as in English, and those are called kind predicates (cf. Lyons 1977: 196; Carlson and Pelletier 1995: 10).

The authors also draw attention to the similarity of Danish and French when it comes to the opposition between generic and non-generic plural references. In Danish, indefinite and bare noun generics cannot occur in 'der' constructions. Moreover, plural nouns in generic contexts do not cause stress reduction on the verb, contrary to the non-referential, non-generic forms (Hansen and Heltoft 2011: 501–502). A similar phenomenon can be observed in French with the use of the so-called kind article, namely the definite article 'les', as in 'on ne peut pas dresser les chats' ['we cannot train cats'], and the partitive article 'des' in 'il dresse des chats' ['he trains cats'] Hansen and Heltoft 2011: 502).

The authors of *Grammatik over det Danske Sprog* raise a number of other aspects connected to genericity, such as the difference between generic and non-generic readings of the same NP types and generics in book titles. The first issue is illustrated with the examples in (63). The difference between the generic reference in (63a) and the specific reference in (63b) is provided by both the context and the subjects in each of the sentences.

(63) a. man bør fælde en birk, men lade en bøg staå (generic)
one should topple a birch but let a beech stand

b. han fældede en birk, men lod en bøg staå (non-generic)
he toppled a birch but let a beech stand (Hansen and Heltoft 2011: 503)

The subject '*man*' in (63a) is by itself generic, which makes the whole sentence generic, irrespective of the forms used. In Sentence 63b the subject '*han*' expresses a specific reference (to a certain person in question), which automatically makes the whole sentence non-generic. The very same context dependence can be observed when it comes to book and chapter titles, where certain forms are not allowed or are simply considered awkward:

(64) a. Elefanten ('the elephant')
b. Elefanter ('elephants')
c. Elefanterne ('the elephants')
d. *En elefant ('an elephant')   (Hansen and Heltoft 2011: 503)

As we read further in the text:

[u]bestemt form singularis forekommer saåledes kun i ægte generiske sætninger. Partielt generiske og ikke-generiske sætninger kræver af et generisk nominal at nominalet og dermed substantivet er pluralt eller har pluralisform. (Hansen and Heltoft 2011: 503)

the indefinite singular form occurs only in truly generic sentences. Partially generic and non-generic sentences require from a generic nominal that the nominal, and therefore the noun, are plural or have a plural form.

Truly generic sentences are sentences with kind-predicates such as 'be extinct', and those cannot refer to single members of a given kind but to whole kinds only. Furthermore, the definite singular form cannot be used with certain nouns and in certain generic contexts. As the authors claim, the definite singular is restricted almost solely to kinds that have hyperonymes, such as 'the saw', which belongs to a larger group of tools (Hansen and Heltoft 2011: 504). It is not crucial whether the speakers are aware of the hierarchy of the species they talk about – certain nouns can occur as definite singulars just because they are perceived as belonging to a subcategory, as with 'the aubergine' in the sentence below.

(65) Ægplanten er spiselig.

The aubergine is edible.

When it comes to definite generics, the definite plural is also allowed in Danish, even though its use is limited to certain contexts. For instance, in most cases the definite plural will be interpreted as anaphoric, deictic, or inferentially definite (Hansen and Heltoft 2011: 506). However, when a speaker wants to refer to a characteristic feature that is shared by all members of a given kind, he or she can express it with definite generics:

(66) Hjerteanfaldene   er   den   hyppigste   dødsårsag   i   denne
      befolkningsgruppe.
      heart.attacks-DEF are   the   most.frequent death.cause in   this
      social.group
      Heart attacks are the most common cause of death in this social group.

Hansen and Heltoft (2011: 506–507) differentiate between countable and uncountable nouns, as well as nexual and inexual nouns, providing a paradigm of generic NP types in Danish. The notions introduce the difference between nouns that describe processes (nexual) and those that describe objects and materials (inexual), Hansen and Heltoft 2011: 172–173. Examples of each noun type are provided below.

(67) a. En violin   er   et   strygeinstrument.
          a violin   is   a   string.instrument
          A violin is a string instrument.
      b. Violins   er   strygeinstrumenter.
          violins   are   string.instruments
          Violins are string instruments.   (countable inexual)

(68) a. Cement   er   opfundet   af   romerne
          cement   is   invented   by   Romans-DEF
          Cement was invented by the Romans.

      b. Cementen   er   opfundet   af   romerne
          cement-DEF   is   invented   by   Romans-DEF
          Cement was invented by the Romans.   (uncountable inexual)

(69) En stopprøve er et politisk styringsredskab.
      a screening.examination is a political tool
      A screening examination is a political tool.   (countable nexual)

(70) Kærlighed   gør   blind.
      love   makes   blind
      Love makes one blind.   (uncountable nexual)

As shown in the examples above, both categories can be divided further into countable and uncountable nouns. In each of the noun groups there are NP types that are not allowed in generic contexts; for instance, we cannot say 'the screening examinations are political tools', as this would imply that each and every such examination plays such a role, which is not necessarily true.

In Hansen (1994) one finds a similar account of Danish generics, including the readings of each of the NP types. As in *Grammatik over det Danske Sprog*, Hansen (1994) also discusses some particularities of genericity, such as the acceptability of some indefinite singular generics and bare plural forms as a default generic form of any noun.

When it comes to the indefinite singular form, it can be used generically in certain contexts, namely when the sentence expresses a statement about all members of a given kind by referring to only one as a kind's model, as *'en hval'* ('a whale') in the sentences below. Moreover, unlike the plural indefinite, the singular indefinite cannot obtain a generic meaning in a non-generic sentence.

(71) a. En   hval   lever   i   vandet.
          a   whale   lives   in   water
          A whale lives in water.

      b. En   hval   lever ikke på landjorden.
          a   whale   lives not on land
          A whale does not live on land.   (Hansen 1994: 139)

Another noun form that does not occur in generic contexts very often is the definite plural form, even though certain contexts promote such readings of definite plural generics (as has been mentioned above), as in (72).

(72) a. Fuglene   har   fjær.
          birds-DEF   have   feathers
          The birds have feathers.
      b. Bakterierne   gør   stor   nytte.
          bacteria-DEF-PL   does   big   use
          The bacteria are of great use.   (Hansen 1994: 143)

The indefinite plural form can be perceived as a default generic form of nearly any noun (Hansen 1994: 143), whereas this cannot be said about any other NP type that can be generic in certain contexts. There are a number of restrictions when it comes to using singular forms, definite plural forms, and bare nouns.

As Hansen (1994) points out, the fact that some forms are accepted as generic in certain contexts and incorrect/awkward in others proves that genericity is rather a pragmatic problem, not a grammatical one. Similar conclusions were drawn by Carlsson (2012) in her study on genericity in Swedish texts (see Section 3.3.).

3.2. Norwegian

Not much of the literature is devoted solely to Norwegian generics. The subject is discussed, for instance, as a part of cross-linguistic studies – as in Skrzypek and Kurek (2018) – as an aspect of definiteness (Norwegian normative grammar books), or it is mentioned in publications concerning the nominal system of Norwegian (e.g. Borthen 2003; Halmøy 2016). One can also find minor works concerning the article system, as in Dyvik (1979), and publications that mention genericity as an aspect of other phenomena (e.g. the work of Lønning [1987] concerning mass terms and quantification, where a few examples from Norwegian are given). An overview of the available Norwegian literature on the matter can be found in Kurek (2017).

Generics in Norwegian are rather diverse when it comes to the forms of generic NPs. Kulbrandstad (1998: 121) provides the following examples of Norwegian generics:

(73) a. Is   smelter   ved   0 grader.
         ice   melts   at   0 degrees
         Ice melts at 0 degrees.

     b. Du   må   kunne   stole   på   en   venn/venner.
         you   must   can   count   on   a   friend/friends
         You have to be able to count on a friend/friends.

     c. De   skriver   stil   om   katten.
         they   write   essay   about   cat-DEF
         They are writing an essay about a cat.

     d. Samler   du   på   frimerker?
         collect   you   on   post.stamps
         Do you collect postage stamps?

     e. Dinosaurene   døde ut   for 60 milioner år   siden.
         dinosaurs-DEF   died out   for 60 millions years   ago
         The dinosaurs died out 60 million years ago.

The author comments on the examples in the following way:

I tilfeller hvor substantivet ikke refererer til noe spesifikt eksemplarer, men til hele arten, brukes dels bestemt, dels ubestemt form (Kulbrandstad 1998: 121).

In cases where the noun does not refer to some specific entities but to the whole kind, sometimes the definite form is used, sometimes the indefinite one.

This rather vague explanation surely cannot be of much help for non-native speakers of Norwegian who would like to understand the differences in meaning among the examples in (73). However, certain guidelines do exist when it comes to article use, including in generic contexts.

There are a number of publications on Norwegian grammar, some of which are meant for non-native speakers, such as Strandskogen and Strandskogen (1995), MacDonald (1997 and 2009), Hagen (1998), Golden et al. (2008), and others. Apart from that, *Norsk referansegrammatikk* by Faarlund et al. (1997) is the most detailed work on Norwegian grammar, meant for both native speakers of Norwegian and L2 learners.

In handbooks for foreigners, one finds rather scarce information on definiteness and the use of articles in Norwegian. Most of the books focus on the obvious, namely connecting indefinite articles with unknown information and the definite form with topics that have already been mentioned in the discourse. A slightly more elaborated comment on the use of Norwegian articles is proposed by Strandskogen and Strandskogen (1995: 52), where the authors say that 'the definite article is used in a connection with a particular type or species of animal or object.'

Most of the Norwegian grammar books also mention different types of references. In some publications they are called 'special' and 'general' references (Strandskogen and Strandskogen 1995; MacDonald 1997), in others 'specific' and 'general/generic' references (Faarlund et al. 1997; Kulbrandstad 1998; Golden et al. 2008; MacDonald 2009). The lack of consistency when it comes to the use of notions that denote basically the same phenomenon is also known in the English literature on the subject (cf. Lyons 1977; Carlson and Pelletier 1995).

Golden et al. (2008: 15) illustrates the difference between specific and general reference with the following examples:

(74) a. Fisk   er   godt.
        fish   is   good
        It's good to eat fish.   (generic)

     b. Fisken   er   god.
        fish-DEF   is   good
        The fish is good.   (specific)

     c. Grønnsaker   er   bra.
        vegetables   are   good
        Vegetables are good.   (generic)

     d. Grønnsakene   er   bra.
        vegetables-DEF   are   good
        The vegetables are good.   (specific)

The bare noun 'fisk' and the indefinite plural form 'grønnsaker' take a general (generic) reading, whereas the definite forms are used as a specific reference. The notion of genericity and generic references is developed in more detail in Faarlund et al. (1997: 52), where generics are said to occur in both singular and plural forms, as well as definite and indefinite forms, which is illustrated in (75).

(75) a. Ulven   er   et   rovdyr.
        wolf-DEF   is   a   hunting.animal
        The wolf is a hunting animal.

b. En ulv   er   et   rovdyr.
    a   wolf   is   a   hunting.animal
    A wolf is a hunting animal.

c. Ulvene   er   rovdyr.
    wolves-DEF   are   hunting.animals
    The wolves are hunting animals.

d. Ulver   er   rovdyr.
    wolves   are   hunting.animals
    Wolves are hunting animals.

No clear difference between the NP types is given, except for the fact that they are all generic and that in this particular example the predicate 'to be a hunting animal' can be used with all four NP types. Furthermore, the authors provide an example (Faarlund et al. 1997: 292, as cited in Barth 1980) where a bare noun is used generically. The example is quite unfortunate due to the fact that kinship terms are often used without articles in many different languages (Dahl and Koptjevskaja-Tamm 2001).

(76) Hos baktamenene spiser aldri   **mor,**   **far**   og   **barn**eteneste
      måltid sammen
      with Bushmen   eat   never   mother, father   and   children
      a single meal together
      In Bushmen's families, mother, father, and children rarely eat together.

Norwegian bare nouns can be kind-referring or generic,[10] when it comes to both countable and mass nouns. Borthen (2003) provides an analysis of Norwegian bare nouns, focussing solely on singulars,[11] also in generic contexts. In her PhD dissertation, she makes a number of claims concerning Norwegian bare singulars, stating that bare nouns are rather unlikely to occur in generic contexts, with a few exceptions (Borthen 2003: 30) which will be discussed later. The examples provided by Borthen (Sentences 77a–f) are based on her intuition as a native speaker of Norwegian.

---

[10] The difference between the two references is a lot more pronounced than in English for instance.

[11] According to Borthen, Norwegian BNs are singular, even though other researchers do not agree with such classification of BNs (cf. Halmøy 2016).

(77) a. En   katt   har   myk   pels.
      a   cat   has   soft   fur
      A cat has soft fur.

   b. */??**Katt**   har   myk   pels.
      cat   has   soft   fur
      A cat has soft fur.

   c. En   bil er laget av metall.
      a   car is made of metal
      A car is made of metal.

   d. */??**Bil**   er laget av metall.
      car   is made of metal
      A car is made of metal.

   e. Ola misliker jenter.
      Ola dislikes girls
      Ola dislikes girls.

   f. */??Ola   misliker **jente**.
      Ola   dislikes girl
      Ola dislikes girls.

The author calls such examples for sentences with *quasi-universal* generic readings (Borthen 2003: 30), where the subject or the object cannot occur as a singular bare noun and refer to the whole kind. However, the author does not claim that bare-noun generics are completely unavailable in Norwegian. She provides a number of examples where the BN is fully acceptable and might even be considered the most suitable NP type (Borthen 2003: 31).

(78) a. **Bil** er et kjøretøy.
      car is a vehicle
      A car is a vehicle.

   b. **Datamaskin**   er et nyttig   hjelpemiddel.
      computer   is a useful   tool
      A computer is a useful tool.

The sentences in (78) are correct, as they have a quasi-universal generic reading (Borthen 2003: 32), meaning that one could insert the determiner 'any' in each of the sentences and the meaning would remain the same. This cannot be said about the sentences without the quasi-universal reading in

(79) that express regularities rather than general truths (cf. habitual sentences, e.g. Carlson and Pelletier 1995; Mari et al. 2013b).

(79) a. Småbarn   spiser   med   **skje.**
         small.children   eat   with   spoon
         Small children eat with a spoon.

     b. Kari kjører (alltid) **bil** til jobben.
         Kari drives (always) car to work-DEF
         Kari always drives a car to work.

     c. Man bør bruke **jakke** om vinteren.
         one should use jacket in winter
         One should wear a jacket in winter.

The examples show that bare nouns can occur in generic contexts, not only as subjects (even though the majority of them do) but also as objects and complements. However, in most cases the (un)acceptability of the sentences is based on the speakers' intuition and their own interpretations, as is the case in many of the theoretical studies on genericity. As Borthen puts it herself:

> Norwegian bare singulars can be generic. However, in generic statements of the type discussed in Carlson (1977), where the nominal in question gets a quasi-universal generic interpretation, Norwegian bare singulars are either out or highly exceptional, depending on how one interprets the examples in (19) [here (78)]. (Borthen 2003: 32)

Some of the claims made by Borthen (2003) were later reevaluated by Rosén and Borthen (2017) in their empirical study based on data from the NorGramBank corpus. The authors refer to the original claims and examples, but they also provide a new take on bare singulars in Norwegian. One of the aspects of the study is bare singulars in generic contexts, as presented in the examples in (80).

(80) a. **Hest** er et koselig   dyr.
         horse is a nice   animal
         The horse is a nice animal.

     b. **Taxi**   er dyrt.
         taxi   is expensive
         Taking a taxi is expensive.

Both sentences, (80a) and (80b), are *classic* generic sentences with bare nouns in the subject position. While the example in (80a) can be translated into English with the use of the definite singular, the subject in (80b) can only be rendered with the phrase 'taking a taxi' (Rosén and Borthen 2017: 221).

Rosén and Borthen (2017: 224) discuss different construction types with bare singulars in Norwegian, introducing the 'taxonomic' construction, as in (81). This means that the bare singulars in (81a) and (81b) can be perceived as belonging to a broader group of similar objects, other tools, and other vehicles, respectively (cf. hyperonyms, mentioned by Hansen and Heltoft [2011]).

(81) a. Det hjelpemiddelet som   er   mest brukt er **datamaskin**.
          the tool   that   is most used is computer
          The type of tool that is used the most is the computer.

      b. **Buss**   er   et naturvennlig   kjøretøy.
          bus   is   a nature.friendly   vehicle
          A bus is a non-polluting vehicle.

A similar type of construction where bare singulars can occur are 'covert infinitival clauses' (Rosén and Borthen 2017: 224), as in (82), where we can see that BNs can be subjects (*'sykkel'*) as well as objects (*'telt'*).

(82) a. **Sykkel**   er kult.
          bike   is cool
          To ride a bike is cool.

      b. Jeg   vil   anbefale   **telt**.
          I   will   recommend   tent
          I will recommend (having/using) a tent.

The similarity between the examples in (81) and (82) is that both constructions can be interpreted generically, as they do not refer to any particular computers, busses, bikes, or tents. It is rather the idea or a prototype of each of the objects that is expressed by a bare noun. In this sense, BNs become concepts of a computer, a bus, and so on.

Borthen (2003) and Rosén and Borthen (2017) discuss only bare singulars, giving some examples of generic uses of this form. A slightly more detailed analysis was proposed by Halmøy (2016), who describes the nominal system of Norwegian. One of the many aspects of Norwegian nouns analysed by Halmøy is genericity, which can be expressed with the use of all available NP types.

The work by Halmøy (2016) can be considered groundbreaking due to the fact that the author confronts the existing theories on generics and kind-reference with data from Norwegian. The data in the book are based on the author's intuition and illustrate that what has been thought of as generics and kind-reference in English and related languages seems to function differently in Norwegian. The main claims made by Halmøy concern Norwegian bare nouns and indefinite plurals, and they stand in stark opposition to Borthen's claims:

> I will argue that the truly bare Norwegian Nouns **do not carry the features singular and indefinite** as is traditionally assumed, but **that they are marked for general number and are neutral with regard to definiteness.** I will furthermore propose that the Norwegian Indefinite Plural Noun is a true indefinite, not just neutral with regard to definiteness as is commonly suggested. (Halmøy 2016: 45; emphasis added)

These claims are revolutionary considering the scholarly literature on indefinites and generics (for an overview, see Chapter 2). Being marked for general number means that Norwegian BNs are countable but are in a way perceived as mass nouns or prototypes of a given kind (cf. 'sykkel' and 'telt' in Example 82).

Furthermore, the author opposes the common claim that generics are directly triggered by kind-reference (a theory proposed by Chierchia [1998], among others) and provides a number of examples from Norwegian that seem to support this assumption. She also denies the possibility of indefinite plurals in Norwegian having three possible readings, as is the case with English bare plurals (Halmøy 2016: 62):

> [T]he Norwegian Indefinite Plural is especially interesting in that it exhibits the rare property of distinguishing between generic and (true) kind predicates. While the English (bare) Plural has been famous since Carlson (1980) for receiving three interpretations as weak indefinites, generics, and kinds, the Norwegian Indefinite Plural may only receive the two former readings.

This is illustrated with the following English (83) and Norwegian (84–86) examples (Halmøy 2016: 66–68), where the kind reading of Norwegian bare plurals is either unavailable or questionable:

(83) a. Elks are not on the verge of extinction. (Kind)

    b. Elks are magnificent animals. (Generic)

    c. I saw elks and bears around the campsite. (weak indefinite)

(84) a. Det   er   elger   i   hagen.

         there   are   elks   in   garden-DEF

         There are elks in the garden. (weak indcfinitc)

    b. Kjøpte du lyspærer?

         bought you light.bulbs

         Did you buy light bulbs? (weak indefinite)

(85) a. Elger   er   flotte dyr/ pattedyr /   har   fire bein.

         elks   are   pretty animals/ mammals /   have   four legs

         Elks are pretty animals/ mammals/ have four legs. (generic)

    b. Lyspærer avgir mye varme.

         light.bulbs give a.lot warmth

         Light bulbs produce a lot of heat. (generic)

(86) a. #Elger   står   i   fare   for   å   bli   utryddet.

         elks   stand   in   danger   for   to   be   extinct

         # Elks are threatened with extinction. (kind)

    b. #Lyspærer   ble   oppfunnet   av Edison.

         light.bulbs   were   invented   by Edison

         # Light bulbs were invented by Edison. (kind)

    c. ?Poteter kom til Norge først på 1600-tallet.

         potatoes came to Norway first in 16th.century

         Potatoes were first introduced in Norway in the 17th century.

         (kind)

The difference between (85) and (86) is that the former contains predicates that hold for all individuals of a given kind (all elks are mammals, all lightbulbs give light, etc.), whereas the latter shows typical kind-predicates. We cannot say that each individual elk is threatened with extinction or that each and every lightbulb was invented by Edison (Halmøy 2016: 68). This approach clearly contradicts the popular view that kind reference is directly connected to generics.

Halmøy (2016: 92) also discusses mass nouns in generic contexts, which again differ from English uncountable nouns when it comes to their form.

In Norwegian (Sentences 87a–d), the preferred form of generic mass nouns is the definite form, whereas in English (Sentences 88a–c) mass nouns occur as BNs.

(87) a. (...) siden   før   mennesket oppfant stålet/*stål
          (...) since   before   man-DEF invented steel-DEF/steel
          ...since before the man invented steel.

     b. Risen   kom til Norge   på midten av 1600-tallet.
         rice-DEF   came to Norway   on middle of 16th.century
         The rice came to Norway in the middle of the 17th century.

     c. Vann er livsviktig for alt velende på jorda.
         water is vital for all living on earth
         Water is vital for all life on earth.

     d. Gull er ikke   bare sjeldent   og meget vakkert...
         gold is not   only rare   and very beautiful
         Gold is not only rare and very beautiful...

(88) a. Man invented (*the) steel.

     b. (*The) water is becoming scarce.

     c. (*The) gold is rare.

As shown in (87c) and (87d), the bare form of mass nouns is also correct when it comes to generic contexts. The difference between the definite forms in the first two sentences of (87) and the bare forms in the latter two is that the former can access sub-kinds (types of steel and rice), whereas the latter cannot. A similar mechanism can be observed when it comes to the use of definite plurals in generic contexts (Halmøy 2016: 78).

(89) a. Dinosaurene/?#dinosauren   er utryddet.
         dinosaurs-DEF/dinosaur-DEF   is extinct
         The dinosaurs are/ the dinosaur is extinct.

     b. Hvalene/?#hvalen   er ytrydningstruet.
         whales-DEF/whale-DEF   is extinction.threatened
         The whales are/the whale is threatened by extinction.

     c. Pattedyrene/?#pattedyret   er ytrydningstruet.
         mammals-DEF/mammal-DEF   is extinction.threatened
         The mammals are/the mammal is threatened by extinction.

(90) a. Dinosaurene, både tyrannosaurus rex, velociraptor etc, er utryddet
  alle som en
  dinosaurs-DEF both tyrannosaurus rex velociraptor etc are extinct
  all as one
  The dinosaurs, tyrannosaurus rex, velociraptor, etc. are all extinct.

  b. *Dinosauren, både tyrannosaurus rex, velociraptor etc, er utryddet.
  dinosaur-DEF both tyrannosaurus rex velociraptor etc is extinct
  *The dinosaur, tyrannosaurus rex, velociraptor, etc. is extinct.

As Halmøy points out, definite plural generics can denote super-kinds as in (89) or sub-kinds as in (90), which cannot be said of indefinite plural or definite singular forms. The definite singular form can access kinds, but in such cases 'the reference is mass-like and the members of the class are conceived as homogeneous' (Halmøy 2016: 79):

(91) a. Elgen   er drøvtygger.
  elk-DEF   is ruminant
  The elk is a ruminant.

  b. Elgen   er sjelden   på våre kanter   av landet.
  elk-DEF   is rare   on our parts   of country
  The elk is rare in our parts of the country.

Norwegian, as with Danish and Swedish, expresses generics in multiple ways, each of them having certain restrictions when it comes to predicates and context. Normative grammars of Norwegian do not provide these, but the available literature (in particular Borthen [2003], Halmøy [2016], and Rosén and Borthen [2017]) gives an overview of all generic NP types and the contexts in which they can occur.

3.3. Swedish

In *Svenska Akademiens Grammatik* (SAG), one can find the following notions connected to generics: *artbetydelse, sortbetydelse, typ, generell referens*, and others. The first notion can be translated as kind-reference, the second as sub-kind-reference, and the third notion, *typ*, is class/kind (Teleman et al. 1999: 155, 234). The notion of general reference is a term widely utilised in the scholarly literature on reference and generics.

One noun can refer either to one member of a class, a whole kind, or a sub-kind, e.g. singular nouns usually refer to prototypical members of a given kind (Teleman et al. 1999: 22), as in the examples below:

(92) a. Diskmaskinen är sönder.
dishwasher-DEF is broken
The dishwasher is broken.

 b. I större hushåll   sparar diskmaskinen mycket arbete.
 in larger households   saves dishwasher-DEF much work
 In larger households the dishwasher saves a lot of work.

In Swedish, as with Danish and Norwegian, NP-level generics can be expressed with the use of four or five[12] different NP types. When it comes to countable nouns, the following NP types can be utilised in generic contexts (Teleman et al. 1999: 108):

(93) En katt/ Katten/ Katter/ Katterna   har vassa klor.
a cat/ cat-DEF/ cats/ cats-DEF   have sharp claws
A cat/ The cat/ Cats/ The cats has/have sharp claws.

Each of the sentences above can be paraphrased as 'all cats have sharp claws'. Generic reference can therefore be expressed with both definite and indefinite nouns, either in singular or plural (cf. Norwegian and Danish). However, certain restrictions apply:

- Indefinite singular generics imply that the generalisation concerns each and every member of the kind.
- The indefinite singular cannot be used as a kind-reference.
- The definite singular form can access sub-kinds.
- A bare plural can in almost all cases express a generic meaning, but not necessarily a kind-reference.
- Certain fixed expressions and predicates favour the use of definite generics (e.g. *Priserna stiger igen*' ['The prices are rising again'] [Teleman et al. 1999: 108–110]).

---

[12] The use of a bare noun with countable nouns is somewhat limited compared to Norwegian, but it can occur in certain expressions and/or with certain predicates.

The use of different NP types in different contexts is not caused solely by the context or the predicates used in a given sentence. The type of reference and its interpretation is also one of the key factors that allows speakers to differentiate between different meanings. One of the distinctions concerns the use of indefinite singulars in generics.

In Swedish, plural forms can take two different plural suffixes, of which -er is used with kind-references (*sortbetydelse*; Teleman et al. 1999: 23) – as in '*många frö-er*' (many seeds) being an equivalent to '*många sorters frö*' (many types of seeds). The expression '*många frön*' refers to many individual seeds, not seed types.

In an article on definite and indefinite forms, Pettersson (1976: 121) divides generic references into 'limited' (*begränsad* +) and 'non-limited' (*begränsad* –) ones. Limited generics are expressed with the use of the definite form, whereas non-limited ones take the indefinite form or bare nouns. The author explains that every non-generic noun always expresses a specific reference, but specific nouns can also be used in generic contexts. An example of this is the generic sentence in (94) with a definite singular noun.

(94) Gärdsmygen   är   en   flyttfågel.
      Eurasian.wren-DEF   is   a   migratory.bird
      The Eurasian wren is a migratory bird.

This example demonstrates the use of the indefinite singular with a sub-kind. The sentence and the NP type conform to the claim that in most Germanic languages sub-kinds are accessed by definite forms, especially singular ones (cf. 'the Berber lion' examples by Lyons [1977]). The Eurasian wren is interpreted by Pettersson as a prototypical bird that represents the whole kind (Pettersson 1976: 124), whereas a sub-kind reference is understood rather as referring to the whole group of entities (in this case all Eurasian wrens) through a definite singular reference.

In the text, Pettersson (1976) describes all references to kinds as generics, not differentiating between a generic reference *per se* and a kind-reference, as has been discussed in *Svenska Akademiens Grammatik*, Halmøy (2016), and other scholarly literature on the topic (see Chapter 2).

What is innovative in the study is the notion of 'established kinds' (*etablerade klasser*; Pettersson 1976: 128), such as professions and nouns that describe one's activities (cf. well-established kinds in Carlson and Pelletier [1995]). These occur without articles when they have generic readings. Using a noun from this group with an article would usually suggest a specific reference and a different meaning.

(95) a. Han är en bödel.
          he is an executioner
          He is an executioner.

     b. Han är bödel.
          he   is executioner
          He is an executioner.

The difference between (95a) and (95b) is that the first sentence implies that the person belongs to the natural kind 'executioner', whereas the latter means that the kind in question is an established class (Pettersson 1976: 129). The difference may seem only stylistic, but it does change the reading of the sentences. As Petterson mentions, the choice of a bare noun in the indefinite form is highly subjective and can often depend on the context in the moment of speaking. Furthermore, the sentence in (95a) implies that being an executioner is not necessarily that person's profession but rather that he or she behaves in a way that a prototypical executioner would behave in (being cruel, ruthless, etc.).

The use of generic bare nouns in Swedish is limited to certain cases, one of them being sentences with '*ha*' ('to have'), as in Example (96) by Pettersson (1976: 130).

(96) a. Anja har bil, men Kennet har bara cykel.
          Anja has car but Kennet has just bicycle
          Anja has a car and Kennet only has a bicycle.

     b. Jag   har   körkort.
          I   have   driver's.license
          I have a driver's licence.

'Car', 'bicycle', and 'driver's licence' are understood here as prototypes or notions, not a particular car, bicycle, or driver's licence. The fact that these are used as bare nouns may suggest that in Swedish certain common nouns can be perceived as well-established kinds.

Fixed expressions and well-established kinds are similar to uncountable generic nouns when it comes to the form they take. Both of these noun types usually occur as bare nouns of definite nouns, each of the two having a slightly different meaning. The bare form suggests a more general and almost prototypical reference (cf. Pettersson's take on that matter), whereas the definite form suggests that the speaker is focussing on what the noun denotes (Teleman et al. 1999: 111). The examples in (97) illustrate this difference.

(97) a. Guldet/?Guld har sjunket   i   pris.
          gold-DEF/?gold has sank   in   price
          Gold has become cheaper.
      b. Guld/?Guldet   fräts   inte av syra.
          gold/gold-DEF   is.taken   not by acid
          Gold doesn't dissolve in acid.

The definite form in (97a) can denote, for example, the price of gold in our time or in a given period, whereas the indefinite form in (97b) implies that being resistant to acid is a characteristic feature of the material (a truly generic reading, Teleman et al. 1999: 111).

Apart from the theoretical work, an empirical analysis of genericity in Swedish is also available. The study of Swedish generics conducted by Carlsson (2012) is probably the largest empirical study on genericity in Mainland Scandinavian languages. It focusses both on NP-level and sentence-level genericity and is based on a corpus consisting of generic texts and a transcription of a film, both of which are descriptions of animal species. The choice of this particular genre might have been dictated by the need to find unambiguous texts that would (in most cases) have only one possible reading, namely the generic one (see Section 2.3.).

Genericitet i text by Carlsson (2012) consists of two main studies: 1) a text analysis of 36 texts about animal species and 2) an analysis of a 47-minute-long film (fully transcribed) about the species *Macaca fascicularis*. In the first study, the author focusses on the distribution of different NP types in generic contexts (Carlsson 2012: 57). The second study is a continuation of the first analysis and its main goal is to examine the context dependency of generic NPs (Carlsson 2012: 125).

What Carlsson (2012) claims even in the introduction to her work is that genericity can no longer be treated as an *all-or-nothing* phenomenon because the context is often crucial in deciding whether a sentence or an NP can be interpreted as generic or not. As her first study shows, the accessibility of non-generic expressions is much greater than that of generics. It is therefore crucial to study the phenomenon in texts which give a wider context instead of studying individual sentences.

Both the advantage and the disadvantage of Carlsson's study lie in the material. She does not rely on her language intuition in providing the data for the analysis, as was seen in the studies of Pettersson (1976), Hansen (1994), Borthen (2003), and Halmøy (2016). Instead, she opts for written texts and a transcription of the spoken language. The two data sets concern biological texts. On the one hand, focussing only on descriptions of animal species narrows the context and possible readings of NPs. On the other hand, the consistency in choosing the material makes it possible to analyse in detail one particular aspect of genericity, which in this case is context dependency.

The existing literature on generics in Mainland Scandinavian languages consists mainly of normative grammar books and a few detailed works on the phenomenon, only one of which is an empirical study. The majority of the publications presented in this chapter focus on sentence analysis, not a broader context of generics – such as analysing generic texts. Apart from Carlsson (2012), all researchers opt for language data created for the sake of their studies. Even though the Norwegian scholarly literature on generics seems abundant at first sight (Borthen [2003], Halmøy [2016], Rosén and Borthen [2017], and to some extent Faarlund et al. [1997]), there is no empirical study that would put the existing theories to test. An attempt to do so was Rosén and Borthen's revised version of the original study of Borthen (2017) based on a Norwegian corpus. However, the main focus of the study was bare singulars, not generics in particular.

4. Survey 1

4.1. Method

The first part of this project was conducted in 2017 and consisted of a survey published online, where the participants had to fill in texts with gaps. Before the study was conducted, a number of different strategies and approaches were analysed in order to choose an appropriate one that would fit the resources available at the time. Many of the studies concerning genericity in English and other widely spoken languages are corpus analyses. There are Norwegian corpora available online, but tagging them for genericity requires a lot of work and is very time-consuming since the texts cannot always be downloaded. The corpus approach was therefore used in the main core of the study and not for this part of the research.

Another option of testing whether a certain aspect of language poses problems for native speakers is to conduct a survey. There are different types of surveys, depending on what is being tested. A survey based on the Acceptability Judgement Task seemed like a good choice for numerous reasons. First of all, this method can shed light on how native speakers of a given language perceive the problem being tested. Moreover, the participants are given quite a lot of freedom when it comes to choosing among the available answers, as they can provide one or many answers to a question. Finally, the respondents can grade each of the answers, showing in this way that certain phenomena may be interpreted in many ways.

When it comes to genericity, speakers' interpretation and language intuition are crucial because genericity is a semantic phenomenon. Among the studies based on surveys, the works of Oosterhof (2008) and Ionin et al.

(2011) were considered as possible models for Survey 1. Oosterhof tested the semantics of generics in Dutch and related languages, including local varieties of Dutch.[13] His study is based on a corpus analysis combined with surveys conducted among native speakers of the chosen languages.

In his study, Oosterhof (2008: 110) conducted a survey that consisted of 64 characterising sentences and 18 kind-sentences. The sentences were then judged by 29 native speakers of local and regional varieties of Dutch and Frisian. The respondents were asked to grade the sentences from 1 (completely unacceptable) to 5 (completely acceptable) (Oosterhof 2008: 114). An important aspect of this survey is that the test items were adjusted to the dialects spoken by the respondents, namely certain kind-predicates were omitted as they do not occur in those dialects or are expressed in a descriptive way (Oosterhof 2008: 112–113). The method proposed by Oosterhof is certainly efficient, especially when combined with a corpus study.

The second possible model for Survey 1 was the analysis conducted by Ionin et al. (2011). The analysis is based on Acceptability Judgement Task and concerns three languages: English, Spanish, and Brazilian Portuguese. The respondents were given 20 texts with gaps. Each of the texts concerned one topic (one NP) and had one gap to fill in. The respondents could fill in the gaps with all possible NP types and in addition grade the answers on a scale from 1 to 4, where 1 meant an unacceptable sentence and 4 an acceptable one (Ionin et al. 2011: 973).

The method proposed by Ionin et al. can check respondents' intuitions and the way genericity functions in a given language. It therefore seemed like a good way to test genericity in Norwegian. However, the method was slightly modified. Only the first part of the study was used, namely filling in the texts with gaps. Also, the rating of the answers was replaced with a box for respondents' comments. This was done in order to obtain more detailed feedback and to be able to analyse the respondents' language intuitions. However, this did not function as planned and was corrected in Survey 2 (see Chapter 6).

---

[13]   There are many local varieties of Norwegian as well, but these are beyond the scope of this study. Further discussion on this topic can be found in Chapter 7.

4.1.1. Structure of survey 1 and the tools used

Survey 1 was conducted in 2017 among native speakers of Norwegian (the respondents are described in Section 4.2. of this chapter). The survey was designed in Google Forms, a free software programme that allows users to create simple surveys and share them with an unlimited number of people. Due to the simplicity and accessibility of the tool, the survey could be designed and published in a short amount of time and without any storage restrictions.

As stated above, the form of the survey was inspired by the study by Ionin et al., with certain modifications. The first part of the study remained the same: it included short generic texts, each one of them with a gap. The texts were written in Norwegian and proofread by a native speaker of Norwegian. The diversity of the texts' topics not only allowed for a wide range of contexts, but it also made it difficult for the respondents to guess the subject of the survey. The part of the research by Ionin et al. that was modified concerned the rating of the answers. Instead of a rating scale, a comment field was added to each of the survey questions. The comments from the respondents were supposed to provide additional information on the chosen answers and their interpretation.

The survey did not include any filler items. Placing additional items in the survey to disguise the participants would only lengthen the time necessary to complete the test and doing so could have resulted in fewer participants. Moreover, the goal was to include as many different test items as possible, without making the survey too long. The number of participants was crucial for the study, so the survey's length and structure had to be adjusted, according to the criteria mentioned above. However, filler items were included in Survey 2 (see Chapter 6).

Since the goal of Survey 1 was to determine which NP types are used generically and in what contexts, the respondents could choose more than one answer in each of the survey questions. This way it was possible to analyse different generic contexts and the grammatical forms used in them. All of the texts were written in *bokmål*, one of the two written standards of Norwegian. The majority of the Norwegian population utilises *bokmål* as their primary written language. Furthermore, choosing only one written standard unified the survey and the collected results.[14]

---

[14]   A similar study could also be conducted on *nynorsk* in order to test for any differences between the two standards. Further discussion on Norwegian, its variants, and local varieties can be found in Chapter 7.

The 30 texts in the survey concerned different nouns and NPs (one NP per text) in order to provide a broader context. The nouns used in the survey were as follows[15]:

1. styrketrening – strength training[16]
2. eple – apple
3. appelsin – orange
4. venn – friend
5. politiker – politician
6. hund – dog
7. religion – religion
8. smarttelefon – smartphone
9. lastebil – lorry
10. sykkel – bicycle
11. melk – milk
12. musikk – music
13. barn – child
14. øl – beer
15. brødmat – *breadstuff
16. lydbok – audiobook
17. ryggsekk – backpack
18. stearinlys – candle
19. dunjakke – down jacket
20. stråhatt – straw hat
21. magefølelse – gut feeling
22. grønn lampe – green lamp
23. hvit kjole – white dress
24. stor trykkskjerm – big touchscreen
25. vanlig ølflaske – regular beer bottle
26. hvit skjorte – white shirt
27. keramisk komfyr – ceramic cooker
28. grått hår – grey hair
29. rødt hus – red house
30. hvitt flagg – white flag

---

[15] The forms are given as BNs. See Appendix A for the survey texts.

[16] 'Strength training' was used as a countable noun in the survey. The case was discussed with a native speaker of Norwegian.

Some of the nouns could be interpreted as well-established kinds, for instance 'white dress' or 'dog'. However, testing for WEKs was not a goal of this study and shall be discussed later (see Chapters 5 and 6).

In the survey, there were four uncountable nouns: 'milk', 'music', 'bread-stuff', and 'grey hair'. Uncountable nouns, in both generic and specific contexts, occur either as bare nouns or as definite nouns. One could theoretically use an indefinite form such as 'a milk', but that would imply that one means one kind of milk, rather than an uncountable substance. The main focus was therefore on countable nouns that can take any of the five NP types in generic contexts.

In order for the survey to show valuable results, a set of control questions was posted in the first part of the online form. These concerned the following aspects:

- age
- sex
- education
- origin
- languages spoken

The first part of the survey was obligatory and it was not possible to proceed to the generic texts without filling in the introductory part. When it comes to the languages spoken by the respondents, both native and second/third languages were taken into account. The respondents were asked which language they count and dream in, in order to verify whether Norwegian was their native language. The respondents who chose any other language to those two questions were not included in the results.

The link to the survey was published on a forum concerning the Norwegian language. This made it possible to reach people of different ages, education, and professions. Even though the forum was meant for people primarily interested in the language, the participants were not only linguists or teachers. The survey was available on the forum for two weeks.

4.2. Respondents

The A total of 630 people answered the survey questions, 599 of which were identified as native speakers of Norwegian. As mentioned above, the participants who chose a language other than Norwegian in questions concerning their first language and the language they dream/count in were not taken into account. Table 4.1. and Figure 4.1. present the age and sex of the respondents.

Table 4.1. Survey 1 – age of the respondents

Age/Gender	Women	Men	Total
16–19	3	1	4
20–25	30	12	42
26–30	50	10	60
31–40	89	21	110
41–50	108	35	143
50+	163	77	240
Total	443	156	599

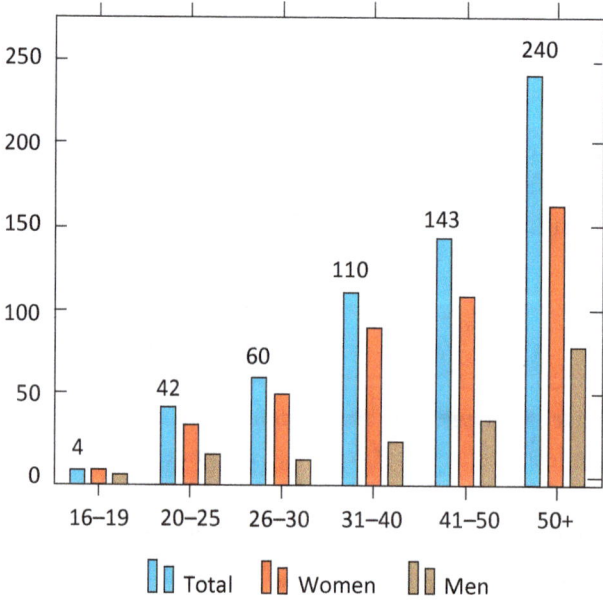

Figure 4.1. Survey 1 – age of the respondents

   The majority of the people who took part in the survey were women over the age of 40. Women were predominant in every age category. The information about the participants' age and sex was collected only for statistical purposes, not in order to analyse whether women would answer differently than men or the other way round. Even though the differences between men's and women's language might be very subtle in Norwegian, this aspect was beyond the scope of this project.

Table 4.2. Survey 1 – education level of the respondents

Education/Gender	Women	Men	Total
Primary school	3	2	5
High school	43	17	61
University	397	137	533

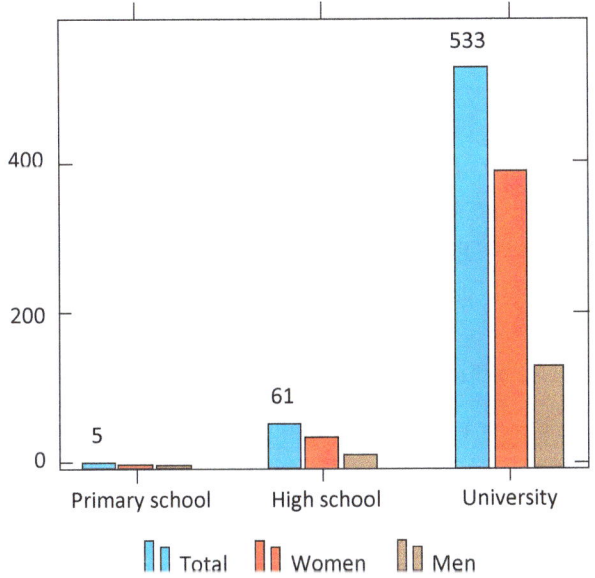

Figure 4.2. Survey 1 – education level of the respondents

When it comes to the participants' education, the majority chose the option 'university' (533 people in total, see Table 4.2.). This however did not indicate whether a person obtained a university degree or not. In Norway, one can take a one-year university course without earning a bachelor's or master's degree and this can still be considered a higher education. Again, this information was collected only for statistical purposes, not to check whether the level of education influences the participants' language in any way. Such an aspect would surely be an interesting subject to study, but was beyond the scope of this survey.

The fact that the majority of the respondents had a higher education is nevertheless interesting. It might just be that people primarily interested in the language would be more willing to take part in such a study than those who only read posts on the forum but do not participate in the discussions. Another explanation is that education and interest in the language correlate, but the results of this survey do not allow for such generalisations. It is safe to assume that people with a higher education were generally more willing to participate in the survey.

Another question in the first part of the form concerned the background of the respondents. In 2017, when the survey was carried out, there were 19 municipalities in Norway. All of them – plus the option 'other' – are listed in Table 4.3. and on the accompanying map. The location 'other' was chosen by only two participants who also marked 'Norwegian' as their primary language. Other respondents who did not choose any of the regions of Norway as their place of origin also chose different languages in the control questions (dreaming/counting in a given language). This made the elimination of non-native speakers of Norwegian much easier and diminished the risk of errors.

Table 4.3. Survey 1 – origin of the respondents

Regions	Respondents
Akershus	57
Aust-Agder	10
Buskerud	26
Finnmark	21
Hedmark	23
Hordaland	41
Møre og Romsdal	30
Nordland	35
Nord-Trøndelag	21
Oppland	21
Oslo	99
Østfold	22
Rogaland	29
Sogn og Fjordane	11
Sør-Trøndelag	32

Regions	Respondents
Telemark	26
Troms	56
Vest-Agder	13
Vestfold	24
Other	2

The map in Figure 4.3. shows the regions where the participants came from. Most of the respondents were from the Oslo region (the municipalities Oslo and Akershus), the north (Troms), and the west (Hordaland), with quite a high percentage of people from the Trondheim region. All of these, apart from the north, are the most densely populated areas of the country. The dialects spoken in those parts of the country belong to the main dialect groups: østnorsk (Eastern Norwegian), vestnorsk (Western Norwegian), trøndersk (Norwegian from the Trondheim region), and nordnorsk (Northern Norwegian).

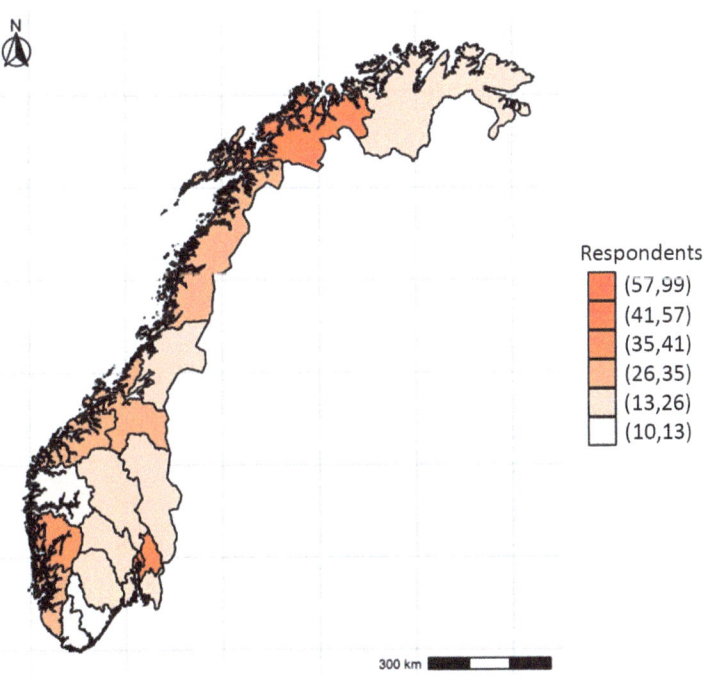

Figure 4.3. Survey 1 – origin of the respondents

As all participants were informed that the survey was written in *bokmål*, we can assume that the dialects did not influence the results. Likewise, the results did not show a large number of outliers that would suggest the influence of dialects on the participants' written language. However, such an influence cannot be completely eliminated without further analysis (see the discussion in Chapter 7).

4.3. Results

Table 4.4. presents the general results of Survey 1 for each of the nouns. The number of answers and the percentages are given next to each noun and each of the grammatical forms. For instance, the BN of the first noun on the list was chosen by 589 respondents, the indefinite singular by five, and so on.

The first impression is that bare nouns are most frequent in generic contexts, whereas definite plural nouns are rather rare (cf. the analysis of the corpus data in Chapter 5). The texts in the survey were not generic in the sense of Behrens' (2005) analysis (see Chapter 2), but their function was to suggest a generic reading of the sentences with gaps to be filled in.

Table 4.4. Survey 1 – results

Noun/Answers (%)	BN	IndSg	DefSg	IndPl	DefPl
1 a strength training	589	5	24	13	1
2 an apple	132	191	3	362	0
3 an orange	374	19	46	373	2
4 a friend	0	203	0	530	18
5 a politician	0	56	17	447	328
6 a dog	64	93	379	293	50
7 a religion	547	47	112	14	9
8 a smartphone	272	98	392	103	30
9 a lorry	0	494	26	266	77
10 a bicycle	360	131	300	177	39
11* milk	555	0	135	–	–
12* music	591	0	35	–	–
13 a child	245	21	54	331	311
14 a beer	78	2	508	82	18
15* breadstuff	585	0	1	–	–

Noun/Answers (%)	BN	IndSg	DefSg	IndPl	DefPl
16 an audiobook	163	259	70	423	27
17 a backpack	433	92	203	146	30
18 a candle	329	26	2	382	5
19 a down jacket	133	457	1	207	1
20 a straw hat	210	520	4	29	4
21 a gut feeling	11	106	512	8	16
22 a green lamp	27	412	2	329	10
23 a white dress	389	85	142	261	59
24 a big touchscreen	309	194	75	278	83
25 a regular beer bottle	16	452	8	368	16
26 a white shirt	199	493	55	29	7
27 a ceramic cooker	320	55	98	336	130
28* grey hair	593	4	6	–	–
29 a red house	24	334	278	98	26
30 a white flag	223	476	78	81	3
Total	7.771	5.325	3.566	5.966	1.300
Total (%)	32.48%	22.25%	14.90%	24.93%	5.43%
Countable (%)	25.43%	24.84%	15.82%	27.85%	6.07%
*Uncountable (%)	92.77%	0.16%	7.07%	–	–

Table 4.5. and Figure 4.4. show how the different NP types were distributed throughout the survey texts. The very low percentage of definite plural nouns contrasts with BNs, which account for over 30% of all answers. However, the proportions differ slightly when we analyse countable and uncountable nouns separately.

Table 4.5. Survey 1 – NP types

Forms	Number	%
BN	7771	32.48
Indefinite singular	5325	22.25
Definite singular	3566	14.90
Indefinite plural	5966	24.93
Definite plural	1300	5.43
Total	23928	100*

* The numbers given in the table are rounded to 0.01. The actual numbers add up to 100%

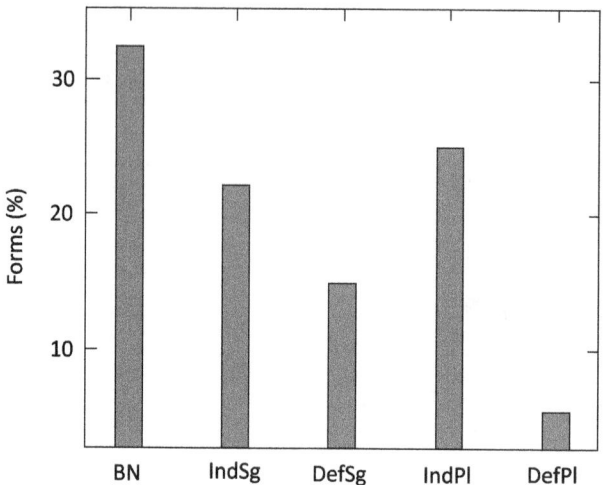

Figure 4.4. Survey 1 – NP types in generic contexts

4.3.1. Countable nouns – general results

The majority of the survey texts concerned countable nouns, as these show more variation when it comes to the use of the five NP types. Twelve of all the texts in the survey included whole phrases, for example, 'a regular beer bottle' in Line 25 of Table 4.4. The other 14 countable nouns did not contain any modifiers. The general results for countable nouns can be seen in Table 4.6. and Figure 4.5.

Table 4.6. Survey 1 – countable NP types

Forms	Number	%
BN	5447	25.43
Indefinite singular	5321	24.84
Definite singular	3389	15.82
Indefinite plural	5966	27.85
Definite plural	1300	6.07
Total	21423	100*

* The numbers given in the table are rounded to 0.01. The actual numbers add up to l00%

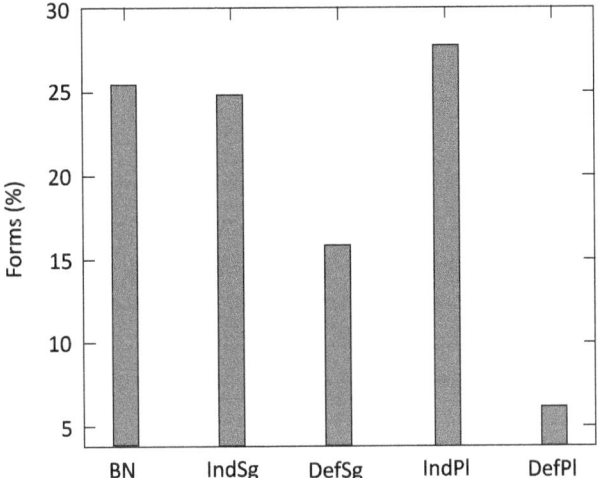

Figure 4.5. Survey 1 – countable NP types

Three forms are surprisingly the most frequent, namely the indefinite plural, BNs, and the indefinite singular. With the indefinite plural being a default generic form in many Germanic languages, including Scandinavian languages (see Chapter 3 and Teleman et al. [1999] for Swedish), the survey has proved that this also holds true for Norwegian. The indefinite singular is also considered very common in English generics, for instance, even though certain restrictions apply (see Chapter 2).

What may be considered surprising is the high percentage of BNs in generic contexts. The distribution of BNs is much wider in Mainland Scandinavian languages than in English; this was also observed in this survey, even in terms of countable nouns. If we look at the results in Table 4.4., we notice that the BN was chosen as a correct form for numerous countable nouns, such as 'orange', 'religion', or 'backpack'.

(98)   Stadig flere sliter med depresjon og angsttilstander som et resultat av stress. For mange kan plikter på jobb og i hverdagslivet være en hovedgrunn til økt stressnivå. Blant vanlige behandlinger og terapier, finner man også en del psykologer som anbefaler alternative behandlingsmetoder. For noen mennesker kan for eksempel a) religion b) en religion c) religionen d) religioner e) religionene være til hjelp.

More and more people suffer from depression and anxiety, which are caused by stress. Too many obligations at work and in everyday life can be reasons for high levels of stress. Among the standard cures and therapies, one can also find some psychologists who recommend alternative treatments. For instance, for some people (a) religion (b) a religion (c) the religion (d) religions (e) the religions can prove helpful.

Certain nouns from the survey, such as 'religion' in (98), may be interpreted in two ways: as a concept – and therefore a mass-like noun – or as a subtype, a particular religion (Catholic, Protestant, etc.). In Example (98), the first interpretation seems more plausible. The use of certain countable nouns without articles, such as 'religion' from the example above, suggests that some nouns can be perceived as abstract or mass-like. The survey results show a high degree of acceptability of BNs, be it with countable or uncountable nouns.

4.3.1.1. Types of generic generalisations

The material from Survey 1 was analysed, according to the cognitive model proposed by Leslie et al. (2011),[17] where six main generalisation types were given, according to the predication type and truth-value. The predications used in such sentences are:

Quasi-definitional	True
Majority characteristic	True
Minority characteristic	True
Majority	True
Striking	True
False generalisation	False

All predication types, except for false generalisations, are true in terms of the truth-value of the generic. The quasi-definitional type does not allow for exceptions and is often used with kind-predicates. A majority characteristic is quite a common type of generic predication that concerns most members of a given whilst allowing for exceptions, whereas minority generics render

---

[17]   It is worth mentioning that the model is strictly descriptive and based on the interpretation of the sentences. It is therefore possible to categorise the examples differently, depending on one's interpretation. This however does not diminish the efficiency of the model in analysing genericity.

generalisation over a whole kind by assigning it a feature characteristic of only the minority (e.g. laying eggs).

The predication type referring to the majority means that a given property is prevalent among the members of a given kind, but is not characteristic of the kind. For instance, we might state that candles create a nice atmosphere, but it is not the main function or a distinctive feature of the object. Striking predication, on the other hand, occurs when a feature associated with a minority of the kind and not very common among its members is presented as generic. The difference between a minority characteristic and a striking predication is that the latter concerns a feature that is considered dangerous.

Table 4.7. presents the classification of the nouns from the survey in terms of the predications they occurred with. Each of the types will be discussed in greater detail in the following sections.

Table 4.7. Survey 1 – types of generic generalisations for the countable nouns

Type	NP	Number
Quasi-definitional	orange, lorry, child, beer	4
Majority characteristic	strength training, apple, friend, dog, bicycle, green lamp, red house, white flag	8
Minority characteristic	politician, audiobook	2
Majority	religion, candle, down jacket	3
Striking	regular beer bottle	1
False generalisation	smartphone, backpack, straw hat, gut feeling, white dress, big touch screen, white shirt, ceramic cooker	8
Total		26

Quasi-definitional

Among the 26 countable nouns in the survey, four of them occurred in the texts with quasi-definitional predications. The text about lorries in (99) is an interesting example since none of the respondents chose the BN among all NP types.

(99)   Antall bilulykker i Europa er på et relativt høyt nivå. Tusenvis av lastebiler som kjører gjennom kontinentet bidrar til stor trafikk på motorveier og i byer. For å kjøre trygt og unngå ulykker er det viktig å huske at **lastebil/ en lastebil/ lastebilen/ lastebiler/ lastebilene** veier flere tonn og trenger derfor lang tid til å bremse.

The number of car accidents in Europe is relatively high. Thousands of cars that drive across the continent contribute to the traffic on the motorways and in the cities. In order to drive safe and avoid accidents, one should remember that truck/ a truck/ the truck/ trucks/ the trucks weigh(s) several tonnes and therefore need(s) more time to brake.

The NP types used most often by the respondents in this example included the two indefinite forms (singular and plural), followed by the definite plural and the definite singular. The most frequent NP type, chosen 494 times, suggests that 'a lorry' was interpreted as a prototype. And since quasi-definitional generics do not allow for exceptions, a prototype with a given feature can be used when referring to the whole kind.

Interestingly enough, the definite plural form was preferred over the singular one in this example, proving once again that in Norwegian delimited generics are not limited to people, as is the case in English (cf. Radden 2009). The use of the definite plural form can also suggest that lorries are understood to be a subtype of a broader category, 'vehicle'. This way the feature assigned to the sub-kind in the text applies to lorries only and not to all vehicles in general.

In the texts about children and oranges, the choices were distributed between the BN and the indefinite plural. Additionally, the noun 'child' also scored high in the case of the definite plural. The noun denotes people, so that choice is not surprising. Another possible explanation may be that children, as with lorries, are perceived as subtypes of the general, larger category. This dependency can be observed in a simple test: a subtype can also be described with the name of the main type, whereas the opposite is not possible. That is, children are people, but it is not possible to say that people are children because that would be qualified as a false categorisation.

The text about beer in (100),[18] even though it falls into the same category as the previous nouns, yielded slightly different results.

(100) Det ei blitt lettere å være entreprenør i Norge. Blant de nye prosjektene som støttes er det flere små bryggerier rundt omkring i landet. Nybegynnere i bransjen ser det som en sjanse til å komme inn på ølmarkedet. For disse entreprenørene betyr øl/ et øl/ ølet/ øl (pl.)/ ølene de selger en liten, men fast inntekt.

---

[18] In Norwegian, 'beer' is used either as a general name for alcoholic drinks with the article 'et' or in the meaning 'a glass of beer' with the article 'en'. It was therefore clear that the example concerned beer in general, not a particular type or quantity of it.

It has become easier to be an entrepreneur in Norway. Among the many projects that receive funding are many small breweries in the country. Beginners in the business see it as a chance to enter the beer market. For those entrepreneurs, beer/ a beer/ the beer/ beers/ the beers they sell mean a small but stable income.

The most frequently chosen NP type was the definite singular, followed by the indefinite plural and the BN. Nevertheless, the vast majority of the respondents chose the definite singular form, suggesting that 'the beer' was perceived as a prototype. Similar, quasi-definitional generics were discussed by Pettersson (1976) in his account on definiteness and generics in Swedish. The examples show that in Norwegian as well prototypes can occur as definite singulars. However, BNs are also common in this function, as has been shown in previous examples.

Majority characteristic

Among all the survey texts with countable nouns, eight were classified as a majority characteristic, namely generics that allow for exceptions but still refer to the majority of a given group. This type of predication occurred in examples such as (101a) and (101b).

(101) a. Det er mange faktorer som må tas hensyn til når man skal pusse opp et kontor. Gode og komfortable møbler må man selvfølgelig ha, men tilbehøret er også viktig. Flere undersøkelser har for eksempel vist at grønn lampe/ en grønn lampe/ den grønne lampen/ grønne lamper/ de grønne lampene hjelper til å fokusere bedre.
There are many factors that need to be considered when one wants to renovate an office. Good, comfortable furniture is a must, but accessories are also important. Many studies have shown that, for example, green lamp/ a green lamp/ the green lamp/ green lamps/ the green lamps help(s) one to focus better.

b. Norsk arkitektur og interiørdesign har gått gjennom flere endringer i de siste årene. Det som var typisk norsk for tjue år siden ikke nødvendigvis er det i dag. Men noen ting blir alltid knyttet til den norske kulturen som for eksempel/ textbfrødt hus/ et rødt hus/ det røde huset/ rød hus/ de røde husene i skogen.

Norwegian architecture and interior design have changed much in recent years. What was typically Norwegian twenty years ago is not necessarily so today. But some things will always be connected to Norwegian culture, for example, red house/ a red house/ the red house/ red houses/ the red houses in the forest.

The fact that green lamps might have a positive effect on people does not mean that any green lamp would have the same function. The example with red houses refers to a noun phrase that could be considered familiar or a well-established kind – it is a characteristic element of Norwegian culture and therefore is recognisable for most people from that country. However, in certain regions of the country, white wooden houses are considered typical; therefore, this predication falls into the category of a majority characteristic.

Minority characteristic

A minority characteristic is the opposite of the previous predication category: it considers a feature shared by a minority of the population and projects it over the whole kind. Among the survey texts, only two were classified this way – the examples in (102).

(102) a. Verdenspolitikken har i det siste vært i krise. I mange land, blant annet Norge, minsker samfunnets tillit til politikere og offentlige organisasjoner. Flere og flere mennesker innrømmer at de ikke tror på det de store politiske partiene påstår. Bortsett fra det mener mange at **politiker/ en politiker/ politikeren/ politikere/ politikerne** har relativt stor makt i det moderne samfunnet.

Recently the international political situation has been in crisis. In many countries, also in Norway, society's trust of politicians and public institutions is deteriorating. Many people admit that they no longer believe what the main political parties claim. Apart from that, many say that politician/ a politician/ the politician/ politicians/ the politicians are relatively powerful in the modern society.

b. I en digitalisert verden der nesten alt foregår på nettet, står papirlitteraturen overfor den største krisen noensinne. Det er flere som velger å laste ned en app istedenfor å lese en bok i fritiden. Mange mener også at vanlige papirbøker er i ferd med å forsvinne helt fra markedet.

I stedet kan imidlertid **lydbok/ en lydbok/ lydboken/ lydbøker/ lydbøkene** være en god litterær opplevelse.

In a digitised world where almost everything happens on the internet, paper books are facing the worst crises ever. Many people choose to download an app instead of reading a book in their free time. Many people also say that regular books will completely disappear from the market. Instead, audiobook/ an audiobook/ the audiobook/ audiobooks/ the audiobooks can be a good literary experience.

Minority generics may be difficult to recognise since such generalisations are often widely accepted, such as the example provided by Leslie et al. (2011): 'Ducks lay eggs.' In the survey, the texts identified as minority characteristic concerned the nouns 'politician' and 'audiobook'. The predications refer to minorities – in fact only a small number of politicians have real power and a good literary experience can be also provided by e-books, regular paper books, or poetry readings.

Majority

Majority predication, as with a majority characteristic, also refers to a feature held by the majority of the population, but the feature in question is not considered distinctive of the kind. An example of such predication can be observed in Sentence 103, where the feature of candles is projected onto the majority of the kind but is not essential.

(103) I høstmånedene er det mange som velger å kose seg hjemme om kvelden med et glass vin og en god bok. Lurer du på hvordan du kan skape den koselige høststemningen i ditt eget hjem? Det er relativt enkelt og krever ikke veldig mye tid. Først og fremst er det fint med **stearinlys/ et stearinlys/ stearinlyset/ stearinlys[pl.]/ stearinlysene** hjemme.

In the autumn months many people choose to stay cosy at home in the evening, with a glass of wine and a good book. Are you wondering how you could create that cosy autumn atmosphere in your own house? It is relatively easy and does not take much time. First of all, it is a good idea to have candle/ a candle/ the candle/ candles/ the candles at home.

The idea that candles create a cosy atmosphere is a popular opinion, especially in the Scandinavian context, where such notions as *kos* and *hygge* are popular. However, the main characteristic of a candle is to provide light, so the statement about its cosiness is very objective. Also, a candle that does not create a cosy atmosphere still fulfils all the essential criteria needed for it to be recognised as a candle (being made of certain material, giving light, etc.).

The majority of the answers in the text about candles were BNs and the indefinite singular, again conforming to the main tendency of the whole survey that those two forms were used most often. Moreover, majority predications often occur in generic sentences where generalisations are made in reference to non-essential features of a kind, so the fact that such forms were chosen is not surprising. Referring to a prototype can be expressed with a BN, whereas kind-reference in the meaning 'the majority' or 'most' is often rendered with the indefinite plural.

Striking

Striking generics are based on predicates that are considered shocking and not typical of a given kind. In Survey 1, the text about a regular beer bottle was considered such predication, as can be observed in (104).

(104) Interiørdesign endrer seg stadig og kan noen ganger bli litt overraskende. Moderne designere bruker ofte gamle kopper og keramikk til å pynte kjøkkenet og stuen. Man kan for eksempel bruke vanlig ølflaske/ en vanlig ølflaske/ den vanlige ølflasken/ vanlige ølflasker/ de vanlige ølflaskene til å pynte kjøkkenet.

Interior design is changing constantly and can sometimes be surprising. Modern designers often use old mugs and ceramics to decorate kitchens and sitting rooms. For instance, one can use regular beer bottle/ a regular beer bottle/ the regular beer bottle/ regular beer bottle/ the regular beer bottles to decorate the kitchen.

An unusual and shocking use of an everyday object, often considered rubbish, falls into the category of striking predications. Such predications refer to a minority of the kind and render improbable and/or surprising characteristics. It rather safe to say that beer bottles are not usually considered good decorations.

Among the NP types chosen in this text, the indefinite singular and the indefinite plural were most common. The adjective in the NP certainly influences the more frequent use of the indefinite form than the BN, as compared to the examples with nouns only. The indefinite plural form, the second most chosen option, expresses reference to some beer bottles that represent the kind in question.

False generalisation

False generalisations are the only predicates in the model by Leslie et al. (2011) that have false values. This means that such generalisations are perceived as generic, but they lack truth-value, as can be seen in the examples in (105).

(105) a. Kjøkkenutstyr er noe alle må velge en gang i livet. Kommer du til å møblere ditt eget kjøkken snart, er det lurt å sammenligne forskjellige typer komfyr før du bestemmer deg. Blant alle de tilgjengelige komfyrene
er det **keramisk komfyr/ en keramisk komfyr/ den keramiske kom-
fyren/ keramiske komfyrer/ de keramiske komfyrene** som anbefales
oftest.

Kitchen equipment is something everyone needs to choose once in
their lives. If you are going to furnish your kitchen soon, it is smart to
compare different types of cookers before you make a decision. Among
all available cookers, ceramic cooker/ a ceramic cooker/ the ceramic
cooker/ ceramic cookers/ the ceramic cookers is/are recommended
most often.

b. I dagens verden er det viktig å være online døgnet rundt. Dette gjør
at telefonprodusentene kommer med stadig nye funksjoner i produktene sine. Ifølge brukerne er det i dag bare **stor trykkskjerm/ en stor
trykkskjerm/ den store trykkskjermen/ store trykkskjermer/ de store
strykkskjermene** som teller.

In today's world it is important to be online 24 hours a day. Because of
that producers are inventing new functions in their products. According to users, nowadays only big touchscreen/ a big touchscreen/ the big
touchscreen/ big touchscreens/ the big touchscreens counts/count.

Interpreting a given predication as a false generalisation requires that there be a corresponding counterpart of equal importance. For instance, the fact that ceramic cookers are often recommended is a generalisation based on current trends from a certain place and time. There are many cooker types that constitute a counterpart for ceramic cookers and that could be used when referring to current trends in other parts of the world.

The example about smartphones with big touchscreens also represents one aspect of mobile technology that can be easily contrasted with other important features of such devices. Even though it is believed that big touchscreens are essential nowadays, such a generalisation is false because a key feature of every mobile device is its ability to connect to different networks. However, this feature is taken for granted and often overlooked, leading to such statements as seen in Example 105b.

When it comes to the NP types used in false generalisations, BNs and indefinite plurals prevailed in three of the survey texts from this category ('white dress', 'big touchscreen', and 'ceramic cooker'). In the text about the NP 'white shirt', the indefinite singular form was chosen most often, followed by the BN.

4.3.2. Uncountable nouns – general results

Uncountable nouns, though they make up a minority of all NPs in the survey, are also somewhat diverse (see Table 4.8. and Figure 4.6.). In the text about grey hair (Line 28 in Table 4.4.), some respondents chose the indefinite NP type ('a grey hair'). However, such a low percentage (0.16%) does not exactly influence the general tendencies for mass nouns.

Table 4.8. Survey 1 – uncountable NP types

Forms	Number	Percentage
BN	2,324	92.77
Indefinite singular	4	0.16
Definite singular	177	7.07
Total	2,505	100

Let us look at Table 4.4. again. The nouns in 11, 12, and 15 follow a general pattern similar for all Germanic languages, that is, they occur as either BNs or definite nouns. The noun phrase 'grey hair' however, was chosen four times with the indefinite article. Only in six answers was the definite form chosen, whereas the majority opted for a bare noun. As mentioned above, all participants were able to choose more than one answer in each of the survey questions. Therefore, the numbers of answers for each of the NP types in all test items vary. Furthermore, due to the number of participants it is not possible to analyse the answers of each and every one of them separately.

Main tendencies are discussed in the analysis, as they provide an overview of the phenomenon, and this was the main point of this survey.

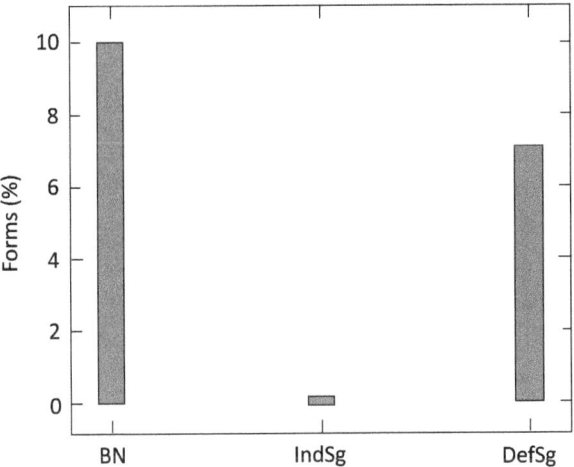

Figure 4.6. Survey 1 – uncountable NP types

Even though the indefinite form accounts for less than 1% of all answers in Example 106 below, it is nevertheless an interesting case. It is rather unlikely that the respondents chose this answer by a mistake, but this possibility cannot be ruled out completely due to the design of the survey. If we assume that the choice of the indefinite singular was intentional, another question arises: what interpretation could such a sentence have? Apart from a specific reference to one particular strand of hair,[19] 'a grey hair' can also be understood as a prototype. The first grey hair symbolises a certain age or the ageing process in general. Since the text in the example explicitly suggested ageing, the latter interpretation seems plausible. Interpreting 'a grey hair' as a prototype implies that the phrase may be understood as familiar by certain speakers (Borthen 2007).

(106) Det blir stadig vanligere å endre litt på utseendet når man blir eldre. I dag tilbys plastiske operasjoner og ulike kurer som skal utsette aldringsprosessen. Mange velger friske farger når de begynner å få a) **grått hår**; b) **et grått hår**; c) **det grå håret**.

---

[19]   The indefinite article '*en*' ('a') developed from the number 'one', and in Modern Norwegian the article and the number are homophones.

It is more and more common to modify one's image as one gets older. Nowadays, there are many plastic surgeries and different cures that can delay the ageing process. Many people choose hair dyes in vibrant colours when they start to get a) grey hair b) a grey hair c) the grey hair.

An argument against such a reading of the example is the presence of the aspectual verb 'to begin'. It suggests a whole process and not a certain point in time. Nevertheless, 'a grey hair' which symbolises ageing does not deny the fact that ageing is a process; rather, it is quite the opposite – 'a grey hair' is the first sign of the process beginning. The other survey texts with uncountable nouns did not yield surprising results as all respondents opted either for the BNs, the definite form, or both. BNs dominated in the case of all mass nouns, which was expected.

4.3.2.1. Types of generic generalisations

The uncountable nouns in the survey included 'milk', 'breadstuff', 'grey hair', and 'music'. The texts about the first three nouns are written in a way that suggests the generic meaning of the last sentence which, when interpreted in isolation, could also have a specific reading. The generic sentence in the text about music could be interpreted as generic in isolation as well.

Table 4.9. Survey 1 – types of generic generalisations for the uncountable nouns

Type	NP	Number
Quasi-definitional	–	0
Majority characteristic	grey hair	1
Minority characteristic	–	0
Majority	music, bread	2
Striking	milk	1
False generalisation	–	0
Total		4

Among the four nouns in this category, there were three different types of generic generalisation: majority characteristic, majority generics that occurred twice, and striking generics.

Majority characteristic

Example 107 shows a majority characteristic, namely grey hair is a biological sign of ageing, but certain exceptions occur. For instance, some people might lose their hair early or they may get grey hair at an early age. A majority characteristic allows for such cases, being anomalies to the general tendency.

(107) Det blir stadig vanligere å endre litt på utseendet når man blir eldre. I dag tilbys plastiske operasjoner og ulike kurer som skal utsette aldringsprosessen. Mange velger friske farger når de begynner å få a) grått hår; b) et grått hår; c) det grå håret.

It is more and more common to modify one's image as one gets older. Nowadays, there are many plastic surgeries and different cures that can delay the ageing process. Many people choose hair dyes in vibrant colours when they start to get a) grey hair, b) a grey hair, c) the grey hair.

Majority generics

The text in (108a) presents a majority generic, where a certain behaviour (having bread as one's main food in a cabin) is assigned to the majority of the members (people who have or stay in cabins). Such a property, even though it is associated with most members of a kind, does not characterise the whole kind (Leslie et al. 2011: 19).

(108) a. Det er typisk norsk å dra på hyttetur. Uansett om du reiser alene eller med venner må du ikke glemme det som er viktigst på slike turer, nemlig maten! Taco og varme retter kan være fristende, men det er også greit med noe mer tradisjonelt. Derfor bør man alltid ha **brødmat/ en brødmat/ brødmaten** på hytta si.

It is typically Norwegian to stay in cabins. Whether you travel alone or with friends, you mustn't forget the most important thing on such trips, namely the food! Tacos and warm dishes can seem tempting, but something more traditional is also a good idea. Therefore, one should always have breadstuff/ a breadstuff/ the breadstuff in their cabin.

b. Autistiske barn har det vanskelig med å tilegne seg grunnleggende kunnskaper som lesing og skriving. Gjennom årene har man jobbet med nye opplæringsteknikker og verktøy som kan brukes på skolen. Det har blitt bl.a. påvist at **musikk/ en musikk/ musikken** hjelper barn med autisme til å fokusere bedre på skolen.

> Autistic children struggle with learning new skills, such as reading and writing. For years people have been working on new teaching strategies and tools that could be used in schools. For instance, it has been proved that music/ a music/ the music helps autistic children to focus better at school.

In the text about music in (108b), the generic sentence with a gap is unambiguous and could also be interpreted generically without a broader context. According to the classification proposed by Leslie et al. (2011: 19), the text presents majority generics. This means that a given property (the ability of music to help people concentrate) is prevalent in a kind, but it cannot be perceived as a principled connection for the whole kind. There may exist certain musical genres that do not help people concentrate.

Striking generics

The text about milk is an example of striking generics (Leslie et al. 2011: 19), where a quality that is commonly believed to be true of the whole kind (dairy strengthens bones) is presented in a negative light in reference to certain members of the kind. As in the example provided by Leslie et al. ('Pit bulls maul children', meaning that not all dogs maul children and not always), here milk is also only one type of dairy product that may cause osteoporosis, whereas the same could not be stated abut cheese, for instance. The feature of causing bone disease is shocking and dangerous, as was classified by Leslie et al.

(109) Bør man spise meieriprodukter for å få i seg nok kalsium? Og kan kalsium fra meieriprodukter styrke bein i kroppen? De nyeste undersøkelsene viser at i land der det spises mest meieriprodukter forekommer benskjørhet mye oftere enn vanlig. Er det faktisk slik at **melk/ en melk/ melken** forårsaker dette?

Should one eat dairy products in order to get enough calcium? And can it be that calcium from dairy strengthens bones? The latest studies show that in the countries where the most dairy is consumed, osteoporosis is much more common. Can it in fact be that milk/ a milk/ the milk causes it?

The examples discussed above show that through the classification provided by Leslie et al. the texts can be divided into categories based on the predications they occurred with. All of the predication types were represented in the survey, allowing for a relatively diverse set of texts in Survey 1.

Respondents' comments

As mentioned above, the participants were able to add comments to each of the survey texts. However, the majority of these comments did not concern the survey subject, but the use of commas, for instance.[20] This also suggests that the subject of the survey was unknown to the respondents, so their feedback on the texts mostly concerned spelling and general language use.

The very few comments that proved useful for the survey were those in which the participants listed other possible answers without marking them in the test items. Even though it was possible to mark more than one answer in each of the survey questions, certain participants chose only one NP type and listed alternative ones in the comment section. Such answers were manually corrected in order to count all of the possible NP types in the final results.

The survey was designed in this way in order to obtain more detailed feedback on the phenomenon under study. Unfortunately, this strategy did not prove successful and was therefore changed in the main survey of this project. Despite the lack of comments from the respondents in this survey, the results still represent the main tendencies in the choice of different NP types in generic contexts.

4.3.3. Statistical analysis

The data collected in Survey 1 was analysed in order to test for statistical significance of the results. First, all survey nouns were analysed with regard to data distribution, which can be seen in Table 4.10. The minimal and maximal values for each of the forms were calculated, as well as median and mean values.

The minimal value of 0 for the definite singular means that there was at least one survey question where none of the respondents chose that option. If we look at Table 4.4. again, we'll see that in the text with the noun 'friend', none of the respondents chose the definite singular form. Comparing the minimal values of all NP types shows that the two definite forms were a lot less frequent than the BNs and indefinite plural forms.

The maximal values, as the name implies, show the highest count of the answers for each of the NP types in all of the test items. For instance, the

---

[20]   All of the texts were proofread and edited by a native speaker of Norwegian, so the comments concerning the use of commas or definite/indefinite NP types could be a result of variation within the *bokmål* standard itself.

maximal value of 593 for BNs means that in at least one of the survey texts 593 respondents chose this NP type. As can be seen in Table 4.4., 593 people chose the BN in the text about grey hair when both countable and uncountable results are considered.

The division of the data into quartiles shows the distribution of each NP type throughout the survey texts. When it comes to indefinite and definite plural forms, they were unavailable in four texts where mass nouns were used. These are marked as 'NA' in Table 4.10.

Table 4.10. Survey 1 – descriptive statistics

	BN	IndSg	DefSg	IndPl	DefPl
Min.	0.00	0.00	0.00	8.00	0.00
1st Quartile	67.50	22.25	6.50	86.00	5.50
Median	234.00	99.50	54.50	263.50	18.00
Mean	259.00	177.50	118.90	229.50	50.00
3rd Quartile	385.20	315.25	140.20	355.50	47.25
Max.	593.00	520.00	512.00	530.00	328.00
				NA: 4	NA: 4

Figure 4.7. shows a graphic representation of the data. Bare nouns, the most frequently chosen in the survey, have the largest range between the minimal and maximal values, followed by the indefinite singular and the indefinite plural. No outliers were observed with these three NP types, due to the wide range of values.

Outliers, presented as small circles on the boxplot, represent answers that were out of the main tendency. For instance, the definite plural had a rather narrow range of answers (relatively low minimal and maximal values in comparison to the other NP types, with few outliers). The division of the data into quartiles revealed low values in Q1 (5.50), Median [Q2] (18.00), and Q3 (47.25), compared to BN, IndSg, and IndPl.

As in the case of the definite plural, the definite singular also had a narrow range of answers (the minimal vs the maximal value). It is slightly larger than with DefPl, but the division of the data into quartiles still shows low numbers compared to BN, IndSg, and IndPl (Q1: 6.50, Median [Q2]: 54.40, and Q3: 140.20).

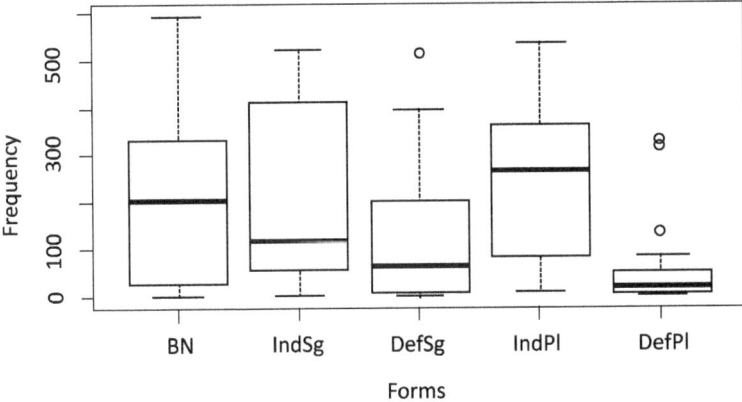

Figure 4.7. Survey 1 – boxplot

The distribution of the data and descriptive statistics let us see which of the NP types were chosen most often by the respondents and how they compare to each other. Such a simple comparison of the data already shows where the differences between the forms are distributed. However, in order to analyse the collected material in even more detail, a set of statistical tests was conducted. The methodology of all tests utilised in this project is presented in Chapter 1. In the empirical chapters (4–6), only the results and their interpretation will be presented.

The next step of analysing the data from the survey consisted in verifying whether ANOVA could be performed. In order to meet the requirements of ANOVA, the homogeneity of variances and the normality of the data need to be tested.

Levene's test was utilised to check the homogeneity of variances; it resulted in a p-value of less than 0.05. The significance of this test is at 0.001 level, so a parametric test such as ANOVA could not be performed. The p-value of 6.68e-06 obtained through the Shapiro–Wilk test also confirmed that the data were not normally distributed, which again prompted the use of non-parametric tests, such as Kruskal–Wallis.

Table 4.11. Survey 1 – Levene's test

	Df	F value	Pr(>F)	
Group	4	5.30	5.32e-04	***
	137			

The Kruskal–Wallis test resulted in a p-value of 3.87e-05, which proved to be statistically significant. This suggests that there were differences between the groups (i.e. NP types). In order to locate these differences, Dunn's test was performed (see Table 4.12.).

Table 4.12. Survey 1 – Dunn's test

Mean comparison	BN	IndSg	DefSg	IndPl
IndSg	1.45			
p-adjust	1.00			
DefSg	2.69	1.24		
p-adjust	0.07	1.00		
IndPl	–0.11	–1.51	–2.71	
p-adjust	1.00	1.00	0.07	
DefPl	4.17	2.78	1.58	4.14
p-adjust	0.00	0.054	1.00	0.00

The values marked in bold in Table 4.12. designate differences between the groups. Significant differences were observed in two pairs of NP types: 1) BN – definite plural and 2) indefinite plural – definite plural. The differences between these NP types indicate that BNs were used in different texts (contexts) than definite plural nouns. When it comes to the difference between the two plural forms, indefinite and definite, one can expect that indefinite plural did function as a *default* kind-reference, whereas the definite plural was considered for delimited generics. If we look at Table 4.4. again, we will see in which texts the definite forms appeared most often. The topic of those texts were 'politician', 'child', and 'ceramic cooker'. The first two nouns are in accordance with the theory of Radden (2009), where delimited plural generics are always connected with people. The example with 'ceramic cooker' suggests that in Norwegian delimited generics may also be extended to *familiar* everyday objects, such as the cooker mentioned in the example. Nevertheless, the data from this survey do not allow for such conclusions and only suggest that the statistically significant differences between the forms may in fact be a result of differences in interpretation of the examples.

Countable nouns

Let us now look at countable nouns only, which constituted the majority of the survey material. As stated before, mass nouns do not exhibit such diversity when it comes to the NP types used in generic contexts, so the main focus of this study remained on countable nouns. However, certain nouns in the survey could be perceived both as countable and mass nouns (e.g. 'beer' or 'strength training'). These were presented in the survey texts as countable nouns with a possible interpretation as mass nouns, allowing for a broader contexts in those texts.

Table 4.13. shows the distribution of the data in questions concerning countable nouns. The minimal and maximal values were counted and the material was divided into quartiles. Since there were only four mass nouns in the survey, the results for countable nouns do not vary much from the general results presented above. However, certain values did change and this is particularly visible in the case of the maximal value for the indefinite singular, which was expected since this form is very rarely used with mass nouns.

Table 4.13. Survey 1 – descriptive statistics for the countable nouns

	BN	IndSg	DefSg	IndPl	DefPl
Min.	0.00	2.00	0.00	8.00	0.00
1st Quartile	36.25	55.25	10.25	86.00	5.50
Median	204.50	118.50	62.50	263.50	18.00
Mean	209.50	204.65	130.35	229.50	50.00
3rd Quartile	326.75	392.50	187.75	355.50	47.25
Max.	589.00	520.00	512.00	530.00	328.00

The boxplot in Figure 4.8. presents the distribution of each of the NP types. We can observe that only in the case of the definite singular and plural forms are there some outliers, whereas other NP types are rather homogeneous. Three NP types have a very wide range of values, namely BN, indefinite singular, and indefinite plural, which is the reason for the lack of outliers. The forms with a smaller range of values, namely the two definite forms, are the only ones with answers that are out of the main tendency. When it comes to the indefinite plural form (the default generic form), the minimal value of 8 is the highest among all NP types. The values are relatively high in the quartiles as well, ranging from 86.00 for Q1, through 263.50 for the median, to 355.00 for Q3.

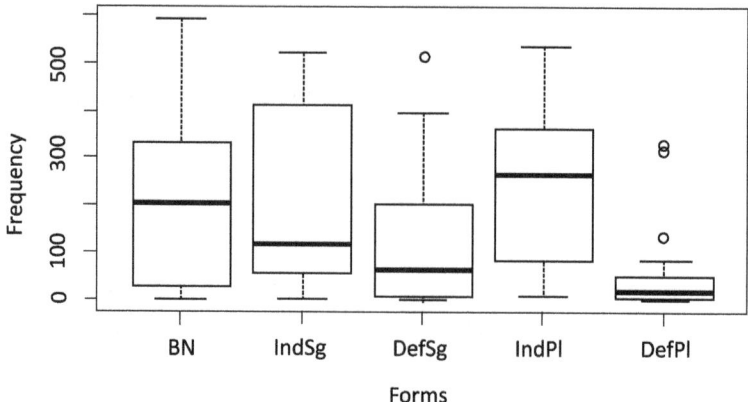

Figure 4.8. Survey 1 – boxplot for countable nouns

Table 4.14. Survey 1 – Dunn's test for the countable nouns

Mean comparison	BN	IndSg	DefSg	IndPl
IndSg	−0.21			
p-adjust	1.00			
DefSg	1.68	1.89		
p-adjust	0.94	0.59		
IndPl	−0.81	−0.60	−2.49	
p-adjust	1.00	1.00	0.13	
DefPl	3.55	3.76	1.87	4.36
p-adjust	0.004	0.002	0.61	0.00

Further analysis of countable nouns was similar as with all nouns: the homogeneity of variances and the normality of the data were checked. The assumption of normal distribution of the data was not met, so the Kruskal–Wallis test was conducted, resulting in a p-value of less than 0.05. This indicates that there are differences between the groups of countable nouns.

The post hoc test indicated where the differences lie (see Table 4.14.). The main differences were observed in the following pairs of grammatical forms: 1) BN – definite plural, 2) indefinite singular – definite plural, and 3) indefinite plural – definite plural. In each of the pairs, delimited generics (the definite plural) were different from other NP types that are often used in generic contexts, namely BNs and the two indefinite forms – singular and plural. These differences are in accordance with the data presented in the part on general statistics above.

Uncountable nouns

The data concerning uncountable nouns from the survey were separated and analysed in a similar manner as for the countable nouns. Due to the fact that mass nouns usually occur as BNs or definite nouns, little diversity in the data was observed, as shown in Table 4.15. and Figure 4.9.

Table 4.15. Survey 1 – descriptive statistics for the uncountable nouns

	BN	IndSg	DefSg
Min.	555.00	0.00	1.00
1st Quartile	577.50	0.00	4.75
Median	588.00	0.00	20.50
Mean	581.00	1.00	44.25
3rd Quartile	591.50	1.00	60.00
Max.	593.00	4.00	135.00

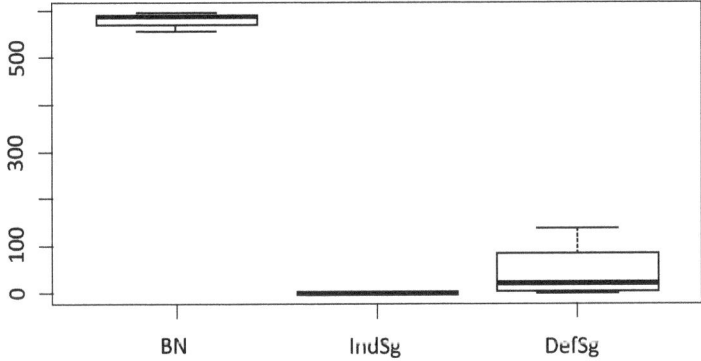

Figure 4.9. Survey 1 – boxplot for uncountable nouns

The minimal and maximal values of the data were estimated for each of the three NP types. The values in Table 4.15. show that there are major differences, especially in the use of the indefinite singular – its minimal value falls way below the maximal one, resulting in a wide range that can also be observed in the boxplot in Figure 4.9. The very few answers with the indefinite singular form occurred in the text about 'grey hair'. As discussed above, such an interpretation would suggest that the respondents understood it as 'the first grey hair', which symbolises ageing. However, those answers were in the minority and in the other three texts about 'milk', 'music', and 'breadstuff' only BNs and the definite form were used.

The distribution of the data in the quartiles was also relatively consistent, due to the very limited diversity of the data. The values of Q1, Median, and Q3 lie rather close to each other in the case of BN (555.0, 588.0, and 591.50, respectively), whereas the definite form shows slightly larger differences between the values, with 1.00 for Q1, 20.50 for Median, and 60.00 for Q3, with a maximal value of 135.00.

Further statistical analysis of the uncountable nouns from the survey were not possible due to the limited amount of data. Moreover, mass nouns in generic contexts do not show such a high degree of diversity as countable nouns, which can be observed in Table 4.15. – the indefinite form has very low values, whereas the BN and the definite form have much higher values. Also, in the case of BN, both the minimal and maximal values are very high, which implies that the form is in some way the default when it comes to generics of mass nouns.

4.4. Conclusions

The results collected in this survey have shown that all five NP types can indeed be used generically in Norwegian, but the forms are not always freely interchangeable. The general results indicate that BN, the indefinite plural, and the indefinite singular were the NP types most often chosen to render a generic meaning. When it comes to mass nouns, as expected, the BN and the definite forms were preferred; there was very limited use of the indefinite form.

The results were interpreted with the use of the cognitive model proposed by Leslie et al. (2011), where different predication types used in generic texts were described. In Survey 1, all predication types were present and the distribution of the NP types in each of the groups was analysed. As in the case of the general results, the cognitive analysis showed that BNs and indefinite plurals can be considered the default forms in the case of Norwegian generics. However, the high percentage of other forms chosen in a few of the survey texts indicates that other factors influence the choice of form. These factors can be the topics of the texts, the predications present in the texts, the predicates in individual sentences, or the interpretation of the NPs (familiar or WEK). These aspects will be analysed further in the following empirical parts of this project.

The statistical analysis performed in this study also show that there are significant differences between certain NP types. The analysis was performed in two ways: first on all of the survey texts, and then only on the texts with countable nouns. Mass nouns constituted only a small part of the material, as their distribution is rather regular in a generic context. Therefore, only simple descriptive statistics were performed on the mass nouns.

5. Corpus data

5.1. The choice of the source texts

As stated in the previous chapters, genericity is a language phenomenon that can be challenging to define. One does not simply need to decide whether a given noun phrase, sentence, or text is generic or not – the way of expressing genericity differs depending on the context, text type, and sometimes the noun itself. While studying genericity, the choice of research material can be a challenge, and it can influence the results if not done properly.

Whereas most of the existing studies rely on sentence analysis where the material consists of sentences created for the purposes of the research, there are a number of works that include corpus research. The choice of this type of material, namely longer texts instead of individual sentences, has obvious advantages. One can observe how the phenomenon functions in a language as well as how the broader context influences the way genericity is expressed. Certain drawbacks of this method should also be mentioned: How should one choose a corpus/corpora for the study? How does one manage the data? Can a given corpus be downloaded and tagged manually for genericity? What genres should be taken into account? In this section I shall try to answer those questions and present the reasons for choosing to build a specialised corpus of generic texts for this project.

The choice of the study material was one of the main challenges in the project. Norwegian has two written standards, *bokmål* and *nynorsk*,[21] the former

---

[21] Spoken language is not taken into consideration in this book. It is only worth mentioning that there is no official standard for spoken Norwegian and that the majority of the population uses one or more of many Norwegian dialects.

being used by the majority of the Norwegian population. The two variants of the language are equal and have the same status in politics, culture, education, and the media. Furthermore, the Norwegian government has introduced many programmes in order to maintain the two languages and to ensure that both are present in the public domain. Choosing only one of the variants for analysis can therefore be controversial. There are reasons, however, for such a choice of research material.

First of all, as mentioned above, *bokmål* is a widely used language variant and the vast majority of texts are written in it. Secondly, the two languages are not very different from each other when it comes to grammar and vocabulary. The main differences between *bokmål* and *nynorsk* concern morphology and not necessarily sentence structure (cf. Faarlund 1988). Nevertheless, one cannot assume that genericity functions in exactly the same way in both variants since *bokmål* is an Eastern Scandinavian language (closely related to Danish), whereas *nynorsk* shares many features with Western Scandinavian languages. Choosing the more common variant of the language maximises the chances of describing the main tendencies in the language, while still leaving open the possibility of repeating the study on *nynorsk* later.

Once the dilemma concerning the written standard of the language has been solved (or at least diminished), the choice of corpus material needs to be considered. There are a number of Norwegian corpora that are either freely available or that have limited access, for instance 1) Oslo-korpuset, 2) norsk aviskorpus, or 3) NoWaC. The majority of the Norwegian corpora comprise texts in *bokmål*, but it is of course possible to find texts written in *nynorsk*.

One of the main challenges with existing corpora is data management. Genericity is not tagged in any of the corpora, whether they are in Norwegian, English, or any other language, since it is a context-dependent phenomenon. Tagging semantic data can be automatised only to a certain degree, and even manual tagging does not guarantee success in 100% of the cases (some of the generic sentences can be ambiguous and therefore tagging them as generic or not depends heavily on the language intuition of the person performing the tagging).

Moreover, none of the corpora that could have been used for the study on genericity were accessible for downloading. Editing a corpus and tagging texts for genericity was therefore impossible this way. Given the resources, scope of the project, and available tools, I decided not to rely on the online corpora and instead to create a specialised data set that could be sorted, stored, and tagged with the use of open-source programmes and packages.

Specialised corpora are rather small, comprising fewer words than general corpora, which can contain billions of words. A specialised corpus is built for a given purpose; it can contain texts on a given topic, of a given genre, or focussing on a given aspect of the language.

A specialised corpus can be annotated and analysed by hand and eye, as it contains less data and is much more manageable than general corpora (McEnery and Hardie 2012: 3). Also, one can test hypotheses and study phenomena that cannot be automatically annotated. Genericity is a language feature that cannot (so far) be automatically recognised and tagged, as it requires an understanding of the text and not simply the ability to recognise a limited number of grammatical forms or parts of speech.

In order for the study to be representative, one must consider the genres of text that should appear in the corpus. Even though there were studies conducted on works of literature,[22] finding texts with many generic references in it is a hopeless task. First of all, the present study concerns only the Norwegian language, so repeating Behrens' study on the Norwegian translation of *The Little Prince* would not reveal how genericity is expressed in everyday language. Likewise, if we considered several literary works, even in the form of e-books, data management would be a challenging task. Popular e-book formats, such as .mobi and .epub, are not easily converted into .txt format, which could then be uploaded into open-source tools.

Should we eliminate *belles-lettres*, another questions arises: why not use newspaper texts or internet texts? There are tools that enable the automatic collection of internet texts (that is how the NoWaC corpus was built), but controlling the type of texts collected can prove challenging, making it a task for an IT project rather than a linguistics project. Manually copying newspaper articles which are available online is also a time-consuming task that may not in fact provide the desired amount of data.

Considering all of those aspects, I decided to look for generic texts in a place that certainly contains many of them. As Carlsson (2012) did, I opted for specialised literature, namely encyclopaedic texts. Carlsson analysed 36 texts about animals, retrieved from two books, whereas the idea behind the corpus created for this project was to collect texts in few different categories, not only botanical or biological ones. What Carlsson's study shows is that it is fully possible to test the functioning of a given language phenomenon with

---

[22] See e.g. Behrens (2005) for the account on genericity from a cross-linguistic perspective based on translations of *The Little Prince* by Antoine de Saint-Exupéry.

the use of a rather small, specialised data set. Her analysis is descriptive and focusses mainly on text and discourse analysis, whereas the study conducted for this project is both quantitative and qualitative. Such a combination of methods and a variety of topics in each of the corpus texts makes the study innovative, even if the data collected was rather homogeneous.

Since genericity expresses generalisations and truths about kinds or groups of objects, the texts in the corpus needed to be scientific and describe, for example, the history and features of a given tool, a piece of furniture, or even the tasks of a given profession. Therefore, the collected data were divided into five main categories. All of the categories and technical details of the corpus are described in Section 5.2. Let us now briefly consider the advantages and drawbacks behind the decision to base the whole corpus on encyclopaedic texts only.

The first and most obvious advantage of an encyclopaedia (even an online edition, as in the case of *Store norske leksikon* [SNL], which was utilised in this project) is that the texts are of high quality, compared to texts collected randomly from the internet. Each of the texts is written by a renowned scientist or a specialist in a given field, as opposed to Wikipedia, for instance, which is also a valuable source of information but lacks the credentials about the authors. Other texts that could be retrieved automatically from the internet include forums, blogs, and articles published on various websites, usually without any editing. In addition to that, the texts from SNL contain a fair amount of data about a given object or phenomenon, which makes the samples representative – each of the texts contains at least one generic reference. The texts were chosen in a way that guarantees the diversity of topics, as well as a proper length of each of them. That would not be possible in the case of random text collection for a larger corpus.

The decision to use online encyclopaedic texts in the corpus construction was also dictated by practical reasons. Utilising any printed sources, such as journals and books, would entail transcribing the texts first and then creating a database that could be processed automatically. Considering the availability of computer tools and linguistic packages for open-source programmes, such a method would be a waste of time and would not necessarily yield better results. Encyclopaedic texts are easily found online nowadays, and some of them have even been transcribed from paper editions. Online encyclopaedia editions are also regularly updated and corrected, which can be traced at the bottom of each page of SNL, where the date of publication and corrections are given. That cannot be said of most of the Norwegian journals that could have been utilised for data collection (for instance, *Illustrert vitenskap* or *Historie*).

One drawback of this choice for the material is the fact that the data set was chosen based on the research question itself. This is in fact true, but considering the points mentioned earlier – namely limited online resources, difficulty in manually tagging genericity, and the scope of the whole project – this solution seemed to be the most reasonable and one that would provide enough material to analyse. A possible risk connected to newspaper texts or literary works is that even a large amount of data might not provide as many instances of generics as shorter texts from an encyclopaedia. One can easily imagine that looking for generics in modern literary works or newspapers would take much more time than analysing the material itself. An optimal solution to all of these issues was therefore to use texts that are easily available, up to date, and written by renowned writers and specialists.

Another problem connected to the genres is that opting for encyclopaedic texts only means that the data are highly homogeneous. Even though each of the texts has a different author and is therefore written in a slightly different manner, the genre remains the same. The homogeneity of data can be both an advantage and a disadvantage of the study. Focussing on one particular genre of text, which additionally contains many generic expressions, makes the collected samples relevant to the study. On the other hand, a set of data that is very homogeneous can also place limitations on the analysis – we can only analyse genericity in encyclopaedic texts, not in written language generally. In order to avoid that problem, an Acceptability Judgement Task (AJT) survey based on the corpus data was designed (see Chapter 6 for further discussion), and it comprises judgements based on language intuition. Referring to language intuition can illustrate how a language's grammar works (Devitt 2010). Combining the two methods can therefore diminish the homogeneity of the collected data.

As has been stated before, genericity does not occur in language as often as, for instance, genitive forms or any other strictly grammatical phenomenon. Generics, being rather a semantic aspect of the language, depend on the context as well as the topic of a given text. Searching for generic expressions in texts that touch on a few subject areas seems therefore more reasonable than searching for it in modern literary works or in the news. One can of course find a generic sentence or two in the news or in a collection of short stories, but such texts may also be devoid of a broader generic context. Relying on texts that concern, for instance, a single animal species or a particular tool guarantees that generic expressions will occur in context and that the generic meaning will not be as ambiguous as it can be in other sources.

Even though many linguistic works are based on sentence analysis, context plays an important role in this study. Tagging the texts for genericity was already a challenging task, and the generic context of the material was certainly of great help. Individual sentences created for the analysis would lack that context and can therefore lead to misunderstandings. What an author of a study thinks of as generic and unambiguous can be a specific reference or an ambiguous sentence for another native speaker of a particular language.

Last but not least, building a specialised corpus implies that a given phenomenon or phenomena will be tested based on the material collected. Specialised corpora are homogeneous as they contain texts of one genre, texts concerning the same topic, or even texts written by the same author (e.g. specialised corpora of literary texts). Therefore the argument that the data are too homogeneous and cannot show all the aspects of genericity is invalid. Genericity tends to occur in specific types of texts, such as scientific texts, so it only seems reasonable to collect and annotate the texts that are very likely to be generic and to contain many generic expressions, rather than looking for genericity in a place where it cannot be found.

As discussed in Section 2.3., generic texts differ from texts that only contain generic sentences. In short, a generic text is a text that concerns one topic and makes generalisations and assumptions about it. A text containing generic sentences is the one where such sentences can occur but they need not be frequent. An example of a generic text can be a description of a plant found in a botanical book, whereas *The Little Prince* analysed in Behrens' study is not a generic text – the novel's topic does not concern only foxes or roses.

Building and annotating a corpus of texts can be a complex task, not only because of the amount of the material that needs to be compiled, but also because of the theoretical questions one needs to face. The choice of the material and genres can influence the analysis and the results. In the case of this study, choosing an online encyclopaedia as a source for all of the corpus texts proved to be a good decision. All of the samples contained generic expressions and all of them were generic, which allowed the material to be analysed on three levels, as mentioned by Behrens (2005).

5.2. Corpus structure and tagging

As mentioned above, the corpus of generic texts was based on the texts retrieved from SNL, a Norwegian online encyclopaedia. The whole data set consists of 170 texts in total (27 761 words) and is divided into five categories. The choice of texts and the categories of the corpus were inspired by the research question: it was necessary to include the texts that concern animate and inanimate objects, countable and uncountable nouns, as well as nouns that describe concepts, activities, and professions.

The corpus data set was collected over six months: from January to June 2018. The texts retrieved from SNL were divided into five main categories: 1) people (n=20), 2) animals (n=25), 3) plants (n=25), 4) tools (n=25), and 5) other (n=75).

The division of the texts into particular categories was done based on a few criteria. First of all, the texts had to concern both well-known nouns, such as 'a dog' or 'a horse', and less known members of a given group, such as 'a rhino' in the case of animals. Second of all, the category 'other' comprises 75 texts, as opposed to 25 and 20 in the rest of the categories. The reason for this is that, apart from main categories such as animals and plants, the nouns could have been classified into many different groups (e.g. vehicles, weapons, everyday objects, etc.), which would have been problematic for data management. In order to avoid diving the corpus into many small categories of topics, one large category of nouns was created.

The category 'people' comprises only names of groups, such as Kuvlunger ('Kuvlung'), and functions, such as *'konge'* ['king'] and *'rabbi'* ['rabbi']. Professions were not included in this category – they are a part of the category 'other'. The reason for this is that professions are considered here as names of certain jobs and in most cases they do not designate the people who perform those tasks. If the references were specific, then the nouns would have been included in the group 'people'; since the references were generic and therefore described generalisations about the professions, they were not considered to designate people. The case with the category 'people' is somewhat different – when we talk about an ethnic group or people with an aristocratic background or who have some special functions in society (e.g. kings, priests, etc.), we perceive them as individuals, not institutions. Such an interpretation was applied throughout the corpus.

The wide variety of nouns in the corpus can also allow for a more detailed analysis than those conducted so far, but it can also provide data that have not been collected in this way before. One aspect of particular interest is dividing the texts into particular categories. This can be done in two ways: according to the text's topic (the five categories of texts) or according to the animacy factor (animate vs inanimate). A third possible factor can be the category of well-established kinds (Carlson and Pelletier 1995). Some of the nouns, especially the ones that are somehow typical of a given culture, occur most often in a definite form or as BNs. This can suggest that they are so well known that they function almost as proper names or abstract concepts. Identifying nouns as WEKs can be ambiguous, though. There are no formal criteria concerning such a division of nouns, so they were not tagged during the data collection and are only briefly discussed as a subcategory of the corpus.

The texts were saved in an .xlsx file, with 170 cells (one cell per text) and no formatting or hyperlinks in it. The file was then uploaded into R software in order to annotate the material. The first step was to automatically mark all of the nouns in the corpus. This was possible with the use of an open-source package, UDPipe.

After all the nouns in the corpus were filtered out, the tagging was done manually. Each of the texts was saved in a separate .xlsx file; the tags which were added included the following[23]:

1. GEN-tag,
2. NP type,
3. position in the sentence,
4. function in the sentence.

After all of the texts were annotated and double-checked, generic sentences were filtered out. Each of the texts contained at least one generic reference, and in the majority of the cases it was an average of 3–4 generic expressions. Some of the texts were short, for instance those concerning well-known and widely used tools or objects. Some of the animal species were described in much greater detail than, for instance, exotic animals that do not live in the Scandinavian climate. Even though it was impossible to find 170 diverse texts

---

[23] The tagging was verified twice in order to minimise the risk of mistakes occurring in the material. A random sample of tagged texts was consulted with a native speaker of Norwegian who confirmed the tagging. Because of the available resources and time constraints, it was not possible to hire another annotator, preferably a native speaker of Norwegian, to check the whole material.

that would be of exactly the same length, the collected material has proved to contain enough instances of genericity to conduct the analysis.

As mentioned above, each of the corpus texts was saved in a separate .xlxs file. Once the tagging was completed, the texts were merged with the use of R software. This was necessary in order to carry out the analysis. The division of the texts into 170 files had also another advantage: it made the tagging process easier and more precise, since each of the files concerned only one noun or one noun phrase. Had all the texts been saved in one .xlxs file, the length of the file might have made it much more difficult to notice and correctly tag all instances of genericity. Moreover, choosing a random sample of texts for the native speaker to inspect was also feasible thanks to this tagging method.

In order to annotate and then filter out generics, all nouns and pronouns in all the texts had to be correctly identified. Thanks to the linguistic package mentioned above, the task was possible, but it is worth mentioning that in a few cases it was necessary to manually annotate the nouns and pronouns. A possible explanation as to why the package did not recognise some of the nouns as nouns is that they were compound nouns or loan words. However, the number of such instances was rather small and the necessary corrections were performed manually and double-checked afterwards. This problem did not occur with pronouns.

5.3. Collected data

The texts collected in the corpus consist of 27 761 tokens[24] in total. 870 nouns and noun phrases were annotated as generic, amounting to 9.34% of all tokens. Each of the texts contained at least one generic reference (most of the time several more than that). The generic nouns and phrases in the collected material were rather straightforward because the topics focus on general information about a given object, species, profession, etc. When it comes to everyday speech and the written language of a different genre, an understanding of the context and its interpretation would play a much greater role in annotating generics.

---

[24] Throughout the book the notion of 'token' is used interchangeably with the more colloquial 'word'.

The nouns and noun phrases annotated as generic were sorted according to the form they occurred in. Norwegian generic nouns can take on all five NP types, namely the bare form, the indefinite and definite singular forms, and the indefinite and definite plural forms. As discussed in Section 3.2., generic expressions can be created with the use of either of the forms, but with slight differences in meaning. These differences depend on many factors, one of them being the context. In the collected material, the most frequent form of generic nouns was the BN, followed by the indefinite plural and definite singular forms, as shown in Table 5.1 and Figure 5.1.

Table 5.1. Corpus – general results

Forms	Number	%
BN	345	39.66
Indefinite singular	31	3.56
Definite singular	185	21.26
Indefinite plural	230	26.44
Definite plural	79	9.08

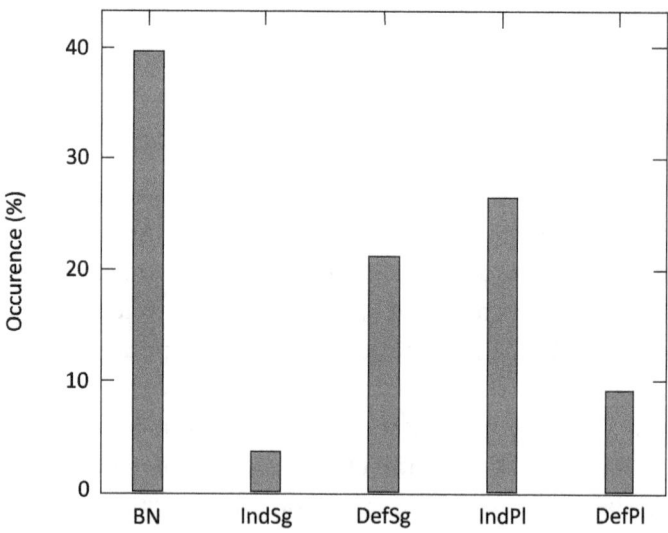

Figure 5.1. Corpus – general results

According to the theory on the matter, bare nouns are not very likely to occur in generic contexts, especially when it comes to countable nouns (see e.g. Borthen 2003; Halmøy 2016). This may prove to be true in the analysis of individual sentences, where BNs are acceptable either in the case of mass nouns or when used with WEKs.

One of the instances where the use of BNs is the most obvious is in the case of encyclopaedic keywords. Such words are often both in the titles of the texts and the first mention of a given subject in the text. Norwegian bare nouns in the corpus are not only keywords but, interestingly enough, the form occurs very often in subsequent mentions, following another form used earlier in the text. This can suggest that Norwegian generic BNs are not only mass nouns or nouns used in the encyclopaedia as entries. Some of them do qualify as WEKs, but a great number of nouns used as BNs throughout the corpus are regular nouns (see the examples in 110).

(110) a. | Sølvsmed | | er | fra | 1995 | ett | lærefag. |
|---|---|---|---|---|---|---|
| silversmith-Ø | | is | from | 1995 | a | subject |

   Silversmith is a subject from 1995.

   b. | Mausoleum | | er | et | monumentalt | gravmæle. |
|---|---|---|---|---|---|
| mausoleum-Ø | | is | a | monumental | gravestone |

   A mausoleum is a monumental gravestone.

   c. | Magnet er | en | | gjenstand som gir | opphav til | et |
|---|---|---|---|---|---|
| magnetisk | felt. | | | | |
| magnet-Ø is | an | | object that gives | origin to | a |
| magnetic | field | | | | |

   A magnet is an object that produces a magnetic field.

The two other NP types that occur most often in generic contexts are the indefinite plural and the definite singular forms. The first one is a form that is typically connected with genericity in Germanic languages (see e.g. Radden and Dirven 2007; Radden 2009). Also, in Norwegian bare plurals refer to an unspecified group of objects or animals, making a reference generic.

(111) a. | skater | er | god | matfisk. |
|---|---|---|---|
| rays | are | good | food.fish |

   Rays are good food.

   b. | Krokodiller | er | en | orden | av | store | krypdyr. |
|---|---|---|---|---|---|---|
| crocodiles | are | an | order | of | big | reptiles |

   Crocodiles are an order of large reptiles.

c. Skruer   har   mange   anvendelser   og   former.
    screws   have   many   uses   and   forms
    Screws have many uses and forms.

When it comes to the definite singular form in generic contexts, it occurred in 21.26% of the sentences marked as generic.

(112) a. Gitaren   kom   opprinnelig   fra   Midtøsten.
          gitar-DEF   came   originally   from   Middle.East
          The guitar originally came from the Middle East.
      b. Mikroelektronikken   har   revolusjonert   kalkulatorteknikken.
          microelectronic-DEF   have   revolutionised   calculator.technique-DEF
          Microelectronics have revolutionised calculator techniques.
      c. I   naturen   finnes   sjiraffen   i   dag bare i   Afrika.
          In   nature-DEF   exists   giraffe-DEF   in   day only in   Africa.
          Nowadays, giraffes live only in Africa.

The last example above shows that generic nouns do not need to occur
at the beginning of a sentence. The position of generic nouns in the corpus
sentences was in most cases initial, but the difference was not significant.
When it comes to the NPs' grammatical functions in the texts, one can observe a certain disproportion, as presented in Table 5.3.

Table 5.2. Corpus – position of NPs in the sentences

Position	Number	%
Initial	443	50.92
Non-initial	427	49.08

Table 5.3. Corpus – function of NPs in the sentences

Functions	Number	%
Subject	577	66.32
Object	146	16.78
Genitive modifier	34	3.91
Other	113	12.99

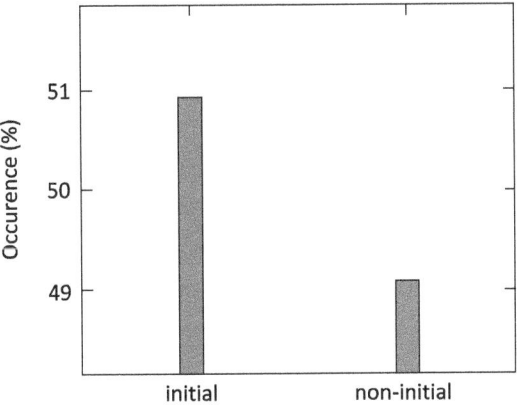

Figure 5.2. Corpus – position of NPs in the sentences

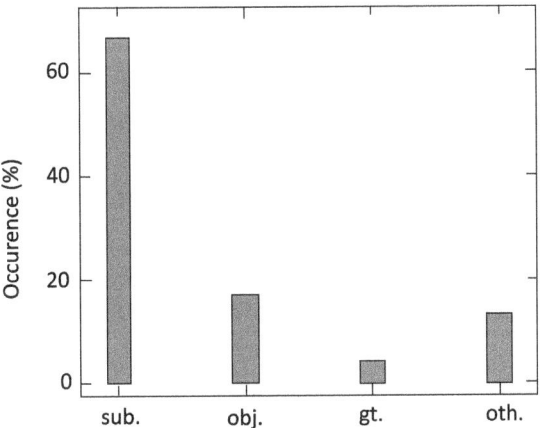

Figure 5.3. Corpus – function of NPs in the sentences

Genericity can occur on different levels. One therefore differentiates between 1) NP-level generics, 2) sentence-level generics, and 3) text-level generics.
NP-level genericity can coincide with sentence-level and text-level genericity
but, in contrary to the latter types, it always contains a generic noun. Sentences with a generic NP in the subject position are regarded in the scholarly
literature as the most common type of generics. These sentences were the
most frequent ones in the corpus, constituting 66.32% of all generic sentences. However, this applies to generic sentences that include a generic NP. As
mentioned before, certain types of generic sentences (e.g. habituals) do not
need to include generic NPs at all. The generic reading might be provided
by a kind-predicate or the context. The former is typical for kind-referring

sentences, whereas the latter applies to all types of generics. In the corpus, the majority of generic sentences were kind-referring, and they therefore had generic NPs.

5.3.1. Thematic categories

The nouns in the corpus (the topics of the texts) were divided into five thematic categories ('people', 'animals', 'plants', 'tools', and 'other'). One of the factors taken into account when dividing the texts into categories was animacy. All the texts in categories 'people' and 'animals' are animate nouns, whereas the nouns in other categories are generally regarded as inanimate. Animacy, however, is a rather complicated notion, as it can be seen from both biological and linguistic point of view. Biological animacy, as the name implies, refers to biological processes that only living organisms can perform. In this sense plants, bacteria, and fungi are animate. In the linguistic sense, only truly animate nouns can occur with control predicates (cf. Comrie 1989: 59–62), which express action taken with will. Plants could occur with certain predicates that express actions (e.g. 'to provide shade' or 'to open the door' as in 'the wind opened the door', etc.), but they cannot occur with control predicates.

Classifying people or animals as animate does not usually pose problems, but when it comes to plants the case is not so simple. Certain languages have very clear-cut classifications and differentiate between humans (animate) and other creatures and objects (inanimate), for example, whereas in other languages the system of identifying something as (in)animate is much more complex (Comrie 1989: 185).

Comrie (1989) proposed a general degree of animacy that applies to a great majority of languages:

human > animal > inanimate

A more detailed model was proposed by Rosenbach (2008: 153), where animate nouns are classified in the following manner:

human N > animal N > collective N

Including collective nouns in this classification allows for a broader interpretation of certain NPs, especially those occurring as BNs in Norwegian.

Comrie (1989: 62) also claims that 'a high degree of animacy is necessary for a noun phrase to be interpreted as having a high degree of control or as an experiencer, but is not a sufficient condition.' According to this description, only creatures that are considered highly animate – namely not only living but also breathing, moving, and so on – have high degree of control (can perform actions or cause others to perform them). Plants clearly do not conform to this description, even though they might be considered biologically animate (living/alive). The ability of such nouns to occur as agents was discussed by Becker (2014: 170), who says that

> plants would be described by adults as 'alive' but they bear none of the prototypical characteristics of animate things: they do not move on their own (save for subtly orienting toward the sun, which small children are unlikely to have witnessed), they lack prototypical animate features like faces, and they lack intentions as far as we know. In short, plants are alive but inanimate, so the label 'alive' does not equate with 'animate'.

Plants can by all means be interpreted cognitively as animate in the sense of 'living/alive' but they cannot be perceived as such in a purely linguistic sense. Other researchers go as far as to simply say that 'plants are always inanimate' (Yamamoto 1999: 48), whereas others refer to 'folk biology' or 'folk taxonomy' (Becker 2014: 288), according to which plants could be perceived as animate in certain contexts. For the sake of this study, plants are considered linguistically inanimate but cognitively and biologically animate, which is also mirrored in the corpus data. The animate nouns in the corpus occurred mainly in two categories: people (ethnic groups and official functions) and animals (names of animal species). As stated before, professions were placed into the category 'other' because they imply something other than descriptions of groups of people.

5.3.1.1. 'People'

The category 'people' consisted of 20 texts that describe ethnic groups and official functions that are not considered professions in the narrow sense, such as 'king' or 'priest'. This category is the smallest of the five groups of topics, since many of the groups of people and ethnic minorities were described in SNL with only one or two sentences. Since each of the corpus texts were at least one paragraph long, the choice of the source material in this category was limited. However, the difference is not significant, and it does not seem to have influenced the general results.

There were 98 generic expressions in the category 'people'. The nouns appeared in all five forms, though the use of the indefinite singular was rather limited (10.20%). The most frequently used NP types were definite singulars, indefinite and definite plural forms, and bare nouns. The definite singular form, used in 31.63% of the cases, might suggest that a number of NPs in this text category function as well-established kinds or that they can be perceived as prototypes of a given social group or people belonging to this class.

As can be seen in Table 5.4. and Figure 5.4., the use of definite plural generics is almost as common as BNs and indefinite plural forms. This may suggest that definite plural generics are in fact most often used when talking about people, as in English. However, they are not limited to this use, in contrast to English plural generics (see Section 2.5. and e.g. Radden and Dirven [2007] for further discussion).

Table 5.4. Corpus – generic NP types for 'people'

Forms	Number	%
BN	19	19.39
Indefinite singular	10	10.20
Definite singular	31	31.63
Indefinite plural	20	20.41
Definite plural	18	18.37

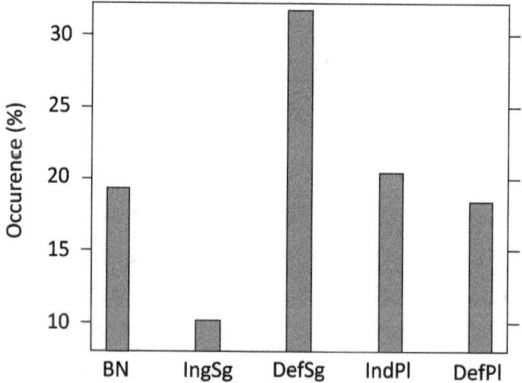

Figure 5.4. Corpus – generic NP types for 'people'

The sentences in (113)[25] show the use of the three most common NP types in the category 'people'. Among these, the BN and the definite plural seem to play a slightly different role than the definite singular, that is, they refer rather to whole social groups, not people of a particular profession. Furthermore, 'the aristocracy' can be regarded as a collective noun (see the classification of collective NPs in the previous section), referring to a certain social background, whereas 'farmers' clearly refers to a group of people.

(113) a. **Adel** er en samfunnsklasse med lovfestede, arvelige politiske og sosiale forrettigheter; forekommer fra de eldste tider i de fleste kulturer.
   The aristocracy is a social class with legal, hereditary, and political privileges; occurs from the oldest times and in most cultures.

   b. **Prester** [priests] får sine oppgaver tildelt enten ved arv eller ved personlig valg (kall).
   Priests receive their tasks either by heritage or by personal choice (calling).

   c. I Tyskland øst for Elben og i de slaviske land ble **bøndene** [farmers-DEF] til og med livegne, og godseierne la helt urimelig arbeidsplikt på dem.
   In Germany, east of the Elbe, and in the Slavic countries, farmers were indentured and the land owners obliged them to do an unimaginable amount of work.

The difference between the reference to an official function and to people who do a certain type of work as a result of the social class they belong to is shown in Sentences 113b and 113c. One might argue whether or not 'priest' denotes a profession, an official function, or even a calling. Nevertheless, the indefinite form 'priests' is unambiguously generic, whereas the definite plural in (113c) might suggest both a specific and a habitual reading of the sentence. On the one hand, the NP refers to farmers from the given region; on the other hand, it denotes a whole social class by giving an example of farmers from Germany and Slavic countries.

(114) a. **En biskop** [a bishop] er den øverste kirkelige lederen i et bispedømme.
   A bishop is the highest church leader in a diocese.

---

[25]   The glosses in English are added in square brackets and to generic nouns only.

b. **Fylkesmannen** [county.governor-DEF] har også en rekke direkte oppgaver i forhold til helsetjenesten, dels med hjemmel direkte i lovgiv-
ningen og dels for eksempel på vegne av Sosial- og helsedirektoratet,
særlig innenfor forebyggende helsearbeid og relatert til helsepolitiske
satsninger.

The County Governor has a number of tasks concerning health care,
which are partially stated in the law and partially an obligation given
by the Norwegian Directorate for Health and Social Affairs, especially
concerning preventive health work and health policies.

The two singular forms – indefinite and definite – in (114) show the reference between what could be considered a call or a life role and an official
function. In (114a), 'a bishop' refers to the tasks such a person performs rather
than people holding this position, whereas the definite form 'the County
Governor' in (114b) implies that the profession is somehow unique. Being
a county governor is not a very common profession and it is therefore seen
as a particular official function, similar to a king or a politician.

When it comes to the place and function of generic NPs in the category
'people', the majority of the nouns were subjects (71%) in the initial position
(53.06%). However, in a number of examples one can observe generic NPs in
an object position (14.29%). Genitive and other grammatical forms occurred
in only 13 sentences. The position and function of nouns in generic sentences
depends on the writing style and topic of the text. However, in all text categories, generic nouns were subjects in the majority of sentences, with other
functions being a lot less common. This may mean that in classic generic
sentences and texts, generic NPs are subjects irrespective of their position
in the sentence (cf. Lyons 1977).

Table 5.5. Corpus – noun position for 'people'

Position	Number	%
Initial	52	53.06
Non-initial	46	46.94

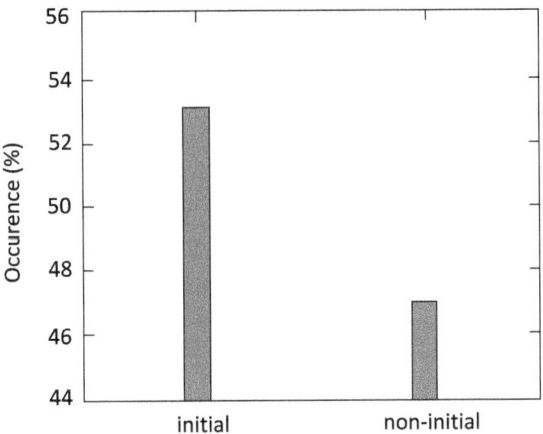

Figure 5.5. Corpus – noun position for 'people'

Table 5.6. Corpus – noun function for 'people'

Functions	Number	%
Subject	71	72.45
Object	14	14.29
Genitive modifier	7	7.14
Other	6	6.12

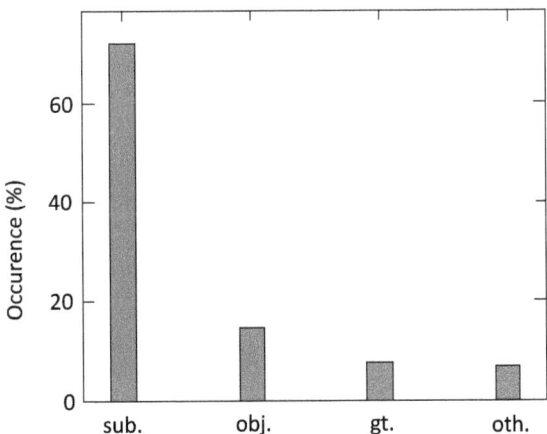

Figure 5.6. Corpus – noun function for 'people'

5.3.1.2. 'Animals'

The other text group that contains animate nouns is the category 'animals', consisting of 25 texts. The description of animal species is one of the most typical generic texts (see the study of Swedish generics by Carlsson [2012]). Among all NPs in this text category, 11.20% were generic references.

Nearly half of all generic nouns denoting animal species were bare plurals (49.66%). Only indefinite singulars were not used in generic contexts to refer to animals, whereas definite singulars, bare nouns, and definite plurals appeared in a number of sentences (21.77%, 17.01%, and 11.56%, respectively; see Table 5.7.).

Table 5.7. Corpus – generic NP types for 'animals'

Forms	Number	%
BN	25	17.01
Indefinite singular	0	0.00
Definite singular	32	21.77
Indefinite plural	73	49.66
Definite plural	17	11.56

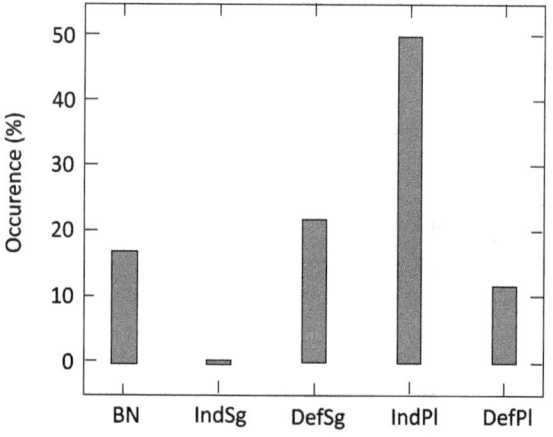

Figure 5.7. Corpus – generic NP types for 'animals'

The sentences in (115) show examples with each of those forms. The bare noun in (115a) is used as a subject in a classic generic sentence describing a kind. The predicate used in the sentences cannot be interpreted as kind-referring. Weighing a certain amount can be a characteristic feature of a species, but not in the same sense as being a mammal, for instance. One can easily imagine dodo birds weighing more than 25 kg or less than 20 kg.

(115) a. **Dronte**, også kalt dodo [dodo-Ø], Raphus cucullatus, på Mauritius veide 20–25 kg og fantes i store mengder da europeerne kom dit i 1598.
Dodo, *Raphus cucullatus*, on Mauritius it weighed 20–25 kg and oc-curred in large quantities when the Europeans arrived in 1598.

b. **Skater** [skates] er god matfisk.
Skates are good edible fish.

c. **Oteren** [oter-DEF] er nattaktiv.
T he otter is a nocturnal animal.

d. **Humlene** [bees-DEF] danner samfunn og betegnes sammen med hon-ningbiene som sosiale bier.
Bumblebees create societies and together with honey bees are regarded as social bees.

The sentence in (115b) is a model kind-reference, where the NP occurs as a bare plural – the *default* generic form (cf. Chapters 2 and 3). 'The otter' combined with the predicate 'to be a nocturnal animal' in (115c) is a generic sentence, but not a kind-reference in the classic understanding of the term. The last example in (115d) utilises the definite plural form, 'the bumblebees', when referring to the species. The predicate is truly generic – it characterises the kind's behaviour.

Moreover, the animal species that occurred as definite plurals in the corpus were either small animals perceived almost as a mass (e.g. insects) or animals considered gregarious – animals that are usually seen in flocks – mainly as a result of folk taxonomy. These nouns included such species as seagulls, crocodiles, bats, and mice. On the other hand, certain animals such as giraffes, which are gregarious animals, occurred in the corpus either as BNs or definite singulars. It is a rather *exotic* animal species from the European point of view, which might be one of the reasons for the use of a singular NP in this case.

When it comes to generic nouns' positions in this category, they were mostly non-initial nouns (53.74%). The majority of the nouns were subjects (63.95%) and nearly 30% of all NPs in this category had grammatical func-tions other than subjects, objects, and modifiers.

Table 5.8. Corpus – noun position for 'animals'

Position	Number	%
Initial	68	46.26
Non-initial	79	53.74

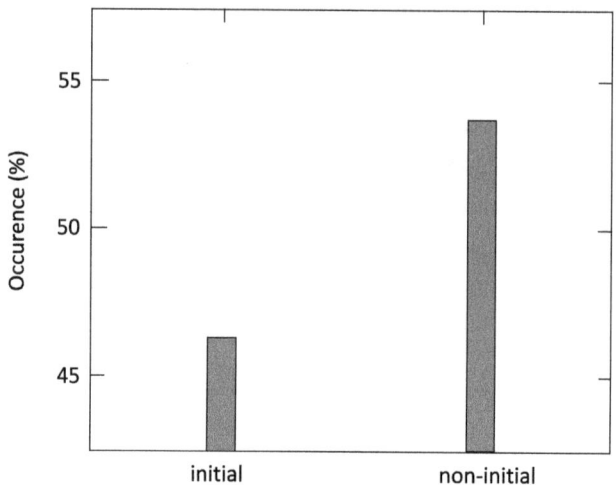

Figure 5.8. Corpus – noun position for 'animals'

Table 5.9. Corpus – noun function for 'animals'

Functions	Number	%
Subject	94	63.95
Object	6	4.08
Genitive modifier	4	2.72
Other	43	29.25

5.3.1.3. 'Plants'

The category 'plants' consisted of 25 texts, each of them denoting one plant. A total of 142 sentences in this category were annotated as generic. Despite the fact that the plants are considered linguistically inanimate, the nouns in this category occurred in similar forms as animals, that is, there was no instance of the indefinite singular (see Table 5.10.). However, the use of BNs was much more prevalent in the category 'plants' (73.24%), with minor use of the definite singular (9.86%), definite plural (8.45%), and indefinite plural (8.45%) forms.

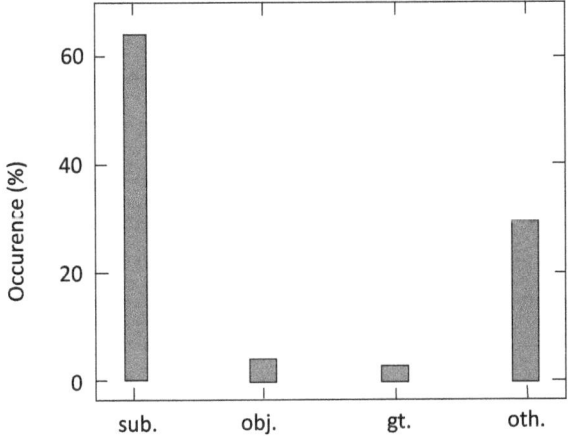

Figure 5.9. Corpus – noun function for 'animals'

Table 5.10. Corpus – generic NP types for 'plants'

Forms	Number	%
BN	104	73.24
Indefinite singular	0	0.00
Definite singular	14	9.86
Indefinite plural	12	8.45
Definite plural	12	8.45

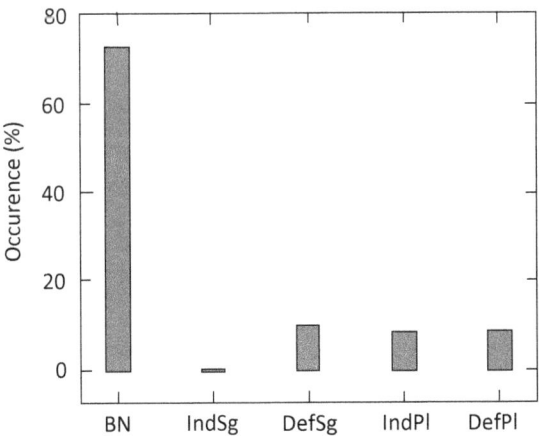

Figure 5.10. Corpus – generic NP types for 'plants'

The examples in (116) demonstrate the use of each of the NP types in descriptions of plants. 'Fennel' in (116a) can be understood as a mass noun, which explains the use of the bare form. It is not a particular fennel or a number of fennels that are used as edible vegetables. The definite singular in (116b) refers to a single tree as a prototype of all oaks. The predicate 'to be spread' can be considered a kind-predicate, as one cannot say that a single tree is spread over an area. The plural forms in (116c) and (116d) express a generic reference in two ways: the bare plural in (116c) means that ferns usually occur in tropical areas of the world, but they can also grow in other areas, whereas 'the agarics' in (116d) expresses a reference to mushrooms of this type. The definite plural generics in this sentence seem to access sub-kinds – there are many types of agarics and all of them have lamellae.

(116) a. **Fennikel** [fennel-Ø] brukes også som grønnsak, rå eller kokt.
          Fennel is also used as a vegetable, raw or cooked.
      b. **Eika** [oak-DEF] hadde da en større utbredelse enn nå.
          The oak was then more widespread than now.
      c. **Bregner** [ferns] er utbredt over hele Jorden, de fleste i tropene.
          Ferns are spread around the whole world, mostly in tropical climates.
      d. **Fluesoppene** [agarics-DEF] er skivesopp med hvite skiver.
          The agarics are mushrooms with white lamellae.

The positions and functions of generic NPs in this category are depicted in Tables 5.11. and 5.12. The majority of the nouns were subjects, with quite a high percentage of object function (22.54%). When it comes to the initial and non-initial positions of generic nouns describing plants, they were equally distributed throughout the texts. A similar regularity was also observed in the category 'tools', which will be discussed below.

Table 5.11. Corpus – noun position for 'plants'

Position	Number	%
Initial	71	50.00
Non-initial	71	50.00

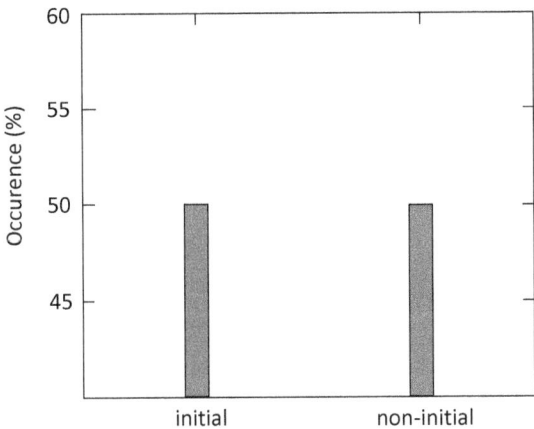

Figure 5.11. Corpus – noun position for 'plants'

Table 5.12. Corpus – noun function for 'plants'

Functions	Number	%
Subject	89	62.68
Object	32	22.54
Genitive modifier	2	1.41
Other	19	13.38

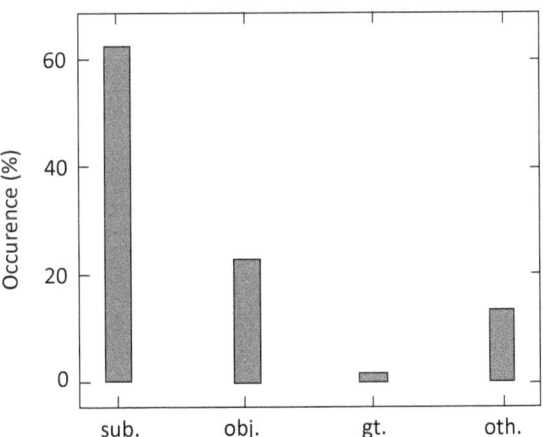

Figure 5.12. Corpus – noun function for 'plants'

5.3.1.4. 'Tools'

The fourth category of corpus texts, namely 'tools', contained 25 texts about different utensils, both everyday objects and specialised devices. The category also contained one mass noun that described an action, namely welding. Among all the nouns and pronouns in the texts, 122 nouns were tagged as generic.

Tools were described with all five NP types available in Norwegian. As in the previous category of texts, BNs were most often used when referring to different objects, representing 52.45% of nouns; the definite singular form was the next most frequent (27.87%). Surprisingly enough, the indefinite plural – which is said to be something of a default generic form in Germanic languages, was used in only 12.30% of the cases, followed by the indefinite singular (4.10%) and definite plural forms (3.28%).

Table 5.13. Corpus – generic NP types for 'tools'

Forms	Number	%
BN	64	52.46
Indefinite singular	5	4.10
Definite singular	34	27.87
Indefinite plural	15	12.30
Definite plural	4	3.28

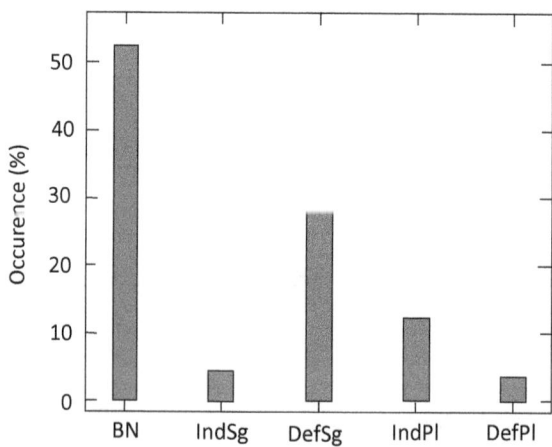

Figure 5.13. Corpus – generic NP types for 'tools'

The examples in 117 show how different NP types function in some of the corpus texts. The use of a BN occurs in a very typical encyclopaedic sentence where the function of an object is explained. This way the noun is interpreted generically but also functions as a prototype, similarly to the indefinite singular in (117b) and the definite singular in (117c). However, the difference between these three forms is that one cannot perceive a BN as singular, contrary to what certain researchers claim (cf. Borthen 2003). Following the view of Halmøy (2016), we shall interpret Norwegian BNs as unmarked in terms of definiteness and number. This makes the noun 'hand net' in (117a) not only a prototype of the device, but also a concept of it (cf. Lyons 1977 and Pettersson 1976).

The examples in (117d) and (117e) are plural nouns. The sentence with the indefinite noun is a generic sentence, describing the main characteristics of screws in general; its content therefore applies to most (if not all) objects from this category. The definite noun 'the gun', referring to spray guns used for different types of painting, refers to a sub-kind – guns designed particularly for powder coating. As in the category 'plants', definite plural generics can access sub-kinds.

(117) a. **Høvel** [hand.net-Ø] er et verktøy til utjevning av treoverflater.
 A hand plane is a tool used to even wooden surfaces.

 b. **En plateskrue** [a plate.screw] er spiss og laget av herdet stål.
 A plate screw is sharp and made of hardened steel.

 c. **Tangen** [pliers-DEF] kan brukes: til å holde fast et arbeidsstykke, til å gjennomskjære det, til å forme det ved pressing.
 Pliers can be used to hold an object one is working on, to cut through it, or to form the piece by pressing it.

 d. **Skruer** [screws] har mange anvendelser og former. Man skjelner mellom skruer beregnet for stål og metalldeler, og for arbeid i tre.
 Screws have many uses and forms. One differentiates between screws meant for steel and metal parts and those meant for working with wood.

 e. **Pistolene** [guns-DEF] kan også være konstruert spesielt for elektrostatisk påsprøyting.
 The guns [powder coating guns] can also be specially made for powder coating.

As stated above, exactly half of the generic nouns in the category 'tools' occurred in the initial position and the other half in a non-initial one. The majority of the nouns (57.38%) were subjects, 25.42% were objects, and the remainder occurred in genitive constructions or had other grammatical functions.

Table 5.14. Corpus – noun position for 'tools'

Position	Number	%
Initial	61	50.00
Non-initial	61	50.00

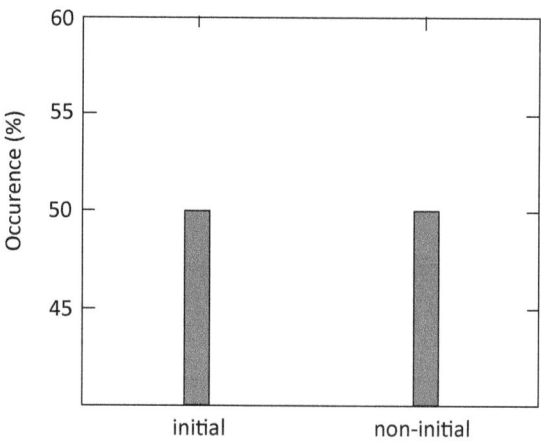

Figure 5.14. Corpus – noun position for 'tools'

Table 5.15. Corpus – noun function for 'tools'

Functions	Number	%
Subject	70	57.38
Object	31	25.41
Genitive modifier	7	5.74
Other	14	11.48

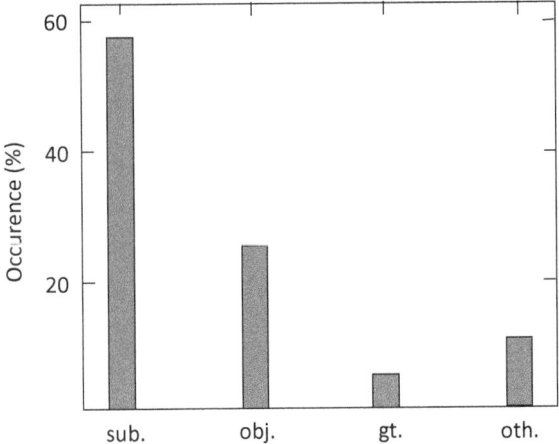

Figure 5.15. Corpus – noun function for 'tools'

5.3.1.5. 'Other'

The last and the largest category of corpus texts is the category 'other'. It comprises 75 texts denoting everyday objects, buildings, notions, and phenomena – as well as professions, which will be discussed in a separate subsection in this chapter. The nouns collected in this category were so diverse that it would be challenging to create a small subcategory for each of them. Therefore, this group of texts is also much larger than the other ones. The category also contains mass nouns, which will be discussed later in the chapter.

Genericity was tagged in 361 sentences. Generic nouns in this category occurred in all five forms, BN being most frequent and representing 36.84% of all generic nouns. The indefinite plural form appeared in 30.47% and the definite singular in 20.50% of cases, so those three forms prevailed in this group. Definite plural and indefinite singular nouns constituted 7.76% and 4.43%, respectively.

Table 5.16. Corpus – generic NP types for 'other'

Forms	Number	%
BN	133	36.84
Indefinite singular	16	4.43
Definite singular	74	20.50
Indefinite plural	110	30.47
Definite plural	28	7.76

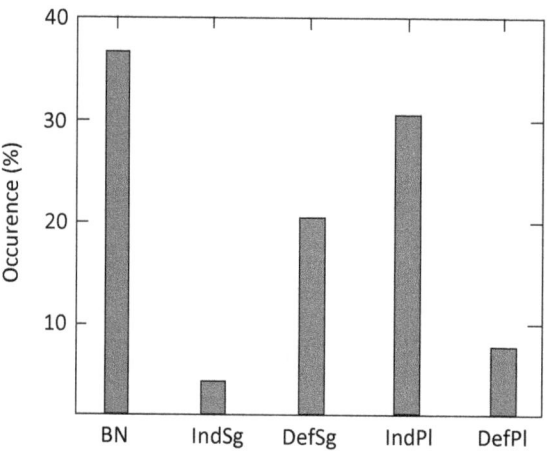

Figure 5.16. Corpus – generic NP types for 'other'

The examples retrieved from this part of the corpus were divided into those concerning objects, such as those in Example 118, and those describing professions in Example 119. As in the previous categories, all five NP types were utilised in generic contexts. The two forms that are of particular interest are the BN and the definite plural, as those have slightly different functions than in English, for example. The bare noun 'stavkirke' in (118a), combined with what could be considered a well-established kind, is not only an encyclopaedic entry but also a concept of this type of church. The sentence describes the characteristics of stave churches, allowing for a truly generic reading.

The definite plural form in (118e) occurs in the past tense and with the adverb 'often'. Again, the definite plural form accesses a sub-kind (a type of tent), whereas the predicate and the adverb make the whole sentence into a characterising expression. The use of a past tense in a generic sentence is not very common, though possible, and it does not influence the generic reading (see Lyons 1977). A similar structure can be observed in 118c, where the past tense is used with definite singular.

The sentences in (118b) and (118d) are again typical generic sentences – they describe the functions and features of certain objects – axles and fish hooks, respectively.

(118) a. **Stavkirke** [stave.church-Ø] er en høyt utviklet kirketype, oppført i reisverk av tre, kjent fra norsk kristen middelalder.
A stave church is a highly developed type of church, constructed with wooden staves and originating in Christian medieval Norway.

b. **En aksel** [an axle] kan også være en stillestående maskindel hvor de roterende deler er lagret, f.eks. foraksel på en bil, og en vanlig vognaksel.
An axle can also be a stationary part of a machine, in which the rotating parts are stored, for instance, a front axle in a car and a regular wagon axle.

c. **Badstuen** [sauna-DEF] var normalt innredet med en oppmurt røykovn av naturstein midt på gulvet uten røykavtrekk.
A sauna was normally furnished with a furnace oven made of natural stone, and without a smoke extractor.

d. **Fiskekroker** [fish.hooks] produseres i 12 000 forskjellige størrelser og varianter, fra 4–5 mm opptil 30 cm.
Fish hooks are produced in 12 000 different sizes and variants, from 4–5 mm up to 30 cm.

e. **Tipiene** [tipis] var ofte dekorert med symboler og tegninger som fortalte om eierens bragder.
Tipis were often decorated with symbols and drawings depicting the owner's feats.

Professions

The difference between professions and words describing official functions is that in order to become a psychologist, for example, one needs to attain a certain level of education in a given subject, whereas being a county governor, for instance, does not imply that has one studied at a given faculty (this is illustrated particularly well in Example 119a). It might be desirable, but it is not obligatory. The division between professions and expressions that describe groups of people (not only ethnicity, but also class, background, etc.) may seem vague, but it was possible to draw the line between the two in the material. This has illustrated how different those two categories are.

The examples listed in (119) describe some of the professions that were included in the corpus. The BN in Sentence 119a describes a person who performs this type of job, whereas the indefinite singular used as a genitival modifier in (119b) directs the main focus to the work connected with the profession. The work of a psychologist is also described with the use of the bare plural in (119d), where a reference to a group of people is expressed. The definite singular form in (119c) has a two-fold function: on the one hand it directs the focus to the profession, and on the other hand, it shows what tasks band leaders are responsible for.

(119) a. **Psykolog** [psychologist-Ø] er en person med utdanning i psykologi.
A psychologist is a person with an education in psychology.

  b. **En bakers** [a baker-GT] arbeid er nær beslektet med det som utføres av en konditor, og mange yrkesutøvere i bransjen har avlagt svenneprøve i begge disse håndverksfagene.
A baker's work is closely related to the work of a confectioner, and many workers in this field choose a certification exam in both of these professions.

  c. **Dirigenten** [band.leader-DEF] instruerer orkesteret eller koret, bestemmer tempo og dynamikk og sørger for at musikkverket blir forsvarlig innøvd.
A band leader instructs an orchestra or a choir, controls the tempo and the dynamics, and makes sure the musical piece is performed correctly.

  d. **Psykologer** [psychologists] arbeider som helsepersonell.
Psychologists work as health staff.

Interestingly enough, none of the professions occurred as a definite plural. The assumption that the professions function differently than notions that describe people was initially confirmed by the corpus data. The texts about groups of people had a slightly different structure than those in the subcategory 'professions': a text about the Bagli party, for example, would concern the origin of that group, their history, etc., whereas describing a profession focusses more on the work and only to a lesser degree on the people performing the given tasks.

Having looked at different nouns from this category, let us now see how the nouns were distributed within the texts. The majority of the nouns in this category were in the initial position (52.91%). Most of the NPs were subjects (70.08%) and only some were objects (17.45%). Genitive constructions and other grammatical functions were tagged in 12.48% of the nouns. Even though the diversity of topics in this category was much greater than in other text groups, the results are not very different from those discussed earlier in the chapter.

Table 5.17. Corpus – noun position for 'other'

Position	Number	%
Initial	191	52.91
Non-initial	170	47.09

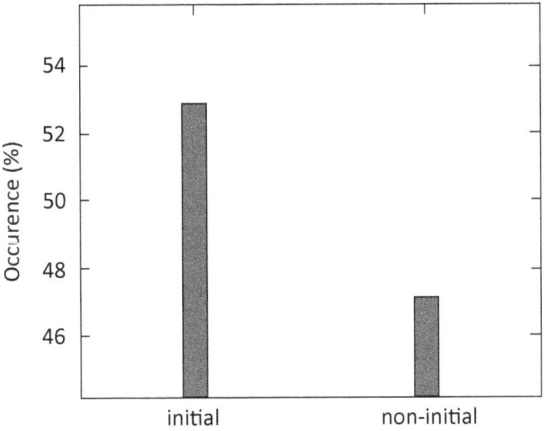

Figure 5.17. Corpus – noun position for 'other'

Table 5.18. Corpus – noun function for 'other'

Functions	Number	%
Subject	253	70.08
Object	63	17.45
Genitive modifier	14	3.89
Other	31	8.59

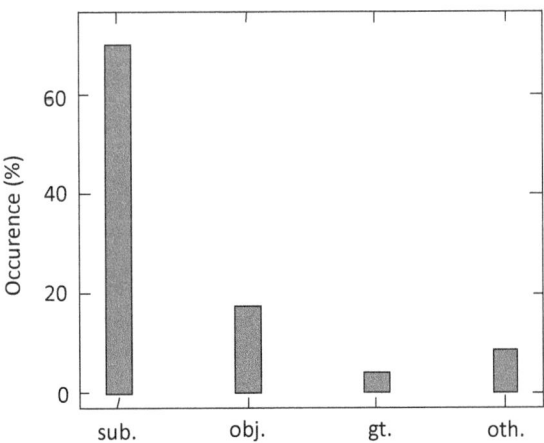

Figure 5.18. Corpus – noun function for 'other'

Mass nouns

As mentioned in Chapter 4, generic mass nouns in Norwegian and other Germanic languages can in fact appear in two forms: the definite form or as bare nouns. However, it is possible to perceive certain mass nouns as semi-countable – for example, 'beer' designates a type of drink, whereas 'a beer' is perceived as a type of beer or one unit of the drink (a glass, a can, etc.). Since Survey 1 included a number of mass nouns and the results were in accordance with the assumptions, only a few uncountable nouns were chosen for this analysis:

- sveising – welding,
- fjernstyring – remote control,
- språkvitenskap – linguistics,
- cellulose – cellulose,
- demokrati – democracy.

As expected, the nouns occurred either as BNs or as definite nouns. Germanic languages do not really allow for other forms to occur with mass nouns. In (120) the noun 'linguistics' is used only as a BN, as it is an abstract noun.

(120) **Språkvitenskap** [linguistics-Ø] er det vitenskapelige studiet av språk. Språk kan studeres fra mange forskjellige innfallsvinkler. Noen språkvitere er opptatt av språk som et typisk trekk ved mennesket, altså språk som kognitivt system som skiller mennesket fra andre dyr på jorda. Innen denne formen for **språkvitenskap** er man mer opptatt av hva som er felles for alle språk enn hva som er forskjellig, fordi man studerer det som gjør mennesket til en art som skiller seg vesentlig fra andre arter.

Linguistics is a scientific study of language. Language can be studied from many different perspectives. Some linguists are interested in languages as a typical feature of humankind, that is, language as a cognitive system which differentiates people from other animals in the world. In this form of linguistics, one is interested in what is common to all languages, not what is different, as one studies factors that make people different from other species.

Other mass nouns that were tagged in the corpus also occurred as BNs and some of them – such as 'welding' – took a countable form as a definite plural compound noun ('*sveisemtodene*' ['the welding methods']).

Familiar nouns and well-established kinds

Certain nouns and noun phrases are sometimes recognised by native speakers as well-established kinds or familiar nouns. Both notions are synonymous to a certain degree, as has been claimed by Borthen (2007: 144), for instance. In the literature on genericity, WEKs are mentioned more often than familiar nouns, but the two refer to the same concept, namely reference to an object or an animal that can easily be recalled by the hearer based only on the discourse.

What one determines as a well-established kind varies from speaker to speaker, but certain tendencies were observed in the corpus material. Apart from the types of nouns mentioned above, the category WEK can also include the following:

1. everyday objects,
2. animals kept as pets,
3. objects characteristic of a given culture (e.g. the Norwegian and Scandinavian/Nordic cultures),
4. objects that are sometimes perceived and/or interpreted as mass nouns, even though they are countable from a grammatical point of view (certain plant types, materials, everyday objects, etc.),
5. objects that are considered familiar as a result of frequent occurrence (e.g. white wedding dress, Coca-Cola bottle, etc.).

Some of the nouns considered to be WEKs in the corpus were 'dog', 'fjord', 'knife', 'stave church', 'cottage', 'guitar', and 'telephone'.

(121) a. **Hunden** var det første husdyret vårt, og er i dag den arten som viser størst variasjon i størrelse, farge, fasong og atferd. (…) Hvordan **ulv** ble til **hund** finnes det flere teorier om, men hypotesen om selvdomestisering står sterkest.

The dog was our first domestic animal and today it is the species that shows the most diversity when it comes to size, colour, type, and behaviour. … There are many theories about how a wolf became a dog, but the most popular one concerns self-domestication.

b. **Fjord** brukes om en større, forgrenet innskjæring av havet, oftest lang og smal og omgitt av fjellsider. Noen ganger blir uttrykket også brukt om langstrakte innsjøer, for eksempel Tunnhovdfjorden. I vitenskapelig

terminologi er fjord betegnelsen på en havbukt dannet ved at en bre
har formet og fordypet en tidligere dal. **Fjordene** har bratte, u-formede
sider og kan være meget dype, men har oftest en grunnere terskel ved
munningen.

[The notion] 'fjord' is used when talking about a larger split of the shore,
most often long and narrow and surrounded by mountains. Sometimes
the expression is used when referring to long lakes, for instance, Tunnhovdfjorden. In scientific terminology, 'fjord' is a name of a bay that
was created when a glacier formed and deepened a valley. The fjords
have steep, U-shaped sides and can be very deep, but most often they
have a shallow threshold by the opening.

In Example 121a, the noun 'dog' appears in the definite form and as a BN.
Likewise, the noun 'wolf' could be perceived as a WEK, even though it is
not the main topic of this text. Furthermore, 'wolf' is also strongly rooted in
Norwegian culture, which can influence its interpretation in generic contexts.
Sentence 121b describes the characteristic properties of fjords, using both
BNs and definite forms. Bare nouns can be interpreted as concepts, in a way
model fjords, whereas definite plural generics give actual fjords as examples
when describing their characteristic features.

At first sight, WEKs do not differ from *regular* nouns when it comes to
the grammatical forms they occur in. The difference is mainly semantic and
pragmatic. The issue has been discussed in several works on genericity (see e.g.
Carlson and Pelletier 1995; Mari et al. 2013a), but the judgment of whether or
not a given noun is familiar always depends on speakers' language intuitions.

The nouns proposed as WEKs in this section were consulted with a native
speaker of Norwegian, but their interpretation is by no means final. This
aspect of the study is only an attempt to identify nouns that do not seem to
follow the same pattern as other nouns in generic contexts. Nevertheless, the
study would have to be designed differently in order to show the diversity
of WEKs and their interpretations. The examples presented here are meant
to show that the phenomenon exists in Norwegian but is highly context-de-
pendant. Moreover, certain predicates and sentence structures might occur
solely with BNs, which then obtain a WEK-like reading (e.g. *'spille gitar'* ['to
play guitar']).

Table 5.19. shows an overview of all the results. When we compare all of
the NP types that appeared in the corpus, we can see that BNs occurred in
every category and with very different values, ranging from as low as 19.39%

('people') to as high as 73.24% ('plants'). BNs are often used when the generic reference is made with a prototypical object.

The indefinite plural also presents a broad spectrum of usage across the texts, ranging from 8.45% ('plants') to 49.66% ('animals'). The results confirm that, especially in the case of kind reference in such categories as 'animals', this form remains the *default* in terms of classic kind-reference.

Table 5.19. Corpus – NP types by category

Forms	Animals	Plants	Tools	Other	People	Total
	Number (%)	Number (%)	Number (%)	Number (%)	Number (%)	Number (%)
BN	25 (17.01)	104 (73.24)	64 (52.46)	133 (36.84)	19 (19.39)	345 (39.66)
IndSg	0 (0.00)	0 (0.00)	5 (4.10)	16 (4.43)	10 (10.20)	31 (3.56)
IndPl	32 (21.77)	14 (9.86)	34 (27.87)	74 (20.50)	31 (31.63)	185 (21.26)
DefSg	73 (49.66)	12 (8.45)	15 (12.30)	110 (30.47)	20 (20.41)	230 (26.44)
DefPl	17 (11.56)	12 (8.45)	4 (3.28)	28 (7.76)	18 (18.37)	79 (9.08)
Total	147	142	122	361	98	
Total (%)	16.90	16.32	14.02	41.49	11.26	

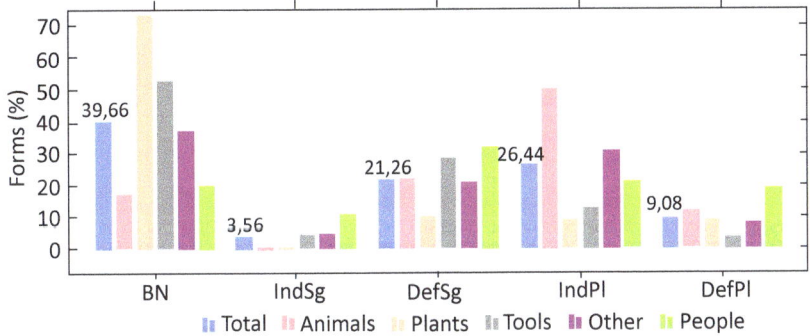

Figure 5.19. Corpus – NP types by category

5.4. Cognitive analysis

The results from the corpus were analysed, according to the cognitive models proposed by Radden and Dirven (2007), and Radden (2009). The types of generic references these authors discussed do not account for BNs; therefore, the model designed by Pettersson (1976) for Swedish was used and modified, according to the data collected.

The types of generic references proposed in the cognitive grammar of English by Radden and Dirven and Radden include the following:

1. indefinite singular generic,
2. definite singular generic,
3. indefinite plural generic,
4. definite plural generic.

When we consider a similar model designed for Swedish, bare nouns occur as one of the possible choices in such contexts (Pettersson 1976). The use of BNs was frequent in this study and they occurred in every text category. It was therefore possible to differentiate between different meanings of BNs used throughout the corpus.

Table 5.20. presents a simplified matrix of NP types and the contexts in which they occurred most often in the corpus.

Table 5.20. Corpus – generic NPs, a simplified matrix

BN	IndSg	DefSg	IndPl	DefPl
1) mass nouns	1) stand-alone objects	1) mass nouns	1) kinds	1) ethnic social groups
2) WEKs, familiar nouns		2) WEKs	2) groups of people	2) gregarious animals
3) quasi mass nouns	2) professions	3) official functions		3) sub-kinds
4) concepts	3) prototypes	4) kinds		4) hyperonymes
5) professions				

The list of contexts in which the different NP types were used is not exhaustive. However, based on the material collected and the analyses conducted, those were the most common contexts, aligning partially with the cognitive models presented in the theoretical chapter.

Bare nouns – which were not taken into account in the two models by Radden and Dirven (2007) and Radden (2009) – were identified in multiple contexts. According to the graph presented by Pettersson (1976: 121), in Swedish bare nouns are used in unlimited contexts (namely the indefinite) and with non-specific nouns (generic). A similar statement can also be said about Norwegian, where reference to kinds can in certain cases be rendered with

BNs, as in Example (115a), repeated here as (122), or in the example provided by Borthen (2003: 31) (repeated here as 123).

(122) Dronte, også kalt dodo [dodo-Ø], Raphus cucullatus, på Mauritius veide 20–25 kg og fantes i store mengder da europeerne kom dit i 1598.
Dodo, *Raphus cucullatus*, on Mauritius it weighed 20–25 kg and occurred in large quantities when the Europeans arrived in 1598.

(123) a. **bil** er et kjøretøy.
car is a vehicle.
A car is a vehicle.

b. **Datamaskin** er et nyttig hjelpemiddel.
computer is a useful tool
A computer is a useful tool.

These examples show two different contexts in which a kind can be referred to with a BN. The noun 'dodo' in (122) functions as an encyclopaedic entry, a keyword of some sort, and therefore its use without any article is dictated by the text's genre. However, the kind reference is clear. In the sentences in (123), BNs have only one function: they denote kinds by referring to unspecific and *unlimited* entities. In this regard, Norwegian follows the Swedish model of Pettersson. In the matrix presented above, such cases are identified as references to concepts. 'Car' and 'computer' in (123) do not refer to any particular entities that would represent the whole kind, but rather they denote kinds through concepts of those two objects. A similar use of BNs was observed in the case of professions, where BNs referred to concepts rather than actual people being teachers, psychologists, etc.

When it comes to other uses of BNs in the corpus texts, namely with *quasi*-mass nouns, WEKs and familiar nouns, the examples were numerous. Quasi-mass nouns are nouns that can be perceived as uncountable, such as 'moss'. In Norwegian, the noun is countable and it is therefore possible to say 'the mosses'. However, BNs were used frequently in such cases.

The last context in which familiar nouns and WEKs occur as BNs was also discussed in the scholarly literature on the Norwegian nominal system (see e.g. Borthen 2003, 2007; Rosén and Borthen 2017; Halmøy 2016). This context depends on speakers' interpretation of a given sentence or text, but certain tendencies can be observed. For instance, with predicates such as 'to have', 'to get', or 'to buy', familiar nouns occur as BNs. One can say, for instance, *Jeg skal kjøpe bil'* ['I will buy a car'], where the noun 'car' would be interpreted as a concept of a car, not a particular entity.

A similar notion to the concept of an object is its prototype, which is most often rendered with the indefinite singular (Radden and Dirven 2007: 108). In such a reference, one entity is chosen by the speaker as a prototype of the whole kind. This form was also used when talking about professions and stand-alone objects such as 'a knife' or 'a screwdriver'.

The definite singular reference occurred most often with mass nouns, WEKs, as well as kinds and official functions, especially those understood as unique (for instance being a kind, a priest, etc.). As has been presented in the model by Radden and Dirven and Pettersson, definite singular reference concerns prototypes or refers to distinctive features of a given kind. Such contexts were indeed present in the corpus.

All models used for this analysis describe the indefinite plural noun form as *default* when it comes to genericity. Indeed, many *classic* generic references, namely kind-references, are rendered with this form. The indefinite plural was also used when talking about groups of people. Moreover, in the corpus one more context was observed, namely general truths. As mentioned in Chapter 2, genericity has two senses: it can refer to kinds or it can express regularly occurring actions in the form of habitual sentences. In the corpus, the second of these senses was also rendered with the indefinite plural, making this form the default generic.

The last of the forms depicted in Table 5.20. is the definite plural, and it occurred in four main contexts. Reference to people was most often rendered with this form, aligning with what Radden (2009) calls a 'delimited generic'. However, in Norwegian the definite plural is not at all limited to only this context; it was also used when referring to animals perceived as gregarious[26] and to sub-kinds. This use of the definite plural contrasts with the cognitive model for the English language, where sub-kinds are usually accessed by the definite singular.

Hyperonyms were also described with the definite plural. This can be interpreted as a hyperonym being the main class of certain objects or animals; for instance, the hyperonym 'vehicle' includes cars, lorries, and many others. The same applies to hyperonyms used when describing kinds – 'horse' can have many sub-kinds and both can be accessed with the definite plural.

---

[26] Some animal species are only perceived as gregarious by the speakers of the language, even though the biological classification might state differently.

Despite a much wider use of definite plural generics in the corpus, the models proposed by Radden and Dirven (2007) and Radden (2009) also apply to Norwegian. Delimited generics remain the default form when talking about groups of people, with a few other contexts, such as sub-kinds and hyperonyms.

The cognitive models proposed in this section and the matrix of the NP types used in different contexts in the corpus show that Norwegian generics are slightly more complex than generic references in English. Nevertheless, the forms were used rather consistently in the corpus texts, proving that even though all five NP types can be used generically, they are not interchangeable in each and every context.

5.5. Statistical analysis

In addition to the qualitative description of the corpus data, statistical tests were performed. In order to see how the NP types are distributed throughout the corpus, the data was analysed with the use of descriptive statistics. The material was first divided into quartiles and the minimal and maximal values were calculated, as were the medians and the means. The results are depicted in Table 5.21.

The minimal value of 0 for each of the forms indicates that there are texts in the corpus where one or more of the forms do not appear at all. For instance, there is at least one text that does not have any BNs, at least one that does not have any indefinite singular nouns, and so on. Minimal values of 0 for the indefinite singular were seen in the category 'animals', where none of the texts contained that form.

The maximal value, on the other hand, as the name implies, shows the maximal values of each of the forms in the corpus texts. For instance, there was at least one text where a BN occurred 15 times, at least one where the indefinite singular occurred three times, etc.

The data were then divided into quartiles, which show a more precise distribution of each of the forms throughout the corpus. The values from the corpus were ordered from the minimum to the maximum. The standard deviation (SD) was calculated; SD shows the dispersion of the data, which differ significantly between the forms. For instance, BNs are a lot more dispersed than indefinite singulars. This may be due to the fact that BNs were generally most frequently used throughout the corpus, irrespective of the text category. The distribution and dispersion of the corpus data can also be seen in Figure 5.20.

Table 5.21. Corpus – descriptive statistics of generic NP types

	BN	IndSg	DefSg	IndPl	DefPl
Min.	0.00	0.00	0.00	0.00	0.00
1st Quartile	1.00	0.00	0.00	0.00	0.00
Median	1.00	0.00	0.00	0.00	0.00
Mean	2.029	0.182	1.088	1.353	0.465
3rd Quartile	3.00	0.00	2.00	2.00	0.00
Max.	15.00	3.00	9.00	12.00	6.00
SD	2.26	0.51	1.58	2.18	1.07

The values depicted in Figure 5.20. show the descriptive statistics: minimal and maximal values, means, medians, and outliers – those values that do not follow the main tendencies.

The next step consisted in conducting statistical tests in order to compare the data distribution for each of the forms. As in the previous chapter, the assumptions of ANOVA were verified. One-way ANOVA could not be performed since the assumptions of the normality of the data and the homogeneity of variance were not satisfied. The normality of the data was checked with the Shapiro–Wilk test, which resulted in a p-value of $<2.2\text{e-}16$. As the p-value fell below 0.05, the data were not normally distributed and the necessary assumption was not verified. The second assumption concerning the homogeneity of variance was verified with Levene's test, which also resulted in a p-value of less than 0.05 (see Table 5.22.). ANOVA was therefore not suitable for this analysis (Rasinger 2013: 140).

Another way of analysing data in such a case is with the Kruskal–Wallis test, a non-parametric test that is used when the assumptions for ANOVA are not satisfied. The analysis resulted in a p-value of $<2.2\text{e-}16$ (below 0.05), indicating that there are differences between the tested groups. The groups in the analysis were the five NP types. However, the Kruskal–Wallis test does not show exactly where the differences are; in order to verify that, a post hoc test is needed. The post hoc test of choice in the case of Kruskal–Wallis is Dunn's test. The results of Dunn's test are depicted in Table 5.23.

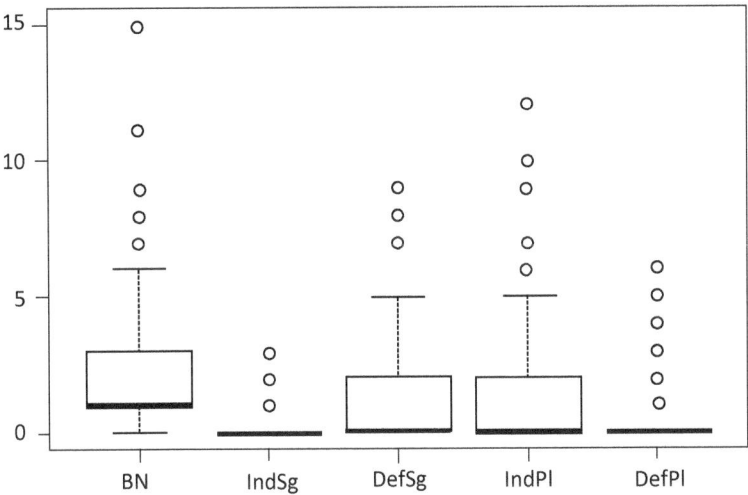

Figure 5.20. Corpus – boxplot of generic NP types

Table 5.22. Corpus – Levene's test

	Df	F value	Pr(>F)	
Group	4	19.58	5.99e-15	***
	845			

Table 5.23. Corpus – Dunn's test

Mean comparison	BN	IndSg	DefSg	IndPl
IndSg	12.47			
p-adjust	0.00			
DefSg	5.83	−6.64		
p-adjust	5.60e–08	3.17e-10		
IndPl	5.93	−6.53	0.11	
p-adjust	2.86e–08	6.70e-10	1.00	
DefPl	10.49	−1.98	4.66	4.55
p-adjust	0.00	0.48	3.12e-05	5.32e–05

Dunn's test is a multiple comparison test that shows the differences be-tween the groups' means. The values marked in bold designate differences between the forms. As can be seen, there were no statistical differences only between two pairs: 1) definite singular – indefinite plural and 2) indefinite singular – definite plural. This indicated that all other pairs of NP types were different from each other, from a statistical point of view. This was also observed in Section 5.4. above, where different contexts were given for each of the NP types. The cognitive interpretation of the results was also confirmed in the statistical analysis, which makes the findings more reliable.

5.6. Conclusions

Generic texts allow the phenomenon to be observed in a wider context, as opposed to sentence analysis. As shown in this chapter, numerous examples confirm that in Norwegian not only are all NP types allowed in generic contexts, but BNs are also quite frequent in generic expressions with countable nouns. Both qualitative and quantitative analyses have shown the diversity of generic nouns and NPs in the corpus. When it comes to animacy, it is a factor that seems to play a role in expressing generics. In the category 'people', definite generics constituted a large amount of the material, with rather limited use of BNs compared to the other text categories. The category 'animals' differed slightly in terms of the most frequently used NP types. There were no instances of indefinite singular, and definite forms were in the minority of all generic expressions. Bare plurals were the most frequent form, which supports the thesis that kind-reference is expressed with the indefinite plural. Interestingly enough, the text group 'plants', even though grammatically inanimate, was very similar to the category 'animals'. The indefinite singular form did not occur in the texts about plants. However, the most frequent NP type was BNs, which may suggest that some plants are considered mass, even though they are grammatically countable. The matrix of NP types in generic contexts presented in this chapter is based on the models designed by Radden and Dirven (2007), Radden (2009), and Pettersson (1976). In order to account for the Norwegian data, the model was adjusted, especially when it comes to BNs and the definite plural (the delimited generic). Most of the functions presented in the models also applied to Norwegian, such as treating the indefinite singular as a concept of an object and the definite singular as its prototype. Moreover, a few more contexts were observed in the corpus and were added to the model. Those contexts included, for instance, using BNs with animals, plants, and objects which are perceived as mass (quasi-mass) nouns or which describe sub-kinds with the definite plural. The last part of the corpus analysis consisted in a number of statistical tests. The tests were performed in order to identify the dispersion of the data and any differences between the NP types. The tests illustrated how the data were distributed and where the main tendencies in occurrences of the forms lay. The statistical part of the chapter complements the cognitive part in that it shows exactly where the differences between different noun forms are and how significant they are for the whole analysis.

6. Survey 2

6.1. Method

After building and analysing the corpus for the project, an AJT survey was conducted among native speakers of Norwegian. The idea of testing speakers' intuitions and contrasting it with the corpus material was inspired by a study by Oosterhof (2008). This way, the corpus served as a basis for the grammaticality judgements utilised in the survey, providing in a way *model* generic sentences. Grammaticality judgements in the form of a survey are widely used in linguistics. They can be used to check speakers' intuitions as well as to compare theory from normative grammar books with the actual usage of a given language. However, many researchers have pointed out that AJT surveys come with a number of issues. One issue is the way a given task is designed. For instance, asking participants for their judgement on a given matter can yield promising results, whereas asking them to justify why they judge a given sentence (in)correct seems futile (Schütze 2016: 56–57). The idea behind most grammaticality judgements is that the answers are very much intuition-driven, which means that it might be difficult for the participants to explain why they think a given sentence is correct or not.

One of the solutions one can apply in order for grammaticality judgements to produce reliable results is to introduce ranking of the test items (Schütze 2016: 58). Such rankings can have different scales or be more or less detailed, but their goal is always the same – to provide the participants with a wider range of answers. This way the participants are able to grade their answers, according to the scale provided, but without the need to explain why they made a given choice.

Many surveys that do employ sophisticated rating scales are conducted on smaller groups of participants (cf. the studies by Oosterhof [2008] and Ionin et al. [2011], among others). Since the first survey was conducted on a large number of participants and did not include a grading scale, the second survey was designed to be slightly different. The main idea was to recruit a smaller number of participants and to be able to prevent non-native speakers from taking part in the survey. A form published online can be answered by anyone, so it is impossible to state with absolute certainty whether each and every answer is an actual answer to the questions or whether it was done haphazardly by someone not even interested in the study. Recruiting participants in person minimised that risk significantly.

As with Survey 1, the test sentences were analysed, according to the model proposed by Leslie et al. (2011). In each of the sentences, a type of generic predication was identified. The types were then analysed together with the judgements from the survey. Since the corpus texts were analysed according to the models proposed by Radden and Dirven (2007), Radden (2009), and Pettersson (1976), the model will also be utilised here, but only in order to develop the matrix of generic NP types and the contexts they are used in. This way, the models originally developed for English (Radden and Dirven and Radden) and for Swedish (Pettersson) can be adjusted to Norwegian and based on empirical data that illustrate actual language use.

6.1.1. Structure of the survey and tools used

The survey based on the corpus material was modified from that of Survey 1. First of all, the number of participants was limited to 100 people, who were chosen in person and not through a website. In the first survey conducted for this project, the respondents received short texts where generic sentences contained gaps. The gaps were filled with a noun in one or more grammatical forms. In the second survey, however, the test items were generic sentences retrieved from the corpus. The test items and filler items were chosen from different text categories. In addition, five filler items were placed in the survey so as not to suggest the actual topic of the study. The test items included the following NPs[27]:

---

[27] All NPs are listed as BNs. For a full survey, see the Appendix.

1. Birkebeinere – the Birkebein Party,
2. diakon – deacon,
3. måke – seagull,
4. skate – batoidea,
5. flaggermus – bat,
6. oter – otter,
7. sjiraff – giraffe,
8. krokodille – crocodile,
9. hai – shark,
10. humle – bumble bee,
11. ål – eel,
12. torvmose – peat moss,
13. kniv – knife,
14. meander – meander,
15. stavkirke – stave church,
16. kulepenn – ballpoint pen,
17. gen – gene,
18. fiskekrok – fish hook,
19. skrue – screw,
20. gitar – guitar.

The sentences with NPs 1–2 were retrieved from the category 'people'; NPs 3–11 were from the category 'animals', 12 was from the category 'plants', 13 from the category 'tools', and 14–20 from the category 'other'. As mentioned above, the sentences chosen for the survey had to be generic without a wider context and their forms needed to be diverse – with generic nouns in both the initial and non-initial positions, for instance. The thematic categories from which the sentences were retrieved were not the main priority.

The filler items in the survey consisted of five sentences with the following NPs:

1. sjefdirigent – leading conductor,
2. husmann – cotter,
3. knivspiss – knife tip,
4. sysselmann – governor,
5. telefon – telephone.

The NPs in the test items and filler items occurred in both the initial and non-initial positions in order to provide more diversity and not to suggest the subject of the survey to the respondents.

Open-source software tools were used to create and publish the survey. The core of the software was R, whereas the graphical interface was designed with the use of the package Shiny. All survey results were saved directly to Dropbox. The choice of such tools over, for instance, Google Forms – which was used to build the first survey – was informed by the need to adjust the design of the form. Google Forms does provide certain options when it comes to customisation, but they are rather limited. Also, the answers from Google Forms are saved in one file and without being divided into columns, which makes the analysis much more complicated. The way of saving the data was customised with R and Shiny.

Using R and Shiny also made it possible to adjust the survey interface for all screen sizes. The grading scale for the sentences was always displayed horizontally, which made it consistent with the grading instructions and therefore more intuitive for the participants. The participants were able to fill out the survey on the provided laptop and tablet or to use a link or QR code to open the survey on their own electronic devices.

The survey was divided into two main parts. The first one contained questions about the participants, such as their sex, age, and education. The second part consisted of a list of sentences with all possible NP types. Each of the forms had a grading scale next to it, ranging from 1 to 3, where 1 meant 'correct', 2 meant 'acceptable', and 3 stood for 'incorrect/awkward'. The grading scale was simplified in comparison to Oosterhof's study. The reason for this was the length and complicity of the survey. Since the survey was relatively long, adding a complex grading scale could have discouraged the participants or even resulted in random answers. It is also worth mentioning that because of the available resources the survey could not be conducted in a laboratory or other isolated area where the participants would not be distracted or interrupted. It was therefore necessary to adjust the design of the survey to the conditions. Nevertheless, two participants chose not to fill in the form, judging it too complex despite the provided instructions. Other respondents did not report similar issues.

6.2. Respondents

The second survey, as with the one utilised in Survey 1, also contained a number of questions about the participants. The respondents had to specify their age, sex, education, origin, and the language they usually swear in. The control question about the language used for swearing was added in order to make sure that Norwegian was the first language of all participants. In the first survey, many participants understood the control question as 'In what languages can you count', often listing all the foreign languages they spoke. Furthermore, swearing is an emotion-driven behaviour and it is therefore much more plausible that a speaker swears in his or her native language. However, especially among the younger generation, it is common to swear in English, so the possibility of such answers to the question was also taken into account. This was verified by the fact that none of the respondents chose the location 'other' as their place of origin, so potential answers about swearing in other languages were not critical in identifying native speakers of Norwegian.

Table 6.1. Survey 2 – age of the respondents

Age	Women	Men	Total
18–19	13	2	15
20–24	32	27	59
25–30	11	12	23
31–40	0	2	2
41–50	1	0	1
Total	57	43	100

Table 6.1. and Figure 6.1. show the age and sex of the respondents. One hundred respondents took part in the survey, mostly aged 18–30 years. People from other age groups were rather reluctant and did not agree to devote their time to the study.[28] As with the first survey, women were also predominant in many of the age categories, excluding the groups aged 25–30 and 31–40.

---

[28] All participants were informed about the duration of the survey (15–20 minutes) and that it concerned the Norwegian language.

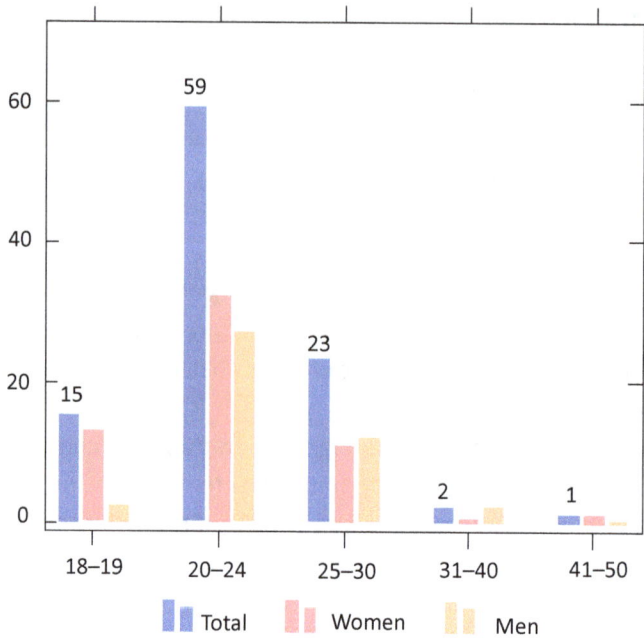

Figure 6.1. Survey 2 – age of the respondents

Table 6.2. Survey 2 – education level of the respondents

Education/Gender	Women	Men	Total
Primary school	3	0	3
High school	31	15	46
University	23	28	51

As can be seen in Table 6.2. and Figure 6.2., 51 respondents stated that they had a higher education, 46 a high school education, and 3 people chose 'primary school' from the answers. Given the high number of young people, who most likely were studying at the University of Tromsø at the time, the choice of 'high school' in so many cases is not surprising – the participants who had not yet completed a university degree chose this option.

Table 6.3. shows the origin of all participants. As can be seen on the map in Figure 6.3.,[29] the majority of the people who took part in the survey were from the north of the country. This was not surprising, given that the survey

---

[29]   In 2019, when the survey was conducted, there were 18 municipalities in Norway, as the country is in the process of merging certain municipalities. See the map in Chapter 4.

was conducted in Tromsø. However, there were a number of people from other regions of the country, e.g. Trøndelag, Vestfold, and Østfold. Nevertheless, the distribution of the various regions of Norway was much less varied than in Survey 1.

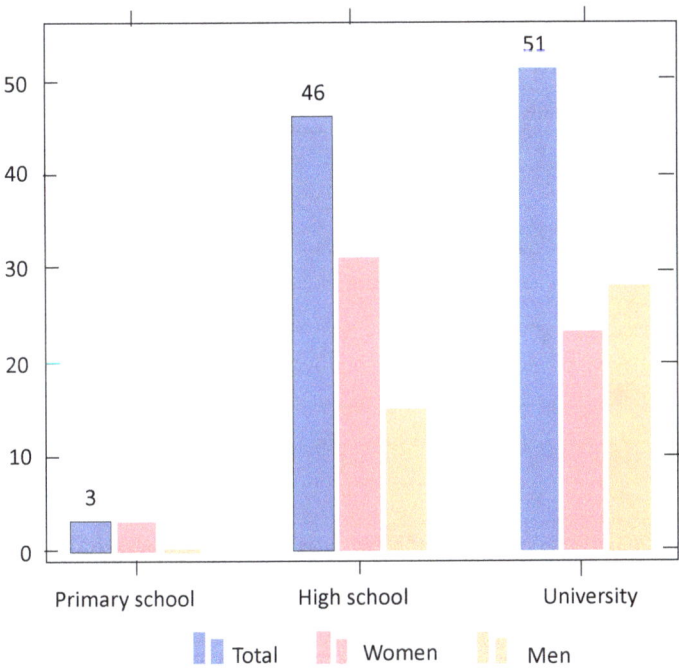

Figure 6.2. Survey 2 – education level of the respondents

As with the first survey, the sentences chosen for this survey were written in *bokmål* and all respondents were informed of the fact beforehand. A few people asked whether they should answer the way they would in their dialects and they were asked not to do so, but rather to opt for more standardised answers. This shows that many participants were aware of the differences between *standard* Norwegian[30] and certain dialects.

---

[30]   I use this term in its colloquial meaning since there is no such thing as 'standard Norwegian'. There are written standards of the language, but those do not correspond to 'RP' English, German 'Hochdeutsch', or Swedish 'rikssvenska'. For further discussion see Chapter 7.

Compared to the first survey, the number of participants was significantly smaller. Since the respondents were recruited in person and not through an online forum, it was possible to verify beforehand whether they were native speakers of Norwegian. This was then confirmed by the places of origin that the participants had chosen.

Table 6.3. Survey 2 – origin of the respondents

Regions	Respondents
Akershus	2
Aust-Agder	1
Buskerud	0
Finnmark	12
Hedmark	1
Hordaland	2
Møre og Romsdal	1
Nordland	12
Oppland	2
Oslo	2
Østfold	4
Rogaland	2
Sogn og Fjordane	1
Telemark	2
Troms	45
Trøndelag	7
Vest-Agder	0
Vestfold	4

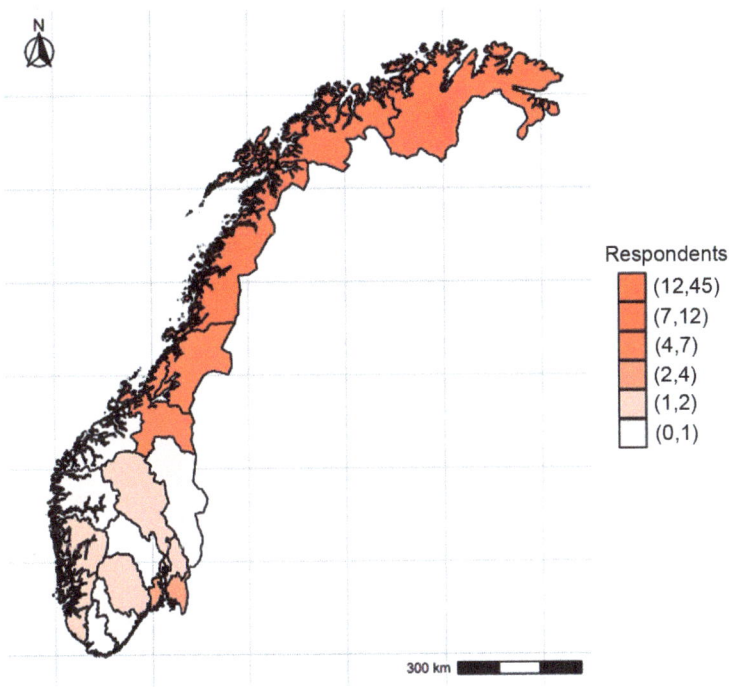

Respondents
- (12,45)
- (7,12)
- (4,7)
- (2,4)
- (1,2)
- (0,1)

300 km

Figure 6.3. Survey 2 – origin of the respondents

6.3. General results

The sentences from the corpus chosen for this survey were in a way model generic sentences, that is, their forms were not significantly different from what previous analyses have shown. One of the nouns chosen for the AJT survey was a well-established kind: 'stave church'. However, stave churches are deeply rooted in the Norwegian culture, so interpreting the noun as familiar is not dependent on context or intuition in this case. The nouns chosen for the study and the forms they originally occurred in are presented in Table 6.4.

As can be seen, only one noun among the twenty chosen for the analysis occurred as a BN, and it is in fact 'stave church', considered to be a *classic* WEK. The majority of the sentences are indefinite plurals, which, as mentioned in previous chapters, can be considered default generics in most Germanic languages. Also, indefinite plurals in Norwegian are very often used when referring to whole kinds (see Chapters 4 and 5). A number of example sentences occurred originally in the corpus with definite plural NPs, such as 'the seagulls' or 'the peat mosses'.

Table 6.4. Survey 2 – chosen nouns

Noun	Form
birkebeinere	indpl
diakonen	defsg
måkene	defpl
skater	indpl
flaggermusene	defpl
oteren	defsg
sjiraffen	defsg
krokodiller	indpl
haier	indpl
humlene	defpl
ålen	defsg
torvmosene	defpl
kniver	indpl
meandere	indpl
stavkirke	BN
kulepennen	defsg
gener	indpl
fiskekroker	indpl
skruer	indpl
gitaren	defsg

The respondents were asked to fill in an online form where all test items and filler items were listed. All sentences had gaps with the possible NP types listed below and the grading scale. The general results can be seen in Table 6.5. and Figure 6.4. The relatively high percentage of plural forms judged to be correct corresponded to the previous analysis in this project. The status 'acceptable' was rarely chosen in all cases, which can mean that the respondents were opting rather for the 'correct–incorrect' scale and ignoring the 'acceptable' judgement. This can be observed in Figure 6.4., where the sum of all judgements in a given category are marked in blue.

Table 6.5. Survey 2 – NP types

Forms	1 – Correct	2 – Acceptable	3 – Incorrect/Awkward
	Number (%)	Number (%)	Number (%)
BN	565 (5.65)	222 (2.22)	1213 (12.13)
IndSg	767 (7.67)	260 (2.60)	973 (9.73)
DefSg	1065 (10.65)	344 (3.44)	591 (5.91)
IndPl	1279 (12.79)	348 (3.48)	373 (3.73)
DefPl	1058 (10.58)	467 (4.67)	475 (4.75)
Total	4734	1641	3625
Total (%)	47.34%	16.41%	36.25%

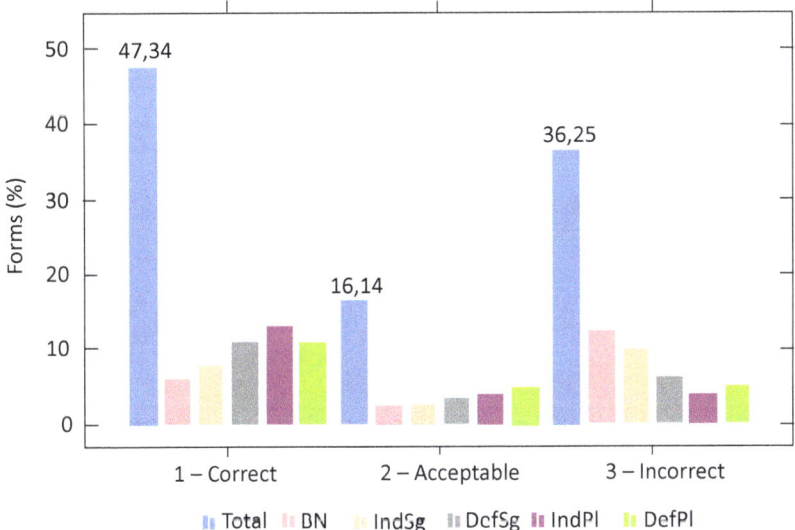

Figure 6.4. Survey 2 – NP types

In the majority of the examples, the participants judged the original corpus forms to be correct and/or acceptable, also providing other options (see Table 6.6.). In just a few of the sentences, the answers differed significantly from the corpus material (see the discussion below). Such close agreement suggests that even though Norwegian generics may be expressed in a number of different ways, certain tendencies can be found. For instance, the limited use of the indefinite singular applied mainly to animate nouns, even though certain participants listed this form as acceptable or even correct. Certain nouns, such as plants perceived to be mass-like and animals considered to be gregarious, often appeared as definite plurals in a generic context – as in the corpus.

Table 6.6. Survey 2 – results

	BN			IndSg			DefSg		
	1 – Correct	2 – Acceptable	3 – Incorrect	1 – Correct	2 – Acceptable	3 – Incorrect	1 – Correct	2 – Acceptable	3 – Incorrect
1-måke	3	6	91	51	24	25	49	25	26
2-skate	48	13	39	30	25	45	38	25	37
3-meander	39	17	44	46	18	36	27	33	40
4-kniv	14	10	76	28	21	51	24	19	57
5-fiskekrok	15	4	81	20	9	71	36	16	48
6-krokodille	10	11	79	46	21	33	69	15	16
7-hai	20	5	75	20	12	68	47	21	32
8-stavkirke	42	17	41	71	12	17	61	15	24
9-kulepenn	9	7	84	89	7	4	82	13	5
10-gen	12	19	69	60	7	33	36	15	49
11-birkebeiner	21	9	70	15	7	78	26	8	66
12-diakon	18	10	72	80	11	9	75	15	10
13-flaggermus	49	14	37	73	9	18	68	13	19
14-oter	44	13	43	20	5	75	74	15	11
15-sjiraff	35	12	53	9	10	81	69	21	10
16-torvmose	52	10	38	26	16	58	64	10	26
17-humle	19	12	69	26	12	62	51	22	27
18-skrue	21	11	68	32	10	58	14	9	77
19-gitar	22	16	62	14	10	76	84	13	3
20-ål	72	6	22	11	14	75	71	21	8
Total	565	222	1213	767	260	973	1065	344	591
Total (%)	5.65%	2.22%	12.13%	7.67%	2.60%	9.73%	10.65%	3.44%	5.91%

	IndPl			DefPl		
	1 – Correct	2 – Acceptable	3 – Incorrect	1 – Correct	2 – Acceptable	3 – Incorrect
1–måke	66	22	12	73	21	6
2–skate	47	24	29	25	26	49
3–meander	65	25	10	30	34	36
4–kniv	80	9	11	58	19	23
5–fiskekrok	77	11	12	37	31	32
6–krokodille	93	7	0	69	25	6
7–hai	88	4	8	70	21	9
8–stavkirke	46	25	29	41	29	30
9–kulepenn	34	24	42	30	28	42
10–gen	72	13	15	62	18	20
11–birkebeiner	62	21	17	79	13	8
12–diakon	18	21	61	24	20	56
13–flaggermus	53	16	31	67	23	10
14–oter	69	24	7	53	25	22
15–sjiraff	82	14	4	66	26	8
16–torvmose	38	23	39	52	21	27
17–humle	79	17	4	84	13	3
18–skrue	90	7	3	42	27	31
19–gitar	56	24	20	47	25	28
20–ål	64	17	19	49	22	29
Total	1279	348	373	1058	467	475
Total (%)	12.79%	3.48%	3.73%	10.58%	4.67%	4.75%

Bare nouns, both in the corpus and in the survey, have an interesting status. In the corpus, many encyclopaedic entries were BNs, as well as nouns considered somehow familiar to native speakers of Norwegian. In the survey, bare nouns were referred to as 'correct' in a number of examples, indicating that it might in fact be another default generic form, together with the indefinite plural. The nouns judged to be correct and/or acceptable as BNs included 'bat', 'otter', 'eel', and 'peat moss'. 'Stave church' is an example of a typical WEK that occurs without any article, in both the original texts and the respondents' answers.

The majority of the examples were judged in a way that corresponds to the model sentences from the corpus. For instance, a number of NPs used in the survey occurred as indefinite plurals and the respondents also graded this form very high, often suggesting that the definite plural could be used as well. Even though the indefinite singular did not appear at all in the texts about animals, the participants often listed this form as acceptable or even correct. The examples will be discussed in greater detail, according to the category they occurred in. The categories with the most nouns in the survey will be discussed first.

'People'

Only one sentence was chosen from the text category 'people': the example presented in (124). The original NP type used in the corpus was the definite plural, being the classic delimited generic used when talking about groups of people, as shown in the model by Radden (2009).

> (124) Birkebeinere [Birkebein.party-PL] var en politisk gruppering i Norge i høy-middelalderen.
> The Birkebein Party was a political group in Norway in the high Middle Ages.

What is interesting in this example is that both plural forms were very often rated as correct and acceptable, whereas BNs and the singular forms scored much lower and were considered incorrect/awkward by many respondents.

The use of both plural forms and low acceptability of BN and the singular forms aligns with the models proposed for English and Swedish, as well as with the model modified for the Norwegian data in the previous chapter. Talking about groups of people in Norwegian, in contrast to professions, is usually connected with plural forms, referring to the collectivity of the subject in question. This was presented in the animacy model by Rosenbach (2008) and is discussed in detail in Chapter 5.

'Animals'

Among the nouns that originally were indefinite plurals in the corpus, certain ones were judged to be correct and/or acceptable with other forms as well, such as the definite singular (correct with the noun 'crocodile' and 'shark'). The results also show that several participants opted rather for *extreme* grades (correct–incorrect), rather than the more neutral 'acceptable' rating in many of the examples.

The examples in (125) show two cases where the respondents provided more correct and acceptable forms than those in the original sentences. The noun 'crocodile', originally a BP, was judged to be correct in this form 93 times, and the definite plural was marked as 'correct' 69 times. None of the participants judged the indefinite plural to be awkward or incorrect. The noun 'shark' was graded in a similar manner, with the BP scoring 88 'correct' answers. The definite plural form 'the sharks' was considered correct 70 times.

(125) a. Krokodiller [crocodiles] lever i vann og finnes i tropiske områder over hele kloden.
Crocodiles live in water and can be found in tropical climates all around the world.

b. Hos haier [sharks] som lever av fisk og lignende er det utviklet skjære- eller gripetenner.
Sharks that live on fish and similar food have developed flattened or needle-like teeth.

Both sentences in (125) that are considered correct as definite plural generics concern animal species. As stated in Chapter 5, this NP type, when used generically, may suggest that the animals in question are seen as gregarious. Sometimes this is true from a biological perspective and sometimes it is just a result of folk taxonomy.[31]

The survey sentence about bats in (126) contained a definite plural form in the original sentence and two other forms were judged to be correct, the

---

[31] In the study by Jacoby et al. (2014) the social behaviour of certain shark species was described.

indefinite and definite singular. In its original form, the sentence can be interpreted in a way that bats – as gregarious animals – are often seen in groups. However, other NP types which the respondents proposed as correct suggest conceptual and prototypical readings of the noun (indefinite and definite forms, respectively).

(126) Flaggermusene [bats-DEF]   har   et enormt næringsbehov.
      The bats   have   an enormous appetite.

A similar interpretation of animals being gregarious was also observed in the example with bumble bees. The two plural forms were most often judged to be correct and the original sentence contained the definite plural.

Reference to kinds seems to have the widest range when it comes to the NP types chosen in such contexts. Another interesting noun from this category is Sentence 127. The species 'eel' is described with the definite singular in the original sentence. This NP type also scored high in the survey and was selected 71 times as correct and 21 times as acceptable. Also, the BN was chosen many times as correct, whereas the two plural forms scored slightly lower. Nevertheless, almost all NP types, except for the indefinite singular, were chosen as correct and/or acceptable.

(127) Ålen finnes i hav og ferskvann fra Nord-Afrika og middelhavslandene i sør
      til Kvitsjøen i nord.
      The eel lives in seas and fresh waters, from North Africa and Mediterra-
      nean countries in the south to the White Sea in the north.

As mentioned in the previous chapter, predicates used in generic sentences influence the choice of possible NP types. The predicate 'to live in seas' from Sentence 127 suggests a kind-reference. Therefore, all forms – except for the BN – were seen as possible in this context. Reference to a kind can be expressed either through a reference to a concept or a prototype (singular forms) or by referring to a certain number of members from the kind (plural forms). Either way, the sentence is unambiguous because of its generic predicate.

Many examples with animals were judged to be correct and/or acceptable with plural forms, whereas singular forms were chosen in fewer cases. This can refer to the interpretation of a given sentence. Again, singular forms can be understood as concepts or prototypes of a given species, making them awkward/incorrect with certain predicates. The lack of singular forms in the category 'animals' in the corpus might have been the result of the predicates chosen by the authors of the texts.

'Plants'

The texts from the category 'plants' followed similar patterns as those about animals in the corpus in that there were no uses of the indefinite singular. In the survey, one example from this category was chosen – the one concerning the NP 'peat moss'. The fact that 'moss', even though grammatically countable in Norwegian, is almost considered an uncountable noun can be seen in (128), where definite plural generics are used.

(128)	Torvmosene [peat.moss-DEF-PL]	har	en eiendommelig bygning.
	Peat moss	has	a homogeneous structure.

'Moss', as a plant of homogeneous structure, can be difficult to count, despite its grammatical countability. On the other hand, the NP from the sentence is a sub-kind, namely a certain type of moss which is rendered with the definite plural in the model sentence. As shown in the cognitive model presented in the previous chapter, definite plural generics can access sub-kinds in certain cases.

When it comes to the respondents' answers, no clear tendencies were observed. None of the proposed NP types was chosen as correct or incorrect more often than the others. This may suggest different interpretations of the example. On the one hand, the plant could have been perceived as a prototype or a concept of 'peat moss', and therefore quite a few respondents opted for the BN and the definite singular. On the other hand, the plant was perceived as consisting of many small elements or even as mass-like by the respondents who chose the plural forms. The predicate used in the sentence 'to have a homogeneous structure' can only refer to a whole kind, not one particular plant. Therefore, singular generic references are interpreted as conceptual or prototypical, as in the models of Radden and Dirven (2007) and Pettersson (1976).

'Tools'

Only one sentence from the category 'tools' was chosen for the survey, and it concerned the noun 'knife'. As can be observed in (129), the generic reference in the sentence is understood as a reference to a sub-kind, namely certain knives produced by different companies. In the original sentence from the corpus, both references are rendered with the indefinite plural.

(129) I Norge har kniver fremstilt ved småindustri på Toten vært av anerkjent kvalitet, likeså kniver fra Geilo.

In Norway, knives fabricated by a small company in Toten have been known for their quality, as with knives from Geilo.

Many respondents graded the BN and singular forms as incorrect/awkward, whereas the two plural forms were preferred by the majority. The indefinite singular was chosen most often, confirming the original interpretation of the sentence. The definite plural form was marked as correct 58 times and acceptable 19 times, suggesting either specific reference or reference to a subkind, namely particular types of knives produced in Toten and Geilo. As discussed in the previous chapter, sub-kinds in Norwegian can be accessed by the definite plural. However, predicates used with the definite plural and the wider context of a sentence might influence the interpretation.

'Other'

Seven sentences in the survey were retrieved from the category 'other' in the corpus. The only noun that occurred as BN in the original material was 'stave church', considered a WEK in Norwegian. In most cases, WEKs take on definite forms or are used as bare nouns in generic texts. However, in the survey many answers of 'correct' and 'acceptable' were given to all five NP types, with the indefinite and definite singular scoring the highest (71 and 61 answers, respectively). The bare noun was marked 'correct' 42 times and 'acceptable' 17 times. The fact that many of the participants opted for the definite singular (and partially BN) confirms that the noun is recognised as familiar.

(130) Stavkirke [stave.church-Ø] er en høyt utviklet kirketype, oppført i reisverk av tre, kjent fra norsk kristen middelalder.

A stave church is a highly developed type of church, constructed with wooden staves, originating in Christian medieval Norway.

The case of 'stave church' is an interesting example of a WEK that is characteristic for of a given culture. Its use is very often conceptual (BN) or prototypical (definite singular), confirming the existing theories on WEKs and familiar nouns (see e.g. Borthen 2007; Rosén and Borthen 2017).

6.3.1. Cognitive model

As in the previous chapter, a matrix of generic NP types from the survey was created, based on the cognitive models of Radden and Dirven (2007) and Radden (2009). Due to the smaller amount of material in this survey, there are fewer contexts available for each of the NP types. However, some of them are the same as in the matrix based on the corpus (see Table 6.7.).

Table 6.7. Survey 2 – generic NPs, a simplified matrix

BN	IndSg	DefSg	IndPl	DefPl
1) WEKs, familiar nouns	1) prototypes	1) prototypes	1) kinds	1) ethnic)social groups
2) concepts	2) *kinds	2) WEKs	2) ethnic)social groups	2) gregarious animals
3) *kinds		3) *kinds		3) mass-like plants

One of the interesting aspects of this model is that, according to native speakers, reference to kinds can be expressed with every NP type. However, the types of kind-reference differ slightly between the forms – this was marked in the table with an asterisk. Reference to kinds can be achieved through concepts and prototypes, namely with the BN and the two singular forms. In the model described in Radden (2009), a kind generic is assigned only to the definite singular and is interpreted as a 'prototypical subtype of a well-established type' (p. 224). In Norwegian, however, this function can be rendered with two singular forms. BNs have a similar role with the difference that they do not rely on prototypes but concepts. Concepts, as with BNs, are neutral when it comes to number marking. Therefore, we cannot say that a kind reference expressed this way is done by referring to an example entity of a kind or a number of such entities.

Kind reference rendered with the indefinite plural is a classic generic reference, and it was often chosen by the respondents in sentences with kind-predicates. When it comes to definite plural generics, kind-reference is also possible, but with certain restrictions. As was observed in both the corpus and in the AJT survey, reference to gregarious animal species was most often expressed with this form. Interestingly enough, such classification of certain animal species is often done in accordance with folk taxonomy, not a biological classification.

Another interesting aspect that can be observed in the model is NP types being used with familiar nouns and WEKs. First of all, BNs are often used in this context, where they function as concepts, as seen for instance in the example (130) about stave churches. Such reference is neither singular nor plural from a strictly grammatical point of view. When it comes to cognitive interpretation, however, one may argue that the concept of a stave church consists of a singular entity that is utilised in a generic reference.

The use of the definite singular with WEKs and familiar nouns is a bit different. On the one hand, it can be connected to prototypes (cf. Pettersson 1976), where a singular entity denotes the whole kind. On the other hand, WEKs rendered with the definite singular are sometimes perceived as proper names (cf. Carlson 1982; Carlson and Pelletier 1995). WEKs such as 'stave church' in Norwegian are well-rooted in the language and culture.

The most significant change from the original model by Radden (2009) concerns the definite plural form. In the model designed for English, de-limited generics can only be used when talking about people. In Norwegian, however, delimited generics – even though they are still limited – can be used in a wider range of contexts. The context concerning social and eth-nic groups remains the same as in English. The two other contexts that are possible in Norwegian concern animals and plants. As in the corpus texts, here the respondents also judged sentences about gregarious animals and mass-like plants to be correct when uttered with the definite plural. Both of these concepts assume that the subject in question contains more than one entity, that is, gregarious animal species imagined as a flock of animals or moss consisting of many strands and thus forming a mass-like plant.

The answers provided by the respondents were in most cases the same as in the original sentences from the corpus texts. Additional contexts provided by the respondents helped develop the proposed model further. A discussion of both models designed for Norwegian, that based on the corpus texts and that based on the AJT survey, will be discussed in greater detail in Chapter 7.

6.3.2. Statistical analysis

The statistical analysis in this chapter is divided into two sections. In the first part, all the answers marked as 'correct' are analysed, and in the second section the answers marked as 'acceptable'.[32] The statistical tests can provide a broader perspective on the values, namely the number of answers in each

---

[32] No statistical tests of the 'incorrect' answers were performed, as they would mirror the results of the other two ratings.

of the survey questions. As in the previous chapter with the corpus data, quantitative analysis can indicate whether there are statistically significant aspects of the data, such as differences between the NP types.

6.3.2.1. NP types marked 'correct'

The first step in analysing the data was to conduct descriptive statistical analysis, which included dividing the data into quartiles and calculating minimal and maximal values, means, and medians. The results are presented in Table 6.8. and Figure 6.5.

Table 6.8. Survey 2 – data for 'correct' forms

	BN	IndSg	DefSg	IndPl	DefPl
Min.	3.00	9.00	14.00	18.00	24.00
1st Quartile	14.75	20.00	36.00	51.50	40.00
Median	21.00	29.00	56.00	65.50	52.50
Mean	28.25	38.35	53.25	63.95	52.90
3rd Quartile	42.50	53.25	69.50	79.25	67.50
Max.	72.00	89.00	84.00	93.00	84.00
SD	18.19	24.70	21.27	20.07	18.22

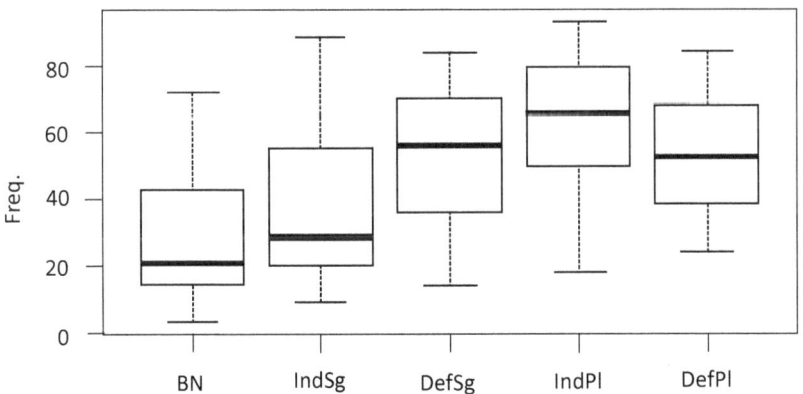

Figure 6.5. Survey 2 – boxplot for 'correct' forms

The minimal and maximal values show the extreme scores for each of the NP types – the lowest and the highest values, respectively. For example, the minimal value of 3 for BN means that in at least one of the survey questions only three people judged this form as correct. When it comes to the maximal value of 72 for BN, it indicates that there was at least one survey question where 72 of the respondents judged the BN as correct. The values for the other NP types are presented in the same manner.

In Table 6.8., Standard Deviation (SD) shows the dispersion of the data in the analysed groups. As can be observed, indefinite singulars marked as 'correct' demonstrate a slightly larger dispersion than the other NP types. Simply put, the values of the indefinite singular rated as 'correct' have a wider range in relation to the mean.

As in the previous chapters, the data were also tested for homogeneity of variances and normality in order to verify which statistical tests could be performed. The first step was to test for homogeneity of variance, which was done with the use of Levene's test (see Table 6.9.). Since the p-value was above the significance level of 0.05, there was no evidence that the variances across the tested groups were significantly different from each other.

Table 6.9. Survey 2 – Levene's test for 'correct' forms

	Df	F value	Pr(>F)
Group	4	0.62	0.65
	95		

After conducting Levene's test, the normality of the data was verified with the Shapiro–Wilk test. It resulted in a p-value of 0.17, proving that the requirement concerning the normality of the data was not violated. In such a case, parametric analysis – ANOVA – can be performed.

Table 6.10. Survey 2 – ANOVA for 'correct' forms

	Df	Sum Sq	Mean Sq	F value	Pr(>F)	
Forms	4	15740	3935	9.244	2.37e–06	***
Residuals	95	40439	426.0			

(***) significant at 0.001

ANOVA revealed statistically significant results with a p-value of less than 0.001. This indicates that there are differences between certain some of the tested NP types. In order to verify where the differences lay, a post hoc test had to be conducted. The post hoc test of choice used throughout this study in the case of ANOVA was Tukey HSD.

Tukey HSD is a multiple pairwise comparison where the groups are compared to each other in pairs – BN vs indefinite singular, BN vs definite singular, and so on. Differences were found between four pairs of NP types – they are marked in bold in Table 6.11., whereas in Figure 6.6. the differences are indicated by the bars that do not cross the reference line at 0.

Table 6.11. Survey 2 – Tukey HSD for 'correct' forms

	BN	IndSg	DefSg	IndPl
IndSg	−10.00			
p-adjust	0.53			
DefSg	**−25.00**	−14.90		
p-adjust	**0.002**	0.16		
IndPl	**−35.70**	**−25.60**	−10.70	
p-adjust	**0.00**	**0.002**	0.48	
DefPl	**−24.65**	−14.55	0.35	11.05
p-adjust	**0.003**	0.18	1.00	0.44

95% family – wise confidence level

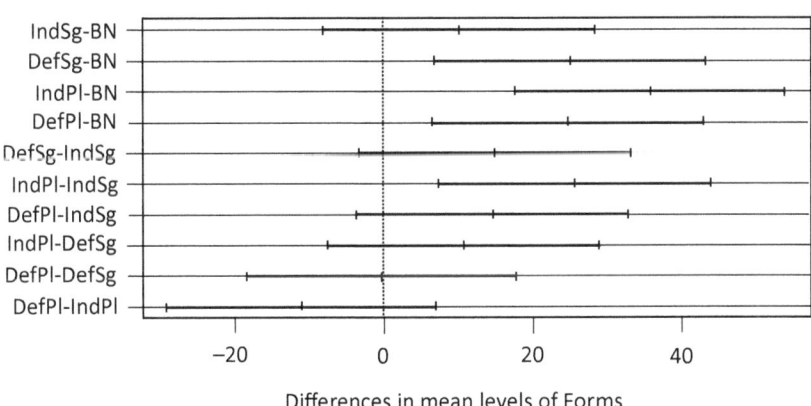

Differences in mean levels of Forms

Figure 6.6. Survey 2 – Tukey HSD for 'correct' forms

The fact that there are statistically significant differences between the tested groups does not tell us in exactly what way they are different – whether some of the NP types are used more often with animate nouns, mass nouns, etc. Statistical analysis takes into account the values (the count of each answer), not the actual NPs from the test sentences.

The results show that statistically significant differences are in many cases similar to those presented in the cognitive analysis. For instance, BNs are significantly different from the definite singular and the two plural forms. Even though certain generic contexts are similar between those forms (e.g. referring to WEKs is possible with both the BN and the definite singular), most of them are different, such as the classic true kind reference with the indefinite plural or delimited generics of the definite plural, which is not compatible with the BN.

6.3.2.2. NP types marked 'acceptable'

The answers selected by the respondents as 'acceptable' were analysed in the same manner: descriptive statistical analysis was performed first, followed by a number of more complex tests. Table 6.12. shows the descriptive statistics of the data marked 'acceptable'. The material was first divided into quartiles. Then, minimal and maximal values were calculated along with means, medians, and SD. The boxplot in Figure 6.7. shows the graphic representation of the data.

Table 6.12. Survey 2 – data marked 'acceptable'

	BN	IndSg	DefSg	IndPl	DefPl
Min.	4.00	5.00	8.00	4.00	13.00
1st Quartile	8.50	9.00	13.00	12.50	20.75
Median	11.00	11.50	15.00	19.00	24.00
Mean	11.10	13.00	17.20	17.40	23.35
3rd Quartile	13.25	16.50	21.00	24.00	26.25
Max.	19.00	25.00	33.00	25.00	34.00
SD	4.22	5.92	6.17	6.92	5.39

As can be observed, the values are much lower than in the case of correct answers. Nevertheless, certain tendencies can be observed. For instance, the SD of all NP types is rather homogeneous, meaning that the range of the values is not very broad in reference to the mean. Moreover, the differences between the minimal and maximal values are much lower for each of the NP types. One of the reasons for this is certainly the smaller data set. However, it is also possible that the 'acceptable' answers are not as clear-cut as those judged to be 'correct'.

The next step of the analysis consisted in verifying the assumptions needed for ANOVA. First, the homogeneity of variances was tested with the use of Levene's test. It resulted in a p-value of 0.28 (see Table 6.13.), proving there was no violation of the first ANOVA assumption.

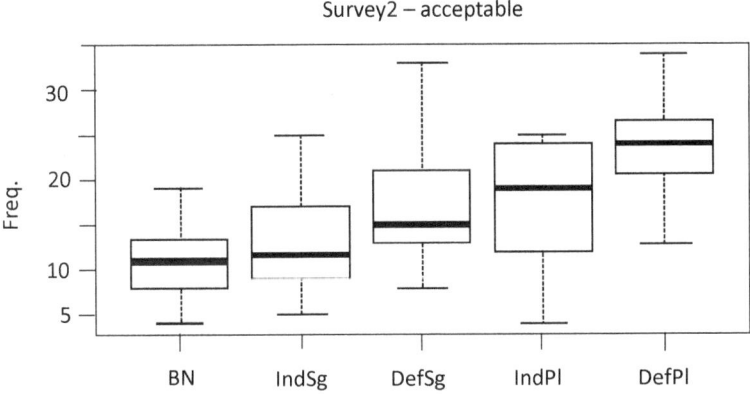

Figure 6.7. Survey 2 – boxplot for 'acceptable' forms

Table 6.13. Survey 2 – Levene's test for 'acceptable' forms

	Df	F value	Pr(>F)
Group	4	1.28	0.28
	95		

The second requirement needed for a parametric test, normality of the data, was checked with the Shapiro–Wilk test. The resulting p-value of 0.69 means that the data are normally distributed and that the analysis of variance can be performed.

Table 6.14. Survey 2 – ANOVA for 'acceptable' forms

	Df	Sum Sq	Mean Sq	F value	Pr(>F)	
Forms	4	1792	448	13.35	1.14e–08	***
Residuals	95	3188	33.60			

(***) significant at 0.001

As can be seen in Table 6.14., ANOVA revealed that there were differences between the tested groups, so a post hoc test needed to be conducted. The post hoc test of choice was Tukey HSD.

Table 6.15. Survey 2 – Tukey HSD for 'acceptable' forms

	BN	IndSg	DefSg	IndPl
IndSg	−1.90			
p-adjust	0.84			
DefSg	−6.10	−4.20		
p-adjust	**0.01**	0.16		
IndPl	−6.30	−4.40	−0.20	
p-adjust	**0.008**	0.12	1.00	
DefPl	−12.25	−10.35	−6.15	−5.95
p-adjust	**0.00**	**0.00**	**0.01**	**0.014**

The multiple pairwise comparison test showed that there were significant differences between six pairs of NP types – these are marked in bold in Table 6.15. and in Figure 6.8., as values which do not cross the 0-line.

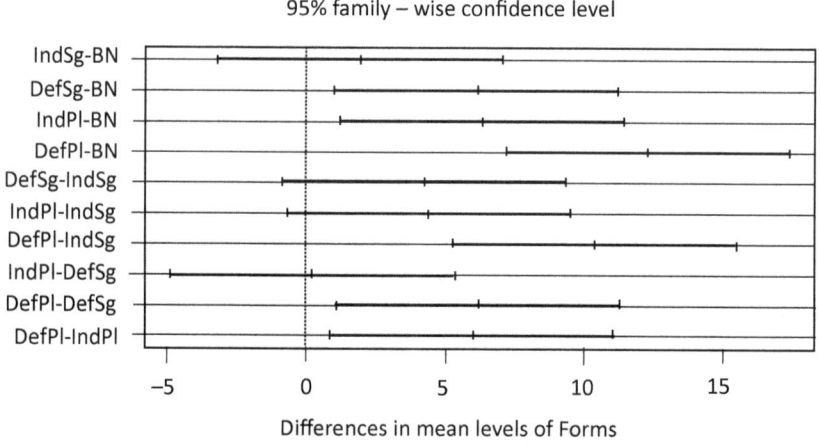

Figure 6.8. Survey 2 – Tukey HSD for 'acceptable' forms

In the case of answers marked as 'acceptable', certain similarities to the cognitive model can be observed. For instance, BNs are significantly different from the definite singular and the two plural forms, which was also confirmed in the previous section on the 'correct' answers. The tendencies of the NP types marked 'acceptable' are very similar to those marked as 'correct', indicating a rather positive reading of this grade in the survey. However, in the case of acceptable answers, the definite plural was recognised as different from every other form, which may confirm its limited use in ambiguous generic contexts.

6.4. Conclusions

The survey conducted with the use of the corpus material was an Acceptability Judgement Task where the participants' intuitions about generic expressions were tested. The survey contained 20 test items and five filler items, both in the form of generic sentences with gaps. The participants rated each of the NP types that could be inserted into the gaps. The rating scale had three levels: 1 – 'correct', 2 – 'acceptable', and 3 – 'incorrect/awkward'.

The majority of the test items were rated in a way that mirrored the original material, namely the NP types judged most often as 'correct' and/or 'acceptable' were in accordance with the forms used originally in the corpus. In each of the examples more than one form was rated as 1 or 2, indicating a high degree of interchangeability of the forms. However, certain NP types, such as the indefinite singular, were not very common in the answers.

The results collected in this survey were used to create a matrix of generic NP types, as in the previous chapter. There were fewer available contexts in this study, due to the smaller amount of material. However, certain generic contexts were confirmed by the respondents, such as conceptual generics expressed with BNs, reference to prototypes rendered with the singular forms, or describing certain gregarious animal species with definite plural generics.

The last part of this chapter consisted in a statistical analysis of the results, where a number of statistical tests verified the distribution of the data. In many cases, the discrepancies in the data confirmed by the statistical tests align with the matrix of generic contexts from this survey. In the following chapter, the results of Survey 1, the corpus study, and the AJT survey are discussed together in order to create a cognitive model of generics in Norwegian.

7. Discussion and conclusions

The project described in this book consisted of three tasks: conducting Survey 1, building and analysing the corpus of generic texts, and conducting Survey 2 based on the corpus material. The first task was performed in 2017 during a 3-month stay in Norway, whereas the two other tasks were conducted in the period 2018–2019. The goal of this project was to investigate and analyse the cognitive status of Norwegian generics, according to the models proposed by Leslie et al. (2011), Radden and Dirven (2007), and Radden (2009). This way, a unified model for Norwegian was created based on the corpus and the AJT survey.

7.1. General results – discussion

Survey 1
The first part of this project consisted in designing and conducting a survey. The survey was inspired by the study of Ionin et al. (2011) in that it contained 30 short generic texts with gaps to fill. The survey was published online and the respondents were asked to choose the NP types that would fit the gaps the best. The goal was to examine as many generic contexts in Norwegian as possible based on the speakers' intuitions. A total of 630 people took part in the survey, of which 599 were recognised as native speakers of Norwegian.

The results of the first survey showed a high percentage of BNs in generic contexts with a somewhat limited use of definite plural generics. The second most chosen form was the indefinite plural, suggesting the similarity to many

Germanic languages when it comes to treating indefinite plurals as *default* generics. Apart from those, all other NP types were used frequently by the participants, though in different texts.

In order to further determine which NP types were chosen by the respondents in generic contexts, the texts were divided into groups based on the types of generic predications they contained. The model proposed by Leslie et al. (2011) was used in order to do this.

The texts contained 26 countable nouns and four mass nouns. When it comes to texts with countable nouns, all types of generic predications were observed, with majority characteristic and false generalisations being the most common ones (eight texts in each of the two categories). The other frequent category was quasi-definitional generics, recognised in four of the survey texts with countable nouns. A majority generic occurred in three texts, a minority characteristic in two, and a striking generic in one. When it comes to mass nouns, two of the texts contained majority predications, one a majority characteristic, and one a striking generic.

In the survey texts, all five NP types were chosen by the respondents, though with different frequency. BNs, indefinite plurals, and indefinite singulars were the most frequent. However, in a number of examples delimited generics were preferred. Apart from the texts about people ('child' and 'politician'), other subjects also occurred in the definite plural (e.g. 'lorry' and 'ceramic cooker'). Definite forms occurred more often in predications classified as quasi-definitional or false generalisations. Those two categories have a lot in common when it comes to the interpretation. Quasi-definitional generics state a truth that is applicable to the whole kind and do not accept exceptions, whereas false generalisations state false truths that have clear counterparts. Nevertheless, both predication types have a form of a definition, just with different truth-conditions.

When it comes to the BNs that were chosen in many of the survey texts, they occurred with all of the predications. According to the scholarly literature on generics in Germanic languages (e.g. Carlson [1977] for English, Pettersson [1976] for Swedish, and Halmøy [2016] for Norwegian), indefinite plurals are considered *default*. Nevertheless, even the first survey demonstrated that bare nouns occur in many generic contexts and with different types of noun phrases (animate, inanimate, countable, and mass). The two other analyses of this project proved the same, as can be seen below.

Corpus analysis

The second and most important part of the study was building a tailor-made corpus of generic texts. In total, 170 texts (27 761 tokens) were retrieved from the online encyclopaedia *Store norske leksikon*. The material was divided into five thematic categories: 'people', 'animals', 'plants', 'tools', and 'other'. The texts were tagged with regard to genericity. The analysis of all text categories revealed that all five NP types were used in generic contexts, with definite plurals being more frequent than in Survey 1. However, one of the forms, namely the indefinite singular, was rather rare throughout the corpus and even absent in two of the text categories ('animals' and 'plants'). Indefinite plurals were again very common in all of the texts, proving the special status of BPs in Norwegian as well. Moreover, a distinction was observed between prototypes and actual representations in generic texts and sentences. For instance, generic expressions referring to professions were slightly more abstract than those describing groups of people or objects.

Also, in the corpus texts BNs were very frequent and occurred in all of the text categories. One reason for such a high frequency of BNs is the encyclopaedic entries which, in many cases, were also the subjects of the first sentences in many of the corpus texts. However, in many cases BNs were also utilised in subsequent mentions of a given topic, indicating that the form has a generic reading in other contexts as well. In Section 7.2., possible contexts for BNs and other NP types will be provided, based on the corpus and the AJT survey.

Survey 2

The third and last part of the project was the AJT survey, built with the use of the corpus material. Twenty generic sentences were chosen from the corpus as test items, along with five accompanying filler items. The judgement scale used in the survey had 3 levels: 1 – 'correct', 2 – 'acceptable', and 3 – 'incorrect/ awkward'. In total, 100 native speakers of Norwegian took part in the study, most of them aged 18–30.

The majority of the participants opted for *clear-cut* answers (grades 1 and 3), leaving out the 'acceptable' option in many of the survey questions. However, the results align to a very high degree with model sentences from the corpus, meaning that despite the lack of a broader context, the participants were still able to interpret the sentences as generic and to grade them accordingly. The main tendencies connected to the use of certain NP types were similar as those in the two previous parts of the project.

The answers from the AJT survey provided further interpretations of the NP types that occurred in generic contexts. For instance, according to the respondents, kind reference can be rendered with four different NP types (excluding the definite plural), with little difference in meaning. As discussed in Chapter 6, reference to whole kinds can be expressed either through denotation of individual entities or through reference to a group of entities. Singular forms are based on prototypes, whereas BNs render a generic reference through a concept. When it comes to the indefinite plural, it refers to a kind by describing the characteristics of a given group.

Definite plural generics, also called delimited generics in the cognitive theory on the subject, also allow for generalisations about kinds, but in a slightly different manner. In the corpus and in the survey, this form was used in relation to gregarious animals, namely those which are usually seen in flocks. When it comes to plants, mass-like plants were most often described with the use of this form, both in the corpus and in the survey.

7.2. Cognitive status of Norwegian generics

The core of the analysis in this project was the cognitive models for English and Swedish. As presented in Chapters 5 and 6, the material collected for the project allowed the model of generics to be reworked and adjusted to the Norwegian data. First, the data were analysed, according to the generic interpretations provided by Radden and Dirven (2007), Radden (2009), and Pettersson (1976). Then, simplified matrixes of generic nouns were created – one for the corpus data and one for the AJT survey answers. The second part of the cognitive analysis consisted in combining the two paradigms of generic NP types and reworking the model proposed by Radden (2009), where different forms and their generic meanings are provided.[33]Both the descriptive and statistical analyses of all parts of the research – Survey 1, the corpus, and Survey 2 – show that the diversity of the forms that appear in generic contexts is by no means random. Based on the corpus material and the judgements of native Norwegian speakers, a simplified matrix of generic NPs was created. One of the categories from Radden's model, 'ex-/inclusiveness' was replaced with the contexts in which the generic NPs occurred. The contexts marked in bold appeared both

---

[33]   For the discussion on the models, the reader is referred to Chapter 2.

in the corpus and in the judgements in the AJT survey. 'Kinds' marked with an asterisk indicate that the reference was recognised as conceptual, whereas the generic meaning marked with italics represents the element of the original model that did not need to be modified.

Table 7.1. Generic NPs – a simplified matrix based on the corpus and the AJT survey

Generic type	Generic form	Context	Generic meaning
conceptual generic	BN	mass & quasi-mass nouns, **WEKs, concepts**, professions, *kinds	concept representing its type
representative (prototypical) generic	indefinite singular	stand-alone objects, professions, **prototypes**, *kinds	arbitrary instance (prototype) representing its type
prototypical & kind generic	definite singular	mass nouns, WEKs, official functions, *kinds, prototypes	*salient proportion of a type's reference mass*
kind generic	indefinite plural	**kinds, groups of people**	majority representing its type
delimited generic	definite plural	**ethnic/social groups, gregarious animals**, sub-kinds, hyperonyms, mass-like plants	delimited set within a given domain

Each of the rows in Table 7.1. contains generic types, generic forms and meanings, and the contexts in which a given NP type was used most often. The proposed classification is based only on the material collected for this project and is by no means exhaustive. A potential expansion of the system could be provided, should other aspects of genericity be analysed (e.g. generics in the spoken language, differences between the two written standards, different source material, etc.). Furthermore, certain generic sentences can sometimes have more than one interpretation, so the matrix may differ slightly depending on one's language intuition.

As can be observed in Table 7.1., certain elements were modified compared to the original model. First of all, the Norwegian model contains five NP types instead of only four, since BNs are widely used in generic contexts in Norwegian. Secondly, generic meanings are slightly different based on the available contexts.

The model is based on empirical material consisting of two parts. However, many of the contexts were the same, both in the corpus and in the AJT survey, and those are marked in bold. Certain contexts were lacking in the corpus but were observed in the respondents' judgements. One such context included a conceptual reference to kinds that was judged to be correct and/or acceptable in the case of BNs. Prototypical reference to kinds was rendered with the two singular forms – indefinite and definite. In Radden's model, the definite singular has exactly the same function, which was marked in italics in the Norwegian model.

The use of BNs in the collected material, apart from its conceptual interpretation, was often connected to mass nouns and those perceived as mass, e.g. 'moss' (grammatically countable in Norwegian). Also, well-established kinds and nouns considered familiar in everyday speech appeared as BNs in both the surveys and the corpus. Concepts such as 'religion' and abstract nouns were also referred to in this way. Interpreting certain professions as concepts is also known in Norwegian and can result in such sentences as the one in (119a), repeated here as (131).

(131) Psykolog   er   en   person med utdanning i psykologi.
      psychologist-Ø is   a   person with education in psychology
      A psychologist is a person with an education in psychology.

Even though the word 'person' appears in the description of the notion, the interpretation is that 'psychologist' is a profession that includes certain tasks, education level, and so on – in other words, it is a prototypical psychologist that has education in the field of psychology, not necessarily a particular member of this group.

The use of indefinite singulars in generic contexts was also interesting, especially that this form did not appear in two of the corpus categories, 'animals' and 'plants', whereas some native speakers judged sentences about animals with indefinite singulars to be correct and/or acceptable, although the percentage of such answers was relatively low (see Chapter 6).

The indefinite singular form was also used when referring to stand-alone objects and tools, such as 'a knife' or 'a pen', namely objects that are usually perceived as individual tools rather than occurring in sets. This interpretation also brings to mind the notion of a prototype, as in the sentence 'A knife is a tool used for cutting.' It is not a certain knife, nor an example of a knife that has this function, but rather a prototype of it. This way, by assigning a characteristic feature to an object, a generalisation about the whole kind is made. In the second survey, certain nouns were judged correct in such contexts: 'a gene' and 'a ballpoint pen', for example. Likewise, professions referring to a prototypical person performing a given task were described this way (e.g. 'a teacher is someone who works at school'). Reference to kinds rendered with the indefinite singular was prototypical (cf. Lyons 1977; Pettersson 1976).

When it comes to definite singulars, apart from mass nouns and WEKs, official functions ('the king' or 'the County Governor') and certain animal species were also described with the use of this form. The animal species that appeared as definite singulars included both *exotic* kinds such as 'the giraffe' and species which are present in the Scandinavian landscape such as 'the eel'. In Radden's model, the definite singular is recognised as kind generic, whereas in Norwegian it also serves as a prototypical generic reference.

Indefinite plurals, as the least controversial of all generic NP types, were frequent in both the corpus and the two surveys. The judgements of native speakers of Norwegian have confirmed the special status of this form, often seen as *default* in many Germanic languages. It is seen as correct almost in any generic context, be it with a kind-predicate or not (see the examples in 132). Studies on generics in other languages have also confirmed this claim (see, for example, the study of Karczewski [2016], where English and Polish generics are compared[34]).

(132) a. Krokodiller lever i vann og finnes i
tropiske områder over hele kloden.
croodile-PL live in water and finds in
tropical climate in whole world
Crocodiles live in water and can be found in tropical climates around the world.

b. Hos haier som lever av fisk og lignende
er det utviklet skjære- eller gripetenner.
with shark-PL that live of fish and similar
is it developed flattened or needle-like.teeth
Sharks that live on fish and similar food have developed flattened or needle-like teeth.

---

[34] In Polish, a language without articles, the plural form was seen as one that corresponds to English bare plurals.

The sentence in (132a) shows what can be considered a classic generic reference that denotes a whole kind. The use of the predicate 'to live in water' makes the reference possible only when it concerns the whole kind. It is not possible that only certain crocodiles would live in water, as it is a characteristic feature for the whole kind. The indefinite plural was judged to be correct by 93 of the respondents – the most frequent among all of the NP types.

The sentence in (132b), on the other hand, shows the use of a regular predicate with an indefinite plural form in a generic sentence. The form was judged to be correct 88 times, making it most widely used form in this example.

Both sentences in (132) show that the respondents chose the same form as in the model sentences from the corpus. Moreover, the predicates used in the two examples confirm the claims of Pettersson (1976), Carlson (1977), Chierchia (1998), and others that bare plurals can be considered a *default* generic form in English and other Germanic languages.

The last of the mentioned NP types, the definite plural, is not very common in generic contexts in English, for instance, but it does appear quite often in Norwegian. In the collected material, definite plural generics were most often used in texts and sentences about people (e.g. 'the Sami') and animal species that are considered to be gregarious or are usually seen in flocks (e.g. 'the bumblebees'). In certain cases, sub-kinds were accessed through this form (e.g. 'the tipis' – a particular type of a tent), whereas in other cases definite plurals denoted hyperonyms (e.g. 'the drilling machines' – a general category). The use of the definite plural in generic contexts in Norwegian is indeed delimited, but it still allows for a wider range of contexts compared to English.

The types of generic references and their meanings presented in Table 7.1. were chosen among those that appeared most often in the corpus and in the AJT survey. Certain contexts, especially in the corpus, depended on the writing style. Encyclopaedic texts belong to a genre where the information needs to be concise and understandable. Also, in many texts the first mention of the text's topic was both an encyclopaedic entry and the subject of the text's first sentence. In such cases, the noun phrase was often a BN. However, the use of BNs was analysed in detail in order to account for other possible contexts and not only those of the first mentions.

Genericity as a part of general knowledge

The idea that genericity is a part of general knowledge is not new (see e.g. Leslie 2007; Karczewski 2016). Furthermore, some studies have shown that the ability to form and interpret generic expressions might be innate or developed at a very young age.[35] The empirical material presented in this book also suggests that despite the normative language rules, cognition itself is a key factor in understanding and expressing generics. General knowledge and interpretation of certain phenomena have an influence on the way genericity is rendered in a language. For instance, understanding whether one is speaking about a prototypical object or a specific one is not only conditioned by the sentence's structure, but also by the context and one's cognitive abilities. 'Generic knowledge' (Karczewski 2016: 19) can be observed when the corpus material (Chapter 5) is compared with the results of the AJT survey (Chapter 6). In many of the cases, the participants intuitively marked the default forms (namely those that occurred in the corpus) as correct and/ or acceptable. Also the recognition of the special status of the noun 'stave church' was observed, indicating that the notion of WEKs might also be a part of one's generic knowledge.

7.3. Implications for further research

Some of the aspects of genericity that were beyond the scope of this project include studying local varieties of the Norwegian language and a contrastive study of generics in the two written standards of Norwegian. The status of the language is rather complicated: as mentioned above, there are two written standards of Norwegian and no spoken standard. Moreover, there are distinct varieties of *bokmål* and *nynorsk* – some are more conservative, others more liberal – and the number of local varieties and dialects in Norway is difficult to estimate, given such a wide diversity and the lack of a standardised language.

The choice of *bokmål* for this project proved effective, though a comparison of the two written standards could provide a broader perspective on genericity in Norwegian. Even though a great majority of the written resources are available in *bokmål*, a set of data in *nynorsk* could be collected, for instance with the use popular science magazines and websites such as forskning.no, where the texts are published in two language variants. Some

---

[35]   The study of Leslie and Gelman (2012) proves for instance that children recognise generic statements before they are able to interpret quantificational ones.

articles from *Store norske leksikon* are available in *nynorsk*, even though they are rarer than the ones written in *bokmål*.

When it comes to analysing generics in local varieties of Norwegian, the case is much more complex. Dialects are mostly spoken, although it is possible to find texts written in non-standard Norwegian, e.g. on a forum or in the comment sections on YouTube. There are certain tools that allow for the automatic extraction of such texts (such an application can be constructed in R or Python, for example). Nevertheless, filtering out the necessary information cannot be automated to such a high degree, since the written versions of the spoken dialects are very diverse and they differ from the standardised *bokmål* and *nynorsk*. Another option for analysing the dialects of the language is to conduct a study similar to Oosterhof's (2008), where a survey was constructed and speakers of certain local varieties of the language were consulted. Such a project could provide insight into generics in Norwegian dialects, but it would certainly require a great deal of time and resources.

As demonstrated throughout this book, the scholarly literature on genericity mostly concerns English and other widely spoken languages. Testing the existing models of generics in other languages, especially less studied ones, would certainly contribute to the development of the models and provide more information on genericity in general.

Appendices

A. Survey 1 texts

1. Det å trene og utvikle muskulaturen har i det siste blitt veldig populært verden rundt, også i Norge. I dag er det ikke bare menn som ønsker å bli sterkere og se strammere ut. De fleste vet at … kan gi gode resultater både hos kvinner og menn.
   (a) styrketrening
   (b) en styrketrening
   (c) styrketreningen
   (d) styrketreninger
   (e) styrketreningene

2. At et sunt kosthold er viktig når man trener, vet alle. Det som skaper uenighet blant personlige trenere og helseentusiaster er hva et sunt kosthold egentlig er. Noen påstår for eksempel at … bør spises daglig for å forebygge mangel på viktige vitaminer og næringsstoffer.
   (a) eple
   (b) et eple
   (c) eplet
   (d) epler
   (e) eplene

3. Blant dagens mange dietter og kosthold finner man forskjellige tilnærminger til næring. Alle har sine egne meninger om hva som bør spises og hva som bør unngås.
   Det er for eksempel enighet om at:

(a) appelsin er en god kilde til c-vitaminer
(b) en appelsin er en god kilde til c-vitaminer
(c) appelsinen er en god kilde til c-vitaminer
(d) appelsiner er en god kilde til c-vitaminer
(e) appelsinene er en god kilde til c-vitaminer

4. Har du lyst til å dekorere huset ditt, er det viktig med en detaljert plan og en god oversikt over budsjettet du har til rådighet. Det kan være vanskelig å bestemme om hvordan leiligheten eller huset skal se ut etter oppussing. Ikke la deg påvirke av design-blader eller selgere i butikker som håper å tjene på deg, for … gir nok de beste rådene.
(a) venn
(b) en venn
(c) vennen
(d) venner
(e) vennene

5. Verdenspolitikken har i det siste vært i krise. I mange land, blant annet Norge, minsker samfunnets tillit til politikere og offentlige organisasjoner. Flere og flere mennesker innrømmer at de ikke tror på det de store politiske partiene påstår. Bortsett fra det mener mange at … har relativt stor makt i det moderne samfunnet.
(a) politiker
(b) en politiker
(c) politikeren
(d) politikere
(e) politikerne

6. Antall bilder og videoer med katter som man finner på nettet er overraskende stort. Katteelskere betrakter sine firbeinte venner som konger. Likevel synes fortsatt mange at det faktisk er … som er det beste selskap.
(a) hund
(b) en hund
(c) hunden
(d) hunder
(e) hundene

7. Stadig flere sliter med depresjon og angsttilstander som et resultat av stress. For mange kan plikter på jobb og i hverdagslivet være en hovedgrunn til økt stressnivå. Blant vanlige behandlinger og terapier, finner man også en del psykologer som anbefaler alternative behandlingsmetoder. For noen mennesker kan for eksempel … være til hjelp.

    (a) religion

    (b) en religion

    (c) religionen

    (d) religioner

    (e) religionene

8. Hver dag bruker man opp til fire timer på internett. De fleste bruker nettet både på datamaskin, nettbrett og telefon. Dekningen her i landet er såpass bra at det ikke er noe problem å surfe på nettet utenfor hjemmet eller arbeidsplassen. Ifølge de nyeste statistikkene er det nettopp … de fleste bruker til å sjekke e-post og sosiale medier.

    (a) smarttelefon

    (b) en smarttelefon

    (c) smarttelefonen

    (d) smarttelefoner

    (e) smarttelefonene

9. Antall bilulykker i Europa er på et relativt høyt nivå. Tusenvis av lastebiler som kjører gjennom kontinentet bidrar til stor trafikk på motorveier og i byer. For å kjøre trygt og unngå ulykker er det viktig å huske at … veier flere tonn og trenger derfor lang tid til å bremse.

    (a) lastebil

    (b) en lastebil

    (c) lastebilen

    (d) lastebiler

    (e) lastebilene

10. Hvert år bygges det nye sykkelveier i mange norske byer og tettsteder. De som bytter sine biler mot sykler påstår at det ikke bare er bra for helsen å sykle, men at det også kan fikse budsjettet og hjelpe å spare litt ekstra hver måned. Det er jo klart at … er billige og økovennlige transportmidler.

    (a) sykkel

    (b) en sykkel

    (c) sykkelen

    (d) sykler

    (e) syklene

11. Bør man spise meieriprodukter for å få i seg nok kalsium? Og kan kalsium fra meieriprodukter styrke bein i kroppen? De nyeste undersøkelsene viser at i land der det spises mest meieriprodukter forekommer benskjørhet mye oftere enn vanlig. Er det faktisk slik at … forårsaker dette?

(a) melk

(b) en melk

(c) melken

12. Autistiske barn har det vanskelig med å tilegne seg grunnleggende kunnskaper som lesing og skriving. Gjennom årene har man jobbet med nye opplæringsteknikker og verktøy som kan brukes på skolen. Det har blitt bl.a. påvist at … hjelper barn med autisme til å fokusere bedre på skolen.

(a) musikk

(b) en musikk

(c) musikken

13. I dagens Norge er tilpasset opplæring og inkluderende skoler de viktigste målene man arbeider mot. Lærere og foreldre kommer stadig med nye idéer om hva som er best for de yngste. Hva om elever selv kunne bestemme hva de vil lære? Det er viktig å huske at … også utgjør en viktig del av samfunnet

(a) barn [sg.]

(b) et barn

(c) barnet

(d) barn [pl.]

(e) barna

14. Det er blitt lettere å være entreprenør i Norge. Blant de nye prosjektene som støttes er det flere små bryggerier rundt omkring i landet. Nybegynnere i bransjen ser det som en sjanse til å komme inn på ølmarkedet. For disse entreprenørene betyr … de selger en liten, men fast inntekt.

(a) øl [sg.]

(b) et øl

(c) ølet

(d) øl [pl.]

(e) ølene

15. Det er typisk norsk å dra på hyttetur. Uansett om du reiser alene eller med venner må du ikke glemme det som er viktigst på slike turer, nemlig maten! Taco og varme retter kan være fristende, men det er også greit med noe mer tradisjonelt. Derfor bør man alltid ha … på hytta si.

(a) brødmat

(b) en brødmat

(c) brødmaten

16. I en digitalisert verden der nesten alt foregår på nettet, står papirlitteraturen overfor den største krisen noensinne. Det er flere som velger å laste ned en app istedenfor å lese en bok i fritiden. Mange mener også at vanlige papirbøker er i ferd med å forsvinne helt fra markedet. I stedet kan imidlertid … være en god litterær opplevelse
    (a) lydbok
    (b) en lydbok
    (c) lydboken
    (d) lydbøker
    (e) lydbøkene

17. Hvordan bør man kle på seg på en jobbtur? Om du jobber i et stort firma der det er en kleskode, kan det være en krevende sak. Det er ikke uvanlig å ta på seg en dress eller en kjole på en slik tur. Problemet kan være tilbehør man må ha med seg. Hvordan reiser man med dokumenter og en pc når man også skal være elegant? … er ikke lenger forbudt i den profesjonelle verden.
    (a) Ryggsekk
    (b) En ryggsekk
    (c) Ryggsekken
    (d) Ryggsekker
    (e) Ryggsekkene

18. I høstmånedene er det mange som velger å kose seg hjemme om kvelden med et glass vin og en god bok. Lurer du på hvordan du kan skape den koselige høststemningen i ditt eget hjem? Det er relativt enkelt og krever ikke veldig mye tid. Først og fremst er det fint med … hjemme.
    (a) stearinlys [sg.]
    (b) et stearinlys
    (c) stearinlyset
    (d) stearinlys [pl.]
    (e) stearinlysene

19. Når vinteren er godt i gang, er det greit å handle vinterklær på salg. Flere butikker tilbyr da salg opp til 50% fra de vanlige prisene. Lurer du på hva som er best å handle om vinteren? De fleste velger … av god kvalitet
    (a) dunjakke
    (b) en dunjakke
    (c) dunjakken
    (d) dunjakker
    (e) dunjakkene

20. Sommerferie er noe de fleste ser fram til hele året. Når sommeren endelig kommer, er det bare kos og gøy man er opptatt av. Da er det enkelt å glemme riktig beskyttelse mot solen. Solkrem har jo de fleste, men man burde også beskytte hodet. Da kan det være både praktisk og stilig med ...
    (a) stråhatt
    (b) en stråhatt
    (c) stråhatten
    (d) stråhatter
    (e) stråhattene

21. Hvordan velger man den rette leiligheten? Det kan være fristende å gå på alle mulige visninger i området, men ekspertene mener at man heller burde velge to-tre leiligheter man liker godt. Til syvende og sist bestemmes gjerne valget av ... man får.
    (a) god magefølelse
    (b) en god magefølelse
    (c) den gode magefølelsen
    (d) gøde mageføleler
    (e) de gode magefølelsene

22. Det er mange faktorer som må tas hensyn til når man skal pusse opp et kontor. Gode og komfortable møbler må man selvfølgelig ha, men tilbehøret er også viktig.
    Flere undersøkelser har for eksempel vist at ... hjelper til å fokusere bedre.
    (a) grønn lampe
    (b) en grønn lampe
    (c) den grønne lampen
    (d) grønne lamper
    (e) de grønne lampene

23. Det å planlegge et bryllup kan ta mye tid og penger. Særlig for kvinner er det vanskelig siden de må velge en spesiell kjole til seremonien. Bryllupsmoten endrer seg like raskt som den hverdagslige moten. I dag er det vel ikke bare ... som velges til bryllup.
    (a) hvit kjole
    (b) en hvit kjole
    (c) den hvite kjolen
    (d) hvite kjoler
    (e) de hvite kjolene

24. I dagens verden er det viktig å være online døgnet rundt. Dette gjør at telefonprodusentene kommer med stadig nye funksjoner i produktene sine. Ifølge brukerne er det i dag bare … som teller.
    (a) stor trykkskjerm
    (b) en stor trykkskjerm
    (c) den store trykkskjermen
    (d) store trykkskjermer
    (e) de store trykkskjermene

25. Interiørdesign endrer seg stadig og kan noen ganger bli litt overraskende. Moderne designere bruker ofte gamle kopper og keramikk til å pynte kjøkkenet og stuen. Man kan for eksempel bruke … til å pynte kjøkkenet
    (a) vanlig ølflaske
    (b) en vanlig ølflaske
    (c) den vanlige ølflasken
    (d) vanlige ølflasker
    (e) de vanlige ølflaskene

26. Et jobbintervju er kanskje det viktigste steget når man leter etter en jobb. Det første inntrykket arbeidsgiveren får av deg er viktig og kan være avgjørende. Pass derfor på at du kler deg riktig. Har du ingen idé om hva du kan ta på deg, kan … passe best.
    (a) hvit skjorte
    (b) en hvit skjorte
    (c) den hvite skjorten
    (d) hvite skjorter
    (e) de hvite skjortene

27. Kjøkkenutstyr er noe alle må velge en gang i livet. Kommer du til å møblere ditt eget kjøkken snart, er det lurt å sammenligne forskjellige typer komfyr før du bestemmer deg. Blant alle de tilgjengelige komfyrene er det … som anbefales oftest.
    (a) keramisk komfyr
    (b) en keramisk komfyr
    (c) den keramiske komfyren
    (d) keramiske komfyrer
    (e) de keramiske komfyrene

28. Det blir stadig vanligere å endre litt på utseendet når man blir eldre. I dag tilbys plastiske operasjoner og ulike kurer som skal utsette aldringsprosessen. Mange velger friske farger når de begynner å få

    (a) grått hår;

    (b) et grått hår;

    (c) det grå håret.

29. Norsk arkitektur og interiørdesign har gått gjennom flere endringer i de siste årene. Det som var typisk norsk for tjue år siden ikke nødvendigvis er det i dag. Men noen ting blir alltid knyttet til den norske kulturen som for eksempel … i skogen

    (a) rødt hus

    (b) et rødt hus

    (c) det røde huset

    (d) røde hus

    (e) de røde husene

30. Ansiktsuttrykk og symboler kan være forskjellige i de enkelte landene. Men noen tegn er universelle verden rundt. For eksempel vises overgivelse i den militære verden alltid med …

    (a) hvitt flagg

    (b) et hvitt flagg

    (c) det hvite flagget

    (d) hvite flagg

    (e) de hvite flaggene

B. Corpus nouns

1 måke – seagull
2 krabbe – crab
3 manet – jellyfish
4 maur – ant
5 øyenstikker – dragonfly
6 humle – bumblebee
7 mygg – mosquito
8 gresshoppe – grasshopper
9 ål – eel
10 skate – batoidea/ray
11 krokodille – crocodile
12 hai – shark
13 frosk – frog
14 høne – hen
15 dronte – dodo bird
16 flaggermus – bat
17 oter – otter
18 vaskebjørn – raccoon
19 hvalross – walrus
20 lama – llama
21 hund – dog
22 esel – donkey
23 sjiraff – giraffe
24 afrikamus – nesomyidae
25 neshorn – rhino
26 solsikke – sunflower
27 nellik – carnation
28 påskelilje – wild daffodil
29 stemorsblom – viola tricolor (Johnny Jump up)
30 nøkleblom – primula
31 valmue – papaver
32 åkertistel – Cirsium arvense
33 løvetann – common dandelion
34 palme – palm
35 skjermbladtre – umbrella pine
36 mammuttre – giant sequoia

37 edelgran – silver fir
38 alm – wych elm/ Scotch elm
39 sørgepil – weeping willow
40 apebrødtre – baobab
41 lind – small-leaved lime
42 bøk – common beech
43 bregne – fern
44 torvmose – peat moss
45 rødalge – red algae
46 fluesopp – amanita
47 valnøtt – walnut
48 eik – oak
49 hengebjørk – silver birch
50 lerk – larches
51 tang – pliers
52 kanyle – cannula
53 intravenøs kanyle – intravenous cannulation
54 sentralt vanekateter – central venous catheter
55 loddebolt – soldering iron
56 lysrør – fluorescent lamp
57 sveising – welding
58 rulle – mangle
59 kniv – knife
60 høvel – hand plane
61 kloakk – sewage system
62 fødselstang – obstetrical forceps
63 spiker – nail
64 våpen – weapon
65 skrue – screw
66 skruetrekker – screwdriver
67 skive – washer
68 mutter – nut
69 støvsuger – vacuum cleaner
70 glasskjærer – glass cutter
71 skrunøkkel – spanner
72 spøytepistol – spray gun
73 kipperøks – axe
74 vaterpass – spirit level

75 sag – saw
76 aksel – axis
77 hodeplagg – headgear
78 gitar – guitar
79 saksofon – saxophone
80 fyllepenn – fountain pen
81 satelitt – satelite
82 fjernkontroll – remote
83 kalkulator – calculator
84 jekk – jack
85 boremaskin – drill
86 bildekk – car tyre
87 forbrenningsmotor – internal combustion engine
88 stridsvogn – tank
89 boreskip – drillship
90 tanskip – tankship
91 ferge – ferry
92 gaffeltruck – forklift
93 dal – valley
94 barkan – barchan
95 dyne – dune
96 permafrost – permafrost
97 savanne – savannah
98 ørken – desert
99 fjord – fjord
100 meander – meander
101 akvarellmaling – watercolor
102 spiseredskap – cutlery
103 gummi – rubber
104 håv – hand net
105 fiskekrok – hook
106 ukulele – ukulele
107 fjernstyring – remote controll
108 lærer – teacher
109 dirigent – bandmaster
110 psykolog – psychologist
111 taksidermist – taxidermist
112 bakkepersonell – aircrew

113 baker – baker
114 butikkslakter – butcher
115 isolatør – insulation installer
116 sølvsmed – silversmith
117 maler – painter
118 maskinist – train driver
119 gevær – gun
120 bazooka – bazooka
121 skriver – printer
122 fritidshus – vacation house
123 stavkirke – stave church
124 badstue – sauna
125 akvedukt – aqeuduct
126 basilika – basilica
127 bu – stall
128 hytte – cottage
129 korskirke – cross-church
130 mausoleum – mausoleum
131 tipi – tipi
132 kulepenn – ballpoint pen
133 blekk – ink
134 akevitt – akvavit
135 fennikel – fennel
136 mynt – coin
137 krone – crown
138 taco – taco
139 smalahove – smalahove (traditional Norwegian dish)
140 gen – gene
141 vitamin – vitamin
142 språkvitenskap – linguistics
143 mølle – mill
144 telefon – telephone
145 magnet – magnet
146 papir – paper
147 cellulose – cellulose
148 fremmedord – foreign word
149 demokrati – democracy
150 grunnskole – primary school

151 kuvlunge – Kuvlung
152 øyskjegge – Øyeskjegg
153 bagler – Bagler
154 birkebeiner – the Birkebein Party
155 konge – king
156 rabbi – rabbi
157 diakon – deacon
158 prest – priest
159 fylkesmann – county governor
160 ombud – public advocate
161 tsar – tsar
162 siktet – accused
163 vitne – witness
164 berserk – berserk
165 adel – man of nobility
166 bonde – farmer
167 biskop – bishop
168 husmann – crofter
169 embetsmann – official
170 sysselmann – sysselmann/ governor

C. Survey 2 sentences

Test items

1. Måkene er hvite, grå og svarte (svartbrune, rosenmåken svakt rosa) med lange vinger og til dels svevende flukt.
2. Skater er god matfisk.
3. Dannelsen av meandere er blitt forklart ved at elvevannet kommer i stående svingninger på tvers av strømretningen.
4. I Norge har kniver fremstilt ved småindustri på Toten vært av anerkjent kvalitet, likeså kniver fra Geilo.
5. Fra steinalderen kjennes fiskekroker i stort antall av flint, skifer, men særlig av ben i høyst ulike former.
6. Krokodiller lever i vann og finnes i tropiske områder over hele kloden.
7. Hos haier som lever av fisk og lignende er det utviklet skjære- eller gripetenner.
8. Stavkirke er en høyt utviklet kirketype, oppført i reisverk av tre, kjent fra norsk kristen middelalder.
9. Når kulepennen føres over papiret, ruller kulen mot en blekkpasta (tørrblekk) fra en beholder i skaftet.
10. Gener er oppskrifter for egenskaper hos levende organismer.
11. Birkebeinere var en politisk gruppering i Norge i høymiddelalderen.
12. Diakonen er leder av menighetens diakonitjeneste.
13. Flaggermusene har et enormt næringsbehov.
14. Oteren er utbredt over store deler av Europa, sør for tundragrensen, samt i Nord-Afrika.
15. I naturen finnes sjiraffen i dag bare i Afrika.
16. Torvmosene har en eiendommelig bygning.
17. Humlene danner samfunn og betegnes sammen med honningbiene som sosiale bier.
18. Man skjelner mellom skruer beregnet for stål og metalldeler, og for arbeid i tre.
19. Gitaren kom opprinnelig fra Midtøsten.
20. Ålen finnes i hav og ferskvann fra Nord-Afrika og middelhavslandene i sør til Kvitsjøen i nord.

Filler items

1. De fleste orkestre og kor har en fast sjefdirigent.
2. For husmennene som ikke bodde langs strandkanten, ble jorda en viktig del av næringsveien.
3. Moten med avrundede knivspisser bredte seg fra det toneangivende franske hoff og har holdt seg siden.
4. Sysselmannen på Svalbard er også politimester, notarius publicus og hjelpedommer ved underretten, og har dessuten andre offentlige funksjoner.
5. Det var imidlertid engelsk-amerikaneren Alexander Graham Bell som 1876 konstruerte en brukbar telefon, og som helt til 2002 ble regnet som telefonens oppfinner.

Bibliography

Becker, Misha (2014). *The Acquisition of Syntactic Structure. Animacy and Thematic Alignment.* Cambridge: Cambridge University Press.

Behrens, Leila (2000). *Typological Parameters of Genericity. (Arbeitspapier 37.).* Köln: Institut für Sprachwissenschaft der Universität zu Köln.

Behrens, Leila (2005). Genericity from a cross-linguistic perspective. *Linguistics*, 43(2), pp. 275–344.

Borthen, Kaja (2003). *Norwegian Bare Singulars.* Ph.D. thesis, Norwegian University of Science and Technology, Trondheim.

Borthen, Kaja (2007). The correspondence between cognitive status and the form of kind-referring NPs. In: Jeanette K. Gundel et al. (eds.), *The Grammar-pragmatics Interface. Essays in Honor of Jeanette K. Gundel*, chap. 7. Amsterdam/Philadelphia: John Benjamins Publishing Company, pp. 143–169.

Carlson, Greg (2010). Generics and Concepts. In: Francis Jeffry Pelletier (ed.), *Kinds, Things, and Stuff. Mass Terms and Generics.* New Directions in Cognitive Science, Oxford: Oxford University Press, pp. 16–35.

Carlson, Greg N. (1977). A Unified Analysis of the English Bare Plural. *Linguistics and Philosophy*, 1, pp. 413–457.

Carlson, Greg N. (1979). Generics and Atemporal 'When'. *Linguistics and Philosophy*, 3, pp. 49–98.

Carlson, Greg N. (1982). Generic terms and generic sentences. *Journal of Philosophical Logic*, 11, pp. 145–181.

Carlson, Greg N. (1983). Logical form: types of evidence. *Linguistics and Philosophy*, 6, pp. 295–317.

Carlson, Gregory N. and Pelletier, Francis Jeffry (eds.) (1995). *The Generic Book.* Chicago–London: The University of Chicago Press.

Carlsson, Yvonne (2012). *Genericitet i text.* Ph.D. thesis, Stockholms universitet, Stockholm.

Chierchia, Gunnaro (1998). Reference to kinds across languages. *Natural Language Semantics*, 6, pp. 339–405.

Comrie, Bernard (1989). *Language Universals and Linguistic Typology*. Chicago: The University of Chicago Press, 2 ed.

Creswell, John W. and Clark, Vicki L. Plano (2018). *Designing and Conducting Mixed Methods Research. [Ebook]*. Los Angeles, London, New Delhi, Singapore, Washington DC, Melbourne: Sage, 3. ed.

Dahl, Östen (1975). On generics. In: Edward Keenan (ed.), *Formal semantics of natural languages*. Cambridge: Cambridge University Press, pp. 99–111.

Dahl, Östen (1985). Remarques sur le generique. *Langages*, 79, pp. 55–60.

Dahl, Östen (2015). *Grammaticalization in the North. Noun phrase morphosyntax in Scandinavian vernaculars*, *Studies in Diversity Linguistics*, vol. 6. Berlin: Language Science Press.

Dahl, Östen and Koptjevskaja-Tamm, Maria (2001). Kinship in Grammar. In: Irene Baron et al. (eds.), *Dimensions of Possession*, *Typological Studies in Language*, vol. 47. Amsterdam/Philadelphia: John Benjamins Publishing Company, pp. 201–226.

Delsing, Lars-Olof (1993). *The Internal Structure of Noun Phrases in the Scandinavian Languages A Comparative Study*. Ph.D. thesis, Lunds universitet, Institutionen för nordiska språk, Lund.

Devitt, Michael (2010). Linguistic Intuitions Revisited. *The British Journal for the Philosophy of Science*, 61(4), pp. 833–865.

Dyvik, Helge (1979). Omkring fremveksten av artiklene i norsk. Språklig markering av referensielle forutsetninger. *Maal og Minne*, 1-2, pp. 40–78.

Faarlund, Jan Terje (1988). *Morfologi. Bøyningssystemet i nynorsk og bokmål*. Oslo: Det Norske Samlaget.

Faarlund, Jan Terje et al. (1997). *Norsk referansegrammatikk*. Oslo: Universitetsforlaget.

Farkas, Donka F. and de Swart, Henriëtte (2009). Stability and variation in article choice: generic and non-generic contexts. In: Anastasia Giannakidou and Monika Rathert (eds.), *Quantification, Definiteness & Nominalization*. Oxford Studies in Theoretical Linguistics, Oxford: Oxford University Press, pp. 188–213.

Galmiche, Michel (1985). Phrases, syntagmes et articles génériques. *Langages*, 79, pp. 2–39.

Gelman, Susan A. and Bloom, Paul (2007). Developmental changes in understanding of generics. *Cognition*, 105, pp. 166–183.

Gelman, Susan A. and Tardif, Twila (1998). A cross-linguistic comparison of generic noun phrases in English and Mandarin. *Cognition*, 66, pp. 215–248.

Golden, Anne et al. (2008). *Norsk som fremmedspråk. Grammatikk*. Oslo: Universitetsforlaget, 3. ed.

Gundel, Jeanette et al. (1993). Cognitive status and the form of referring expressions in discourse. *Language*, 69, pp. 274–307.

Hagen, Jon Erik (1998). *Norsk grammatikk for andrespråkslærere*. Oslo: Ad notam Gylendal.

Halmøy, Madeleine (2016). *The Norwegian Nominal System – A Neo-Saussurean Perspective, Trends in Linguistics. Studies and Monographs*, vol. 294. Berlin, Boston: De Gruyter Mouton.

Hansen, Erik (1994). Generisk substantiv. In: *Språkbruk, grammatik och språkförändring: en festskrift till Ulf Teleman 13.1.1994*. Lund: Lunds universitet, Institutionen för nordiska språk, pp. 137–144.

Hansen, Erik and Heltoft, Lars (2011). *Grammatik over det Danske Sprog*, vol. 1–3. Odense: Syddansk Universitetsforlag.

Hawkins, John A. (2015). *Definitness and Indefinitness. A Study in Reference and Grammaticality Prediction*. London–New York: Routledge.

Hesse-Biber, Sharlene Nagy (2010). *Mixed Methods Research. Merging Theory with Practice*. New York–London: The Guilford Press.

Ionin, Tania et al. (2011). An experimental investigation of the expression of genericity in English, Spanish and Brazilian Portuguese. *Lingua*, 121, pp. 963–985.

Jacoby, David M.P. et al. (2014). Shark personalities? Repeatability of social network traits in a widely distributed predatory fish. *Behavioral Ecology and Sociobiology*, 68(12), pp. 1995–2003.

Kabatek, Johannes (ed.) (2013). *New Perspectives on Bare Noun Phrases in Romance and Beyond, Studies in Language Companion Series (SLCS)*, vol. 141. John Benjamins Publishing Company.

Karczewski, Daniel (2016). *Generyczność w języku i w myśleniu. Studium kognitywne*. Kraków: Universitas.

Krifka, Manfred et al. (1995). Genericity: An Introduction. In: Gregory N. Carlson and Francis Jeffry Pelletier (eds.), *The Generic Book*. Chicago–London: The University of Chicago Press, pp. 1–124.

Kulbrandstad, Lars Anders (1998). *Språkets mønstre. Grammatiske begreper og metoder*. Oslo: Universitetsforlaget.

Kurek, Anna (2017). Hvordan skildres generisitet i norsk faglitteratur? *Folia Scandinavica Posnaniensia*, 22, pp. 4–17.

Langacker, Ronald W. (1997). Generics and Habituals. In: Angeliki Athanasiadou and René Driven (eds.), *On Conditionals Again*. Amsterdam/Philadelphia: John Benjamins Publishing Company, pp. 191–222.

Lakoff, George. (1990). *Women, Fire and Dangerous Things. What Categories Reveal about the Mind*. Chicago–London: The University of Chicago Press.

Lazaridou-Chatzigoga, Dimitra et al. (2015). Genericity is easy? Formal and experimental perspectives. *Ratio*, XXVIII, pp. 470–494.

Leslie, Sarah-Jane (2007). Generics and the Structure of the Mind. *Philosophical Perspectives, Philosophy of Mind*, 21, pp. 375–403.

Leslie, Sarah-Jane and Gelman, Susan A. (2012). Quantified statements are recalled as generics: Evidence from preschool children and adults. *Cognitive Psychology*, 64, pp. 186–214.

Leslie, Sarah-Jane et al. (2011). Do all ducks lay eggs? The generic overgeneralization effect. *Journal of Memory and Language*, 65, pp. 15–31.

Lønning, Jan Tore (1987). Mass terms and quantification. *Linguistics and Philosophy*, 10, pp. 1–52.

Lyons, John (1977). *Semantics*. Cambridge: Cambridge University Press.

MacDonald, Kirsti (1997). *Spørsmål om grammatikk. Når norsk er andrespråk*. Oslo: Cappelen.

MacDonald, Kirsti (2009). *Norsk grammatikk. Norsk som andrespråk. Teoribok*. Oslo: Cappelen Damm.

Mari, Alda et al. (eds.) (2013a). *Genericity*. Oxford: Oxford University Press.

Mari, Alda et al. (2013b). Introduction. In: Alda Mari et al. (eds.), *Genericity*. Oxford: Oxford University Press, pp. 1–92.

McEnery, Tony and Hardie, Andrew (2012). *Corpus Linguistics. Method, Theory and Practice*. Cambridge Textbooks in Linguistics, Cambridge: Cambridge University Press.

Mertens, Willem et al. (2017). *Quantitative Data Analysis. A Companion for Accounting and Information Systems Research*. Switzerland: Springer.

Molnár, Krisztina (2014). *Substantivdetermination im Deutschen und im Ungarischen. Eine sprachtypologisch-kontrastive Analyse*. Berlin, Boston: De Gruyter.

Nickel, Bernhard (2017). Generics. In: Bob Hale et al. (eds.), *A Companion to the Philosophy of Language*. Oxford: Wiley Blackwell, pp. 437–462.

Oosterhof, Albert (2008). *The Semantics of Generics in Dutch and Related Languages*. Amsterdam/Philadelphia: John Benjamins Publishing Company.

Pelletier, Francis Jeffry (ed.) (2010). *Kinds, Things, and Stuff. Mass Terms and Generics*. New Directions in Cognitive Science, Oxford: Oxford University Press.

Pettersson, Thore (1976). Bestämda och obestämda former. In: Eva Gårding (ed.), *Kontrastiv fonetik och syntax med svenska i centrum*. Liber Läromedel, pp. 119–142.

Quine, Willard Van Orman (2013). *Word and Object. New Edition*. Cambridge: The MIT Press.

Radden, Günter (2009). Generic reference in English. A metonymic and conceptual blending analysis. In: Klaus-Uwe Panther et al. (eds.), *Metonymy and Metaphor in Grammar, Cognitive Human Processing*, vol. 25. Amsterdam/Philadelphia: John Benjamins Publishing Company, pp. 199–228.

Radden, Günter and Dirven, René (2007). *Cognitive English Grammar, Cognitive Linguistics in Practice*, vol. 2. Amsterdam/Philadephia: John Benjamins Publishing Company.

Rasinger, Sebastian M. (2013). *Quantitative Reserach in Linguistics. An Introduction*. London–New Delhi–New York–Sydney: Bloomsbury, 2. ed.

Riazi, A. Mehdi (2016). *The Routledge Encyclopedia of Research Methods in Applied Linguistics. Quantitative, qualitative, and mixed-methods research*. London–New York: Routledge.

Rosch, Eleanor. 1978. Principles of Categorization. In: Eleanor Rosch and Barbara Lloyd (eds.), *Cognition and Categorization*. Hillsdale: Lawrence Erlbaum Associates, Publishers, pp. 27–48.

Rosén, Victoria and Borthen, Kaja (2017). Norwegian bare singulars revisited. In: Victoria Rosén and Koenraad De Smedt (eds.), *The very model of a modern linguist, BeLLS*, vol. 8. University of Bergen, pp. 220–240.

Rosenbach, Anette (2008). Animacy and grammatical variation – Findings from English genitive variation. *Lingua*, 118, pp. 151–171.

Schütze, Carson T. (2016). *The empirical base of linguistics. Grammaticality judgements and linguistics methodology, Classics in Linguistics*, vol. 2. Berlin: Language Science Press.

Skrzypek, Dominika and Kurek, Anna (2018). Generics in Mainland Scandinavian languages. *European Journal of Scandinavian Studies*, 48(2), pp. 253–266.

Strandskogen, Åse Berit and Strandskogen, Rolf (1995). *Norwegian. An Essential Grammar*. London–New York: Routledge.

Teleman, Ulf et al. (1999). *Svenska Akademiens grammatik*, vol. 1-4. Stockholm: Norstedts i distrobution.

Yamamoto, Matsumi (1999). *Animacy and Reference. A cognitive approach to corpus linguistics*. Amsterdam/Philadelphia: John Benjamins Publishing Company.

List of tables

List of figures

Summary in Polish

Generyczność w języku norweskim w ujęciu kognitywnym

Tematem książki jest generyczność w języku norweskim w ujęciu kognityw-nym. Zjawisko to występuje w każdym zbadanym dotąd języku, jednak w żadnym z nich nie zidentyfikowano dotąd narzędzia, za pomocą którego można jednoznacznie wyrazić generyczność (Behrens 2005). W zależności od rodziny języków, odniesienia generyczne są wyrażane na różne sposoby. W językach germańskich, do których należy język norweski, paleta możliwo-ści jest szczególnie szeroka. W wyrażeniach generycznych stosowane mogą być zarówno formy określone grup imiennych, jak i nieokreślone, a w nie-których przypadkach również rzeczowniki nagie.

Celem niniejszego badania jest zweryfikowanie, w jaki sposób generycz-ność może być wyrażana w języku norweskim, a także stworzenie modelu opartego na teoriach kognitywnych, który usystematyzowałby użycie po-szczególnych form generycznych fraz imiennych. Głównym założeniem pracy jest wypełnienie luki w badaniach nad generycznością w mniej zba-danych językach, a także przeprowadzenie badania empirycznego języka norweskiego. Pytania badawcze niniejszej publikacji to:

Jakie formy fraz imiennych występują w kontekstach generycznych w ję-zyku norweskim?

Czy i w jaki sposób kontekst wpływa na interpretację generyczności?

Czy i w jaki sposób zdolności kognitywne natywnych użytkowników języka wpływają na wyrażenie odniesień generycznych?

Przeprowadzenie niniejszego badania oraz odpowiedzi na powyższe py-tania pozwoliły na zbudowanie kognitywnego modelu generyczności, który obrazuje występowanie zjawiska w języku norweskim. Podstawę teoretyczną pracy stanowią teorie kognitywne oraz modele wykorzystywane do analizy generyczności (m.in. Radden 2009; Pettersson 1976 i Leslie et al. 2011).

Język norweski jest dość nietypowy, ponieważ nie tylko nie ma żadnego standardu wymowy, ale także posiada dwa warianty języka pisanego – *bokmål* i *nynorsk*. *Bokmål* jest o wiele bardziej powszechny, zarówno w literaturze, mediach, życiu codziennym jak i edukacji. Co więcej, dostępność tekstów napisanych w tym wariancie języka norweskiego jest większa, co również miało wpływ na wybór wariantu *bokmål* do niniejszego badania.

Jak wspomniano, generyczność jest zjawiskiem, które obecne jest we wszystkich zbadanych dotąd językach, jednak nie stwierdzono istnienia elementu, który stosowany byłby jedynie do wyrażenia tego typu odniesienia. Jest to rodzaj odniesienia do całego gatunku lub całej grupy osób/przedmiotów, o których jest mowa w danym zdaniu czy tekście (Lyons 1977).

Według literatury fachowej (zob. np. Carlson, Pelletier 1995; Mari et al. 2013a i Carlson 2010), generyczność może być rozumiana dwojako, a mianowicie jako *klasyczne* odniesienie gatunkowe (*kind reference*), odnoszące się do całych gatunków oraz jako zdanie habitualne (*habitual sentence*), opisujące powtarzające się czynności. Co więcej, generyczność może być wyrażona w języku na trzech poziomach: 1) grupy imiennej, 2) zdania oraz 3) tekstu (Behrens 2005).

Generyczność na poziomie grupy imiennej zakłada, że sama grupa imienna jest interpretowana jako generyczna, bez względu na użyte w zdaniu predykaty. Najczęściej jest to określenie gatunkowe, a więc odnoszące się do wszystkich lub większości przedstawicieli danego gatunku, jak np. podmioty w zdaniach *Psy szczekają* czy *Włosi lubią makaron*. W językach germańskich, a więc także w języku norweskim, funkcję tę pełni najczęściej forma nieokreślona liczby mnogiej, uznawana za *domyślną* formę generyczną grupy imiennej.

Drugim poziomem, na którym może wystąpić odniesienie generyczne, jest poziom zdania. Wówczas to predykat zastosowany w danym zdaniu decyduje o jego interpretacji. Najczęściej są to predykaty gatunkowe lub takie, które nie występują w odniesieniach specyficznych. Na przykład predykat 'być ssakiem' może odnosić się jedynie do całego gatunku. Nie możemy powiedzieć, że tylko niektóre psy lub koty są ssakami, podczas gdy inne nie. W ten sposób każde zdanie, w którym znajdzie się tzw. predykat gatunkowy (*kind predicate*), jest generyczne. Zdania generyczne mogą również zawierać generyczne grupy imienne.

Trzecim poziomem generyczności wyszczególnionym przez Behrens są tzw. teksty generyczne. Teksty te mogą zawierać zarówno generyczne grupy imienne jak i zdania, jednak ich ogólny wydźwięk uzależniony jest od kontekstu. Teksty generyczne to najczęściej teksty naukowe i popularnonaukowe opisujące gatunki, przedmioty lub zjawiska naturalne. Tego typu teksty opisują cechy charakterystyczne dla danego gatunku, przedmiotu czy zjawiska, a więc są generyczne. Jednakże nie wszystkie zdania czy grupy imienne obecne w takich tekstach zostaną zinterpretowane jako generyczne bez szerszego kontekstu. W niniejszym projekcie zostaną zbadane wszystkie trzy poziomy generyczności – ankieta 1 dotyczy głównie poziomu 1 i 2, badanie korpusowe skupia się na poziomie 3, a ankieta 2 na poziomie 2.

Książka została podzielona na siedem rozdziałów. Pierwszy rozdział stanowi ogólne wprowadzenie do badań oraz zarysowanie celów i pytań badawczych projektu. Rozdziały 2–3 to tło teoretyczne dla części empirycznej. Rozdziały 4–6 zawierają opisy przeprowadzonych badań: ankiety 1, badania korpusowego oraz ankiety 2. Ostatni rozdział z kolei jest szczegółowym omówieniem przedstawionych wcześniej wyników, konkluzji oraz perspektyw dalszych badań nad generycznością.

W rozdziale pierwszym przedstawione zostały cele i pytania badawcze, a także wybrana metodologia. Metodologia badań zastosowana w projekcie to tzw. *mixed methods research*, w skrócie MMR. Polega ona na połączeniu metod kwalitatywnych (w tym przypadku modeli kognitywnych) z metodami kwantytawnymi (w tym przypadku są to testy statystyczne).

Rozdział drugi zawiera przegląd najważniejszych publikacji dotyczących generyczności. Omówione prace dotyczą głównie języka angielskiego oraz innych, dobrze zbadanych języków. Zdecydowana większość teorii dotyczących generyczności opiera się na przykładach z języka angielskiego. Zarówno język angielski, jak i norweski należą do rodziny języków germańskich, co umożliwiło zastosowanie omówionych w rozdziale modeli do przeprowadzenia niniejszych badań.

W rozdziale trzecim przedstawiono dostępną literaturę dotyczącą genryczności w językach skandynawskich – duńskim, szwedzkim i norweskim. Jest to ogólny zarys problematyki, oparty głównie na opracowaniach dostępnych w gramatykach wspomnianych języków. Jedynie dla języka szwedzkiego istnieje publikacja dotycząca empirycznych badań nad generycznością przeprowadzonych przez Carlsson (2012). Nieliczne opracowania dotyczące języka norweskiego stanowią jedynie część większych badań dotyczących kategorii określoności lub rzeczowników (m.in. Borthen 2003 i Halmøy 2016), a nie samej generyczności.

Rozdział czwarty opisuje przeprowadzoną w 2017 roku ankietę. Forma ankiety, a mianowicie 30 krótkich tekstów generycznych z lukami do wypełnienia, została zaczerpnięta z badania Ionin et al. (2011). Teksty zostały napisane w odmianie *bokmål* i przeczytane przez natywnego użytkownika języka norweskiego. Ankieta, wraz z pytaniami kontrolnymi mającymi na celu rozpoznanie natywnych użykowników języka, została stworzona za pomocą Google Forms i opublikowana w internecie. Podczas dwóch tygodni, gdy ankieta była dostępna online, 630 respondentów udzieliło odpowiedzi na pytania; 599 z nich zostało zidentyfikowanych jako natywni użytkownicy języka norweskiego.

Badanie to wykazało, że spośród pięciu form rzeczownika w języku norweskim (forma naga, forma określona i nieokreślona liczby pojedynczej oraz forma określona i nieokreślona liczby mnogiej) wszystkie mogą mieć znaczenie generyczne, jednak nie w każdym możliwym kontekście. Co więcej, formy mogą do pewnego stopnia być stosowane zamiennie, jednak i w tym przypadku nie może być mowy o zupełnej dowolności.

Wyniki ankiety 1 zostały przeanalizowane na podstawie modelu zaproponowanego przez Leslie et al. (2011), który zakłada występowanie sześciu różnych typów predykatów generycznych: 1) quasi-definicji, 2) cechy większościowej, 3) cechy mniejszościowej, 4) predykatu większości, 5) predykatu *szokującego* oraz 6) fałszywego uogólnienia (Leslie et al. 2011: 19).

W przeprowadzonym badaniu zaobserwowano występowanie każdego z predykatów generycznych, jednak nie we wszystkich przypadkach respondenci wybierali te same formy grupy imiennej. Również testy statystyczne potwierdziły występowanie znaczących różnych pomiędzy testowanymi grupami, tj. pięcioma formami grupy imiennej. Oznacza to, że kontekst generyczny dyktuje wybór danej formy.

Rozdział piąty jest najobszerniejszym rozdziałem empirycznym i dotyczy przeprowadzonego badania korpusowego. Korpus do analizy został zbudowany za pomocą programu R i oparty na tekstach pobranych ze *Store norske leksikon*, norweskiej encyklopedii online. Korpus liczył w sumie 170 tekstów (27 761 tokenów), podzielonych na pięć kategorii tematycznych: 1) ludzie, 2) zwierzęta, 3) rośliny, 4) narzędzia, 5) inne. Kategoria 'ludzie' zawierała 20 tekstów, kategorie 'zwierzęta', 'rośliny' oraz 'narzędzia' po 25 tekstów, natomiast kategoria 'inne' składała się z 75 tekstów. Każdy z tekstów miał długość przynajmniej jednego paragrafu i był napisany w wariancie języka *bokmål*.

Dane pozyskane w badaniu korpusowym również zostały przeanalizowane na dwa sposoby, zgodnie z metodą MMR. Pierwszy etap analizy zakładał zastosowanie modeli kognitywnych dla języka angielskiego (Radden 2009) i szwedzkiego (Pettersson 1976). Na podstawie tychże modeli pogrupowano dane według typów grup imiennych w każdym z tekstów, a także według kontekstów generycznych, w których występowały. Analiza ta pozwoliła na stwierdzenie, że forma naga przyjmuje często interpretację konceptualną, podczas gdy dwie formy liczby pojedynczej wyrażają generyczność za pomocą odniesień do prototypów. Z kolei forma nieokreślona liczby mnogiej, podobnie jak w języku angielskim, niemal zawsze odnosi się do całych gatunków. Tak zwana ograniczona generyczność (ang. *delimited generics*) ma w norweskim szersze zastosowanie niż w języku angielskim i może być stosowana w większej ilości kontekstów, nie tylko tych dotyczących opisów ludzi. Zebrane dane pozwoliły na stworzenie matrycy form generycznych dla języka norweskiego. Drugim elementem analizy korpusowej było przeprowadzenie testów statystycznych. Testy te wykazały główne tendencje w występowaniu poszczególnych form grup imiennych oraz różnice pomiędzy nimi. Główne tendencje zbadane statystycznie pokryły się w dużej mierze z analizą opisową opartą na modelach kognitywnych.

W rozdziale szóstym opisana została ostatnia część materiału empirycznego, a mianowicie ankieta AJT. Ankieta zawierała 20 zdań generycznych oraz 5 zdań niezawierających odniesienia generycznego. Wszystkie zdania zostały zaczerpnięte z korpusu. Ankieta została zbudowana za pomocą aplikacji Shiny oraz programu R, a następnie umieszczona na serwerze. Badanie zostało przeprowadzone na Uniwersytecie w Tromsø oraz w bibliotece miejskiej w Tromsø, gdzie zrekrutowano w sumie 100 osób.

Respondenci mieli za zadanie dokonanie oceny każdej z form rzeczownika w wybranych do badania zdaniach i z wykorzystaniem skali. Skala ocen poszczególnych form obejmowała 3 stopnie: 1 – forma poprawna, 2 – forma akceptowalna i 3 – forma niepoprawna/nienaturalna. Zebrane w ten sposób odpowiedzi zostały przeanalizowane na podstawie modeli kognitywnych, podobnie jak w rozdziale piątym, oraz za pomocą testów statystycznych.

Badanie wykazało, że w większości przypadków formy grup imiennych w oryginalnych zdaniach korpusowych pokrywały się z odpowiedziami respondentów oznaczonymi jako poprawne (ocena 1). Co więcej, ocena 2 dostarczyła dodatkowych informacji na temat kontekstów generycznych, w których może występować więcej niż jedna forma grupy imiennej. Z kolei ocena 3 pozwoliła na wykluczenie form grup imiennych w danych kontekstach generycznych.

Testy statystyczne zostały przeprowadzone dla odpowiedzi oznaczonych jako 1 i 2, a więc jako formy poprawne i akceptowalne. W ten sposób potwierdzone zostały główne tendencje, widoczne również dzięki analizie kognitywnej. Również dla danych pozyskanych w ankiecie AJT utworzono matrycę form grup imiennych w kontekstach generycznych, która uzupełnia matrycę z rozdziału piątego.

Rozdział siódmy zawiera podsumowanie przeprowadzonych badań oraz syntezę wszystkich danych. W rozdziale uwzględniono wszystkie trzy elementy projektu, a na podstawie dwóch z nich, tj. analizy korpusowej oraz ankiety AJT, zaproponowano model kognitywny form generycznych dla języka norweskiego. Model ten pokrywa się w pewnym stopniu z modelami Raddena i Petterssona, ale także ukazuje konteksty generyczne nieobecne w tychże modelach. Ostatnia część rozdziału siódmego dotyczy perspektywy dalszych badań nad generycznością z wykorzystaniem teorii kognitywnych.

Index

Technical editor
Agnieszka Stęplewska

Editor
Eric Hilton

Proofreader
Agnieszka Toczko-Rak

Typesetter
Hanna Wiechecka

Jagiellonian University Press
Editorial Offices: Michałowskiego 9/2, 31-126 Kraków
Phone: +48 12 663 23 80

GPSR Authorized Representative: Easy Access System Europe, Mustamäe tee
50, 10621 Tallinn, Estonia, gpsr.requests@easproject.com